D0091368

LEARNING TRUE LOVE

LEARNING TRUE LOVE

How I Learned and Practiced
Social Change in Vietnam

CHÂN KHÔNG
Cao Ngoc Phuong

Parallax Press
Berkeley, California

Copyright © 1993, by Chân Không

Printed in the United States of America

Parallax Press
P.O. Box 7355
Berkeley, CA 94707

Cover design by Gay Reineck
Cover photograph by Gaetano Kazuo Maida
All photographs courtesy of Chân Không

LIBRARY OF CONGRESS CATALOGING-IN-PUBLICATION DATA
Không, Chân
    Learning true love : how I learned and practiced social change in Vietnam /
Chân Không Cao Ngoc Phuong
        p.   cm.
    ISBN 0-938077-50-3: $16.00
    1. Không, Chân 2. Priests, Buddhist—Vietnam—Biography. 3. Women
Buddhist priests—Vietnam—Biography. I. Title.
BQ944.02 1993
294.3'092—dc20
[B]   93-31442
                                                                       CIP

Contents

Foreword
Maxine Hong Kingston

Lately, I've been despairing over the deaths and fewness of teachers. The idea of peace has hardly been thought, and its methods difficult to convey. The most famous teachers of peace, Mahatma Gandhi and Dr. Martin Luther King, Jr., were assassinated. As I write, we have bombed Baghdad again, "to deter terrorism" and "using force as a tool for diplomacy." President Clinton and most people believe that the way to stop future war is to kill enemies. I am horrified at the number of people I've met who blame pacifists for causing violence by being unarmed and weak. I have tried to untangle that logic. War is not the way to peace. Peace is the way to peace. But argument is not the way to peace either, nor the way to teach.

Reading Sister Chân Không's autobiography, I learned exacting truths: The pacifist makes peace moment by moment all her lifetime, existentially becoming—being—peace, being Buddhist, being human. Peacefully, lovingly, in the midst of war in Vietnam, Sister Chân Không built communes, "pioneer villages," started schools and taught in them, nursed the wounded and sick, fed the hungry, buried the dead, all the while organizing people to raise funds and to do work that changes the warring world. Most specially, she writes about giving the children a moon festival, and so teaching them a joyful rite of celebration. And all these deeds, all this life were tested in the worst of circumstances, the long, escalating civil war in Vietnam. Sister Chân Không, Thich Nhat Hanh, and twelve other monks and nuns established and held a position that was neither nationalist nor communist, neither North nor South. They were a means and a hope for enemies to communicate and to end the war. This miraculous, strong pacifism did not die though its practitioners were jailed, tortured, murdered.

I am amazed and grateful that Sister Chân Không teaches us how to access strength from the invisible. The Buddhists, trained in non-duality, were able to see that there are not two sides to Vietnam, and thus act wholeheartedly, a vision of the entire country in mind. Another sustenance is poetry. Sister Chân Không gathers and interweaves through this book poems that Thich Nhat Hanh wrote at crucial events. Here are poems—prayers for peace—written in devastated villages and at the Peace Conference in Paris. Here is the poem honoring a monk killed while being interrogated by the police. And "Prayer for Land," a talisman carried by each of 566 boat people on a planned expedition to Australia led by Sister Chân Không. Here are many poems of transition, for journeys and exile, a birthday poem, an ordination poem. And in the context of her life, Sister Chân Không gives us Fourteen Precepts of Buddhism, which state the values that nourish the pacifist—or "social worker," as Sister Chân Không calls herself—and keep her effective and heroic in the real world. With holy words as well as the example of her own life, Sister Chân Không, Cao Ngoc Phuong, heartens and inspires the reader in need of being strong in peace.

Learning True Love stands alongside *The Autobiography of Mahatma Gandhi*, both rare life stories of people who carried out and embodied pacifist values. Moreover, Chân Không tells the considerations and decisions that a woman has to make, should she marry, not marry, cut off her hair, leave her mother, have a room of her own. It is important that we now have this Buddhist woman's point-of-view, and a Vietnamese point-of-view. By meeting the many individuals Sister Chân Không knows and understanding their ways—the book begins on a joyous Têt, a holiday of renewal—we can at last reconcile ourselves with the Vietnamese people and our own history, and put that war to rest.

Maxine Hong Kingston
Grand Canyon, Arizona
June 1993

Foreword
Thich Nhat Hanh

M y students are also my teachers. I learn so much from them. Sister Chân Không (True Emptiness) is among the foremost of these. Please allow me to tell you one of the important lessons she taught me. It was in 1966, when the war in Vietnam had become unbearable, and I was so absorbed in working to end the war it was hard for me to swallow my food. One day, Chân Không was preparing a basket of fresh, fragrant herbs to serve with rice noodles, and she asked me, "Thây, can you identify these *fines herbes*?" Looking at her displaying the herbs with care and beauty on a large plate, I became enlightened. She had the ability to keep her attention on the herbs, and I realized I had to stop dwelling only on the war and learn to concentrate on the fines herbes also. We spent ten minutes discussing the herbs that could be found in the south of Vietnam and the ones in the central regions, and that encounter took my mind off the war, allowing me to recover the balance I needed so badly. In 1968, when I was in the south of France, I sought out the fines herbes of Provence with my full attention and interest.

Years later, a friend from America asked me, "Thây, why do you waste your time planting lettuce? Wouldn't it be better to use the time to write poems? Anyone can plant lettuce, but few people can write such beautiful poetry." I smiled and said, "My dear friend, if I do not plant this lettuce, I will not be able to write poetry." I did not reveal that my answer came from the encounter twelve years earlier with Sister True Emptiness. Even today when I read the manuscript handed to me by Chân Không, I continue to learn from her. A teacher should always be at the same time a student, and a student must always be at the same time a teacher. When we remember this, we benefit from each other.

Sister True Emptiness has a great capacity for joy and happiness. That is what I appreciate most in her life. Her unwavering faith in the Dharma is strengthened each day as she continues to enjoy the fruit of transformation and healing born from the practice. Her stability, joy, and happiness are wonderful supports for many of us in Plum Village and in the circle of the greater sangha. Working for social change and helping people are sources of joy for her. The love and concern that underlie her work are deep. True Emptiness is also true love. Her story is more than just the words. Her whole life is a Dharma talk.

I regret that this book is still too short and that her words could not convey all the depth and reality of her path. Sister True Emptiness could have written a book ten times longer, because she has so much to tell. But she is more an activist than a writer, and for now we must be satisfied with the present work. If you have the opportunity to be with her, please ask her to tell you more about her experiences. You can learn a lot from her. She is a true bodhisattva.

Thich Nhat Hanh
Plum Village, Duras, France
May 1993

Brief Glossary of Vietnamese and Buddhist Terms

ao dai — traditional Vietnamese women's dress.

Avalokitesvara Bodhisattva — the bodhisattva who listens to the cries of the world and offers the gift of non-fear.

bodhisattva — literally "enlightened-being"; One who works to relieve the suffering of others and help bring them to enlightenment.

Heart Sutra (Prajña Paramita) — a first century A.D. Buddhist scripture that teaches the interconnectedness of all things.

sutra — words of the Buddha.

Thây — teacher. It is an informal word used to address a monk, a nun, or any other teacher. Most monks in this book are referred to as "Thây."

Thich — the name given to a Buddhist monk or nun upon being ordained into the family of the Buddha. It is the Vietnamese transliteration of "shak(ya)," the name of the Buddha's clan. Sister Chân Không's full, formal name is Thich Nu Chân Không.

About the Usage of Names

Sister Chân Không's birth name, Cao Ngoc Phuong, is used throughout much of *Learning True Love*. Cao is her family name and Phuong her given name. Chân Không ("True Emptiness") is her Dharma name, as she explains later in the book.

Acronyms

BBC: British Broadcasting Corporation

CIA: Central Intelligence Agency

CMP: Christian Movement for Peace

CRD: Committee for Reconstruction and Development; a UBC committee formed in 1973 to help villages throughout Vietnam

FOR: Fellowship of Reconciliation; an international organization headquartered in Alkmaar, Holland, whose work for peace during the Vietnam War was the most consistently peaceful.

ICCV: International Committee of Conscience on Vietnam

NLF: National Liberation Front; South Vietnamese guerrillas who supported the Hanoi communist government.

OVBA: Overseas Vietnamese Buddhist Association

SYSS: School of Youth for Social Service

UBC: Unified Buddhist Church of Vietnam; established in 1963 when all of the Buddhist congregations united in a nonviolent effort to stop religious oppression.

UK: United Kingdom

UN: United Nations

UNHCR: United Nations High Commissioner for Refugees

UPI: United Press International

U.S.: United States of America

WCC: World Council of Churches

WFB: World Fellowship of Buddhists

WRI: War Resisters International

GROWING UP IN THE LAND OF TÊT
1938-1961

CHAPTER ONE

The Grass Comes Back to Life

I was born in the Year of the Tiger, 1938, the eighth of nine children. My father's ancestors were farmers in An Dinh, a village on the Mekong River Delta, which is known for its immense, fertile rice fields and huge, sumptuous banana and coconut groves. In traditional Vietnam, these villages were run by councils of twelve elders, and my paternal grandfather was treasurer of the council of An Dinh. Because of their integrity, good hearts, and care for the poor, my father's parents were well-respected in their community. In Vietnam, it is said that if you exploit people, your children will have to pay your debt to society, but if you act with kindness, your children will receive many favorable opportunities. I remember Grandfather telling us, "We have no money to leave you, but we bequeath you the merit we earned from helping people in need." My mother's family owned a large market in the city of Ben Tre, and they also gave great love and care to the poor. Mother's father distributed blankets to the homeless, and her brother donated food to prisoners twice each year.

Later, when my father was able to buy some property near his father's land, he invited many people to farm on it. Whenever there was a drought or flood, he waived the rent and allowed his tenants to pay only what they could. Sometimes he even gave them money to support their children. This was rare during French colonialism; usually when poor farmers could not pay a landlord, they had to send one of their children to work as his domestic servant. My father always encouraged his farmers to save money, and he served as a kind of banker for them. When a farmer saved enough to buy his own parcel, my father helped him prepare the papers and then sold it to him at a reasonable price. With my father's support, a dozen farmers bought their own land. When the communists came into power in August 1945, many landlords were killed, but my father was protected by his tenant farmers, who loved him very much.

My extended family. I'm on the right with pigtails.

My father studied painting and house design at the Professional Institute of Painting in Saigon and then settled in Ben Tre City, where he met my mother. Ben Tre City is the capital of Ben Tre Province, in the center of the Mekong Delta. My father taught us never to take advantage of poor farmers when we went to the open market. "If you can afford his produce, buy it, and if you cannot, don't buy it. But never bargain with a poor farmer, because for you a few *dông* may not be much, but for him it is enough to support his children." My mother used to loan money to poor street vendors to set up their own businesses. Only if they succeeded did she ask them to pay her back.

My parents were like oak trees, sheltering twenty-two "birds"— nine children of their own, twelve nieces and nephews who stayed with us while they attended school in Ben Tre City, and one poor girl from Hue. Mother and Father cared for all of us equally, without discrimination. At mealtimes, no one was allowed to say, "I am your daughter, so I deserve more food than my cousins." Feeding twenty-two mouths was a strain, but we were taught to be satisfied with and share whatever we had. When there was fish or pork, for example, my eldest sister Suong would cut it into twenty-two small pieces and place each piece in a circle on a large round tray. Then she would cover the portions with a big lid, put a grain of rice in front of each piece of fish or pork, and ask each child to choose one grain of rice. We had to accept, without complaining, whatever piece of fish or pork we chose.

When I was three, the adults in my family would impress their guests by asking me to "read" from a classic children's book. I opened the book to any page and recited a poem from memory (prompted by the drawing on that page), as I had listened to my elder sisters reading them. At age three and a half, I asked my parents, "Now that I am as tall as the feather duster and long as the longest pillow, can I go to school?" There were no nursery schools in Vietnam at that time, and public schools only accepted children at age six, so, when I turned four, my parents sent me to a private elementary school one kilometer from our home. One day, to look like the other pupils, who were older, I poured ink on my clothes, even though I knew Suong would punish me as soon as I got home.

The girl from Hue who lived with us was named Bê. Her family could not support her, and my parents accepted her into our family and treated her like their own child. Bê got new clothes at the New Year and pocket money just like the rest of us. One of Bê's tasks was to accompany me to school. She was a great companion for me, although I learned more quickly than she, and sometimes I even helped her with reading and writing. In fact, helping classmates became a specialty of mine. In elementary school, I tutored classmates in math and grammar, and, in return, received candies from them to eat during school breaks.

Each child in our family was given one dông each morning to buy a sweet potato for breakfast from one of the schoolyard vendors. The vendors also sold delicious, salty treats, but we never had enough money for them. For lunch, we had rice, soy sauce, and a hard-boiled egg. I saved my egg for the afternoon break, and I ate it very slowly, first the white and then the yolk, dipping each small bite into salt and pepper. It tasted wonderful! I was able to make one egg last the full fifteen-minute break. When the yolk appeared, it was like the sunrise, even more delicious than the white! Later, when I came to the West and saw how people here take eggs for granted, I taught a few friends this way of appreciating a boiled egg, and they called it "eggs à la Phuong."

When Bê turned eighteen, she fell in love with a young neighbor, and my parents gave her a wedding and jewels as if she were their own daughter. When my sisters Suong and Yen were young, they too had poor village girls as companions. Those girls, when they reached eighteen, returned to their families.

As the second-to-youngest child, I often felt lonely and neglected. People respect the eldest child and lavish the youngest with love, but they forget those in between. My youngest sister, Thanh, was extremely cute, and even I had to call her *cung,* "darling." She was always well-dressed, while I wore torn pants, gathered at the waist (I always lost the drawstrings) and rolled up several times. I wasn't at all coquettish or interested in being a "good girl," although when people gave Thanh sweets, I was always sweet enough to her to get her to share some with me.

As long as I can remember, I struggled against authority. Vietnamese culture is strongly influenced by Confucianism, and children are always supposed to obey their elders. But I would often argue with my older sisters. I remember telling my sister Tam over and over, "I don't care about your age or authority! I am right!" Tam would scream and finally hit me, but I would persist until I broke down in tears. To survive in a culture that rewards seniority over truth, I had to develop a kind of toughness. As a result, it has always been easy for me to empathize with those who appear rude or unkind. I know this is the result of their habit energy, and the best thing to offer is love and an open heart, encouraging the person to share his or her story of suffering. On the other hand, I regret that I am still sometimes too stubborn with friends, and, at times, make them suffer.

In the Vietnamese tradition, men are the breadwinners and women the homemakers. In our family of two boys and seven girls, only the boys had the right to receive a higher education. My eldest sister, Suong, was at the head of her class, and when she was not permitted to go on to high school, I knew even then what a shame that was. She could have gone far given the same chance as a boy.

I can see in my mind's eye as clearly as if it were yesterday waking up on New Year's morning when I was a child. I can still hear the early morning temple bells, the piercing cries of roosters, and the lazy bellowing of cows. The beginning of our lunar calendar was in February, and breathing the cool, fresh, morning air, we twenty-two children brushed our teeth and washed our faces on New Year's morning using the coconut shell dipper in the large water basin in front of Grandfather's house. The odors of the earth were still fresh and strong, and the *mai* trees shimmered with bright yellow blossoms. Two weeks before Têt, we had all helped Grandmother remove the leaves from the mai trees so they would all blossom on New Year's Day.

We children all wore our traditional dresses—the girls in beautiful *ao dai* and the boys in their royal blue robes—and we lined up behind Father and Mother in front of the ancestors' altar. Father would begin the ceremony by lighting a large stick of incense while Mother stood at his side, all of us enjoying the light from the huge, red candles reflecting on the copper incense burners. On the altar, our ancestors' photographs smiled back at us through the smoky incense, surrounded by offerings of fresh, huge watermelons, and small strips of red paper with the Chinese characters for "virtue" and "merit" calligraphed on them. The branch of mai flowers on the one side of the altar was balanced by the large plate of fruit on the other. In front, on a small table, were meals for the ancestors.

Before Têt, every family obtained from a calligrapher at the marketplace two sentences of their choice on two long strips of red paper in ancient characters, called *liên*, which they would hang vertically on each side of the main door of the house. The market would not be a real Têt market without calligraphers writing liên, or without mountains of watermelons and mai flowers. Even the poorest people had a watermelon and a branch of mai flowers on their ancestral altars.

Among the many celebrations during New Year's week, there was a ceremony of respectful greetings for the ancestors, who had returned to our house the day before. The god of the hearth, who had been watching the good and bad acts of our family for the past year, went up to the sky on the twenty-third day of the final month of the lunar year to report to the Jade Emperor, and when he returned on the last day of the year, he was greeted with an offering of sweet pudding and many kinds of candies.

During that week, we prepared for the ancestors' return by visiting their graves as a family. Father prepared the paint, shovels, hoes, and brooms, and Mother fixed a picnic lunch of sweet rice, sesame salt, pepper, and roasted chicken. When we got there, Father lit some incense and we children began to hoe around the gravesites. As we pulled the weeds, Mother trimmed the flower bushes, and we could all feel Tết in the air.

On the last day of the year, we shared a traditional meal of caramelized boiled eggs and pork, prawn paté, pork paté, dumplings, stuffed bitter melons, salted fish, pickles, bean sprouts, mustard greens, various salads, and rice cakes, and then we filled our containers with rice and large jugs with water, as signs of plenty to greet the New Year. Mother and my older sisters prepared special cakes—*banh ich* (cone-shaped cakes), *banh chung* (cakes symbolizing the Earth), and *banh têt* (New Year's cakes). My sisters soaked the rice overnight and then ground it to make paste, which they dried in the sun for three days. The result was a remarkably fragrant, sweet rice flour. They made banh ich by folding this flour around sweet bean paste, shaping it into a pyramid, and then wrapping it in banana leaves. Banh chung was made by soaking rice and beans in coconut milk for a whole day, then wrapping that in the greenest banana leaves and cooking it for eighteen hours. When we opened the leaves, we could see a thin, translucent green image of the leaf on the cake, perfumed with these precious gifts of the Earth.

As soon as we turned fifteen, we were permitted to join the adults staying up until midnight to celebrate *giao thua,* the transitional moment between the old and new years. Waiting for the Earthcakes to be cooked was part of the ritual. We sat around the glowing logs that supported the large pots filled with cakes, and listened with joy to the many stories about Tết, such as this one explaining the yellow banner that was flown in front of each house from a long bamboo pole:

At one time, the kingdom of Viet was disturbed regularly by the evil doings of Mara, the tempter. There was much struggle, and it seemed that nothing could stop this interminable conflict. Then one day, the suffering of the people touched the compassion of the

Growing up in Ben Tre.

Buddha, and he decided to speak with Mara directly to find a peaceful solution. "You can have our land," said the Buddha, "to do with as you wish. But can you leave one small spot where we can live in tranquility? This spot can have very clear boundaries, and as long as we stay within them, you will agree to leave us alone. In turn, we will not violate any of your new territory." "How much land do you want?" asked Mara. "Only a piece large enough to stretch my yellow robe over," said the Buddha.

Hearing so easy a proposition, Mara accepted and solemnly promised not to touch the spot of land covered by the Buddha's robe. But when the Buddha stretched out his robe, it extended miraculously far and covered all the land that was habitable and arable. The people's houses, farmland, and cattle were all under the protection of the yellow robe. Frightened by the Buddha's supernatural powers, Mara fled into the forest. The Buddha advised the Viet people to plant a tall bamboo in front of each house, and each year to hang from it a banner of yellow cloth to remind Mara that this is Buddha's land and Mara cannot enter.

This tradition was observed strictly as I was growing up. People always hung yellow banners from bamboo in front of their houses. In addition, to be sure to scare Mara and other evil spirits, people lit many firecrackers!

At midnight, everyone put on his or her best clothes and stood in the living room, silent and relaxed. The whistling of the wind, the barking of the dogs, the crackling of the fire, the laughing of people hurrying to the pagoda—these sounds were all received with full attention, since the first sounds you heard in the New Year were said to forecast the entire year for you. Although people did not still believe this, they nonetheless listened attentively to the first sounds of the year. Father was always the first to break the silence. He went to the altar of the Buddha, said a few words, and then we joined him in reciting prayers of peace. After that, we went to the pagoda to offer incense and gather flowers, buds, and branches to decorate our home. When we returned home, the person with the most fortuitous name was invited to enter first. The names *Phuc* (merit), *Duc* (virtue), *Lôc* (prosperity), *Tho* (longevity), and *May* (good luck) were always the most favored.

On New Year's morning, Father and Mother, our aunts and uncles, and we children presented our wishes to Grandmother and Grandfather. Then, the elders gave red envelopes with small amounts of money to the youngest children to begin the New Year. Red represented luck and happiness.

As I sit here today, looking back at the years of war, repression, human rights abuses, poverty, and desperation in my country, I can also picture Têt the way it was when I was a little girl. I hear the beautiful bells of the village pagoda, and I breathe in the fresh morning air and the pungent odors of the earth. Will you join me as I walk through Grandfather's front yard? Looking up, we see the bright yellow mai flowers in the morning sun; looking down, we notice the tiny blades of grass coming back to life; and we can imagine the land of Têt at peace.

CHAPTER TWO

Communism and Buddhism

Immediately following the Second World War, in August 1945, the Vietnamese army led by Ho Chi Minh seized control of Vietnam, declared independence, and formed a government. Their biggest mistake was to persecute and even murder hundreds of leaders—both those who had cooperated with the French colonial regime and those who had fought with them against the French but had not joined the Communist Party. As a result, many strong and good-hearted people formed a force against them called the "nationalists," who later were supported by the French. Because my father had worked as a house designer under the French regime, the new communist government arrested him in September 1945, together with all former employees of the French regime. At the same time, my eldest brother, Hung, joined the Viet Minh People's Army (the communists) and my mother was left to care for the family alone. In that same month, the British, under General Douglas Gracey, arrived in Vietnam, to disarm the Japanese on behalf of the Allies. Gracey helped several French army units land and hid them with his own British troops. He then gave the order to free all French prisoners in Saigon, and he armed them. In October, the French General Le Clerc arrived in Saigon with an army of 35,000 to recolonize Vietnam by force.

My family received an order from the People's Committee of the Communist Party to leave Ben Tre City, as the French were attempting to recapture it. My eldest sister, Suong, contacted those who had boats for rent and arranged for us to go from village to village with all our possessions, until we finally arrived at our grandparents' home in An Dinh. After being detained for three weeks, my father and seventeen other prisoners were freed by the communists. A hundred other prisoners, including the husband of my grade school teacher, were taken away and executed. My father was able to join us in An Dinh.

When the French troops returned, the communists withdrew to the jungles, and by 1946, Vietnam had two governments—the nationalists, supported by the French, and the communist guerrillas, who controlled the remote villages.

By 1947, the French army had come to An Dinh, and they controlled the village by day while the Viet Minh ruled at night. The French arrested and openly shot in the marketplace those they believed to be Viet Minh, while the Viet Minh kidnapped and murdered those they suspected of working with the French. My father had to live day and night hiding in his rice field or at one of his former tenant farmer's houses, in order not to offend either side. Having seen so many innocent friends killed by the communists, Father did not want to join the communists, but he did not want to cooperate with the French either, as they too were cruel and violent towards those they suspected to be communist.

In May 1948, a pro-French government was formed in Saigon, and our family returned to Ben Tre City for more safety. Our savings had run out, and my mother and sisters could no longer support us by sewing and baking. Shortly after our return to Ben Tre, Suong died from an appendicitis attack. I loved and admired her so, and it has always pained me that she died at such a young age.

My brother Hung left the Viet Minh in 1948, resumed his studies in Saigon, and eventually went to Paris and received a degree in engineering at the University of Paris. Nghiep, my second brother, also went to Saigon and later to the University of Paris to study engineering, but in his second year, he quit and became a nightclub singer. For most Vietnamese families, becoming a singer is considered a disgrace, and my father stopped supporting him. Still, my brother persisted, and finally our family had to accept his decision. He has turned out to be a very successful singer, and, like Father, an "oak tree," a strong support for the whole family.

It was said that if a girl was from a good family, honest and well-educated, she could marry well, and in those days in Vietnam, a girl needed to know French to be considered refined. As I was growing up, the tradition against girls receiving an education became less strong, and my father was able to send his five youngest daughters to private French high schools in Saigon. I attended the well-

known Marie Curie French High School and was among the top
students in my class.

My second eldest sister, Yen, had married and was already settled
in Saigon, and, in the same generous spirit my parents had shown
in welcoming twelve nieces and nephews, my sister invited me to
stay in her home. My parents gave her rice on my behalf, and they
gave me some pocket money, which I usually spent taking street
children to a nearby noodle restaurant. My father was proud of me,
and I tried my best to be worthy of his pride. When I was fifteen, I
tutored several wealthy children in mathematics and used the
money I was earning to give "scholarships" to needy high school
students. I never thought of using that money for myself; giving to
those who needed it came quite naturally to me from the seeds of
sharing that my parents and grandparents had sown in me.

During my last year of high school, I developed a fondness for my
philosophy professor, Madame Simon, who was a sincere Marxist.
Because of her, I had to consider whether Marxism might be the
way to overcome the suffering and injustice I saw everywhere. But I
saw so many North Vietnamese fleeing to the South, and I knew
that if they were abandoning their homes and belongings to escape
from communism, there must be something about it they feared or
hated. I also remembered my father's arrest when I was seven, and
all the killing. The French had arrested and shot those who resisted
them, and the communists were no better. How could the communists liquidate the 100 people who had been imprisoned with my father, including my teacher's husband, our neighbor, and a simple
clerk in the town hall? A policy that did not respect human life
planted grave doubts in me. I remember my parents saying to us,
"Do not buy prawns today. Yesterday the corpses of nationalist soldiers killed by the communists were floating in the river." My family knew that prawns fed on the swollen corpses. The dead always
seemed to be poor farmers who had been drafted into the army, or
simple employees of the local administration. It was obvious that
guns would not help the poor or liberate the country from oppression. It was clear that death and destruction were not solving anything. The men who killed the nationalist soldiers and the soldiers
themselves were all poor farmers, victims of society's ignorance and

injustice. I started to think deeply about justice and about Vietnamese society. I wanted to find a better way than violence to help
those who were oppressed.[*]

Like most Vietnamese, I was raised Buddhist. But growing up, I
never met a good Buddhist teacher. During the resistance against
the French, many bright Buddhist monks and nuns in South Vietnam were jailed or killed for supporting the resistance. The monks
at most temples in my home province, Ben Tre, were not deep practitioners. They just chanted at funerals and received donations—it
seemed to me they were more concerned about death than life.

In 1957, when I was nineteen, two excellent Buddhist monks
came to Ben Tre City. Both had studied at the An Quang Pagoda in
Saigon, and both gave beautiful, moving discourses. I was in Saigon
when they arrived, and I remember Father writing, "Your mother
and I received the Five Precepts from two wonderful monks, and I
want you and the rest of the family to receive the precepts from
them, too." Because I had met only "chanting priests," I resisted
and tried to ignore my father's wish. But I did agree to meet the
monks when I came back to Ben Tre in the summer.

When I met the elder of the two monks, I asked him a number of
questions, and his answers were vague and unsatisfying. Then he
told me, "Young lady, I am really quite busy. Can you discuss these
matters with Thây Thanh Tu?" Everyone had been praising this elder monk, but when I met Thây Thanh Tu, I found him to be much
more impressive. He answered all my questions thoroughly and in a
most gentle way.

After seeing Thây Thanh Tu several times, I asked if I could receive the Five Precepts, as my father had wished. To my surprise, he
said, "I don't think so. It would be better to wait. You are a strong
young woman, and when you do something, you do it completely. I
suggest you take the time to study and understand the precepts
more thoroughly before receiving them."

---

[*] Some years later, I read *Khu Rung Lau* (*The Forest of Reeds*), a novel by one of
Vietnam's greatest writers, Doan Quoc Sy, and I saw the great love and commitment of
my elder brothers' generation for our nation. Many young men had sacrificed their
youths fighting for Vietnam's independence, only to be pushed away or even killed
when they refused to join the Communist Party. The sadness in me deepened as I read
Doan Quoc Sy's experiences.

So during the next year, I studied about Buddhism and the precepts as much as I could. Sometimes I would drive two hours by motorbike to hear one lecture. Then, in December 1958, I formally received the Five Precepts from Thây Thanh Tu. Since the time of the Buddha, these vows have remained the most basic statement of Buddhist morality—not to kill, steal, commit adultery, lie, or take intoxicants. Thây Thanh Tu gave me the Buddhist name, *Diêu Không*, "Wonderful Emptiness." Vietnamese people praise the Bodhisattva Avalokitesvara as a wonderful cloud who protects people from the hot sun, and Thây Thanh Tu had wanted to give me the name *Diêu Vân*, "Wonderful Cloud," because of my love for the poor. But I had often asked him questions about the meaning of "emptiness," so he gave me the name "Wonderful Emptiness."

One time I told him, "Even though Catholics are in the minority in our country, they take care of orphans, the elderly, and the poor. The Buddha left his palace to find ways to relieve the suffering of people. Why don't Buddhists do anything for the poor and hungry?" Thây Thanh Tu answered, "Buddhism changes people's hearts so they can help each other in the deepest, most effective ways, even without charitable institutions." This sounded good, but I did not feel satisfied. "Thây," I said, "I want to go to the slums to provide food for the hungry and help young delinquents get into school." He listened but said nothing.

Then I told him that I wanted to become a Buddhist nun. He said, "I do not think that becoming a nun would suit you, because nuns have to follow the traditional discipline. You might rebel against it." He intimated that the atmosphere in some nunneries was not very inspiring. I asked if he would help me start a nunnery some day, where we could study and practice both Buddhism and social work. He smiled and nodded affirmatively.

But usually when I talked with him about social work, he expressed the folk belief that it was just "merit work" that could never lead to enlightenment. He said work like that was only a means to get reborn into a wealthy household. No notion could have been more alien to me. I didn't care at all about rebirth, especially into a wealthy family. There was so much to do right in the present moment. Thây Thanh Tu's eyes were filled with pity as he said, "You need to study scriptures more and work to become enlightened. Af-

ter you are enlightened, you will be able to save countless beings."
The more he said, the more uncomfortable I felt.

When I introduced Thây Thanh Tu to one friend of mine, she
agreed with him that my work for the poor was "like holding a knife
by the blade. Doing social work when you are not enlightened can
destroy you. You must wait until you are enlightened before you can
be of real help to the poor." Her argument was sincere and logical,
but deep inside I knew they were both wrong, at least in my case.
Since the age of fourteen, buying dinner for street children and
sharing my earnings with poor high school students had given me
more peace and joy than any efforts towards "enlightenment." My
friend's words reminded me of what so many young people in Marie
Curie High School had said: "I will join you in your work for the
poor when I graduate." But when they graduated, they had to get
college degrees, and higher degrees, and they never had the chance
to work for those in need. The enlightenment my friend described
was a kind of Ph.D. we could seek endlessly while refusing to help
those right in front of us.

So I continued to study Buddhism without any enlightenment. I
read beautiful texts, but I felt as though I were standing in front of
a steep mountain with no way of climbing up. The monks and nuns
told us to release our anger, for example, "because life is an illusion," but they never told us how to do it. For me, life was not an
illusion—the injustices and suffering of life in the slums were very
real, and I wanted to learn how to cope with these realities, not
deny them. Many years later, when I finally had a chance to study
Buddhism in depth, I learned that the Buddha did not teach that
life is an illusion in the way that those monks and nuns believed.
He taught that our perceptions about life are often inaccurate, because they are conditioned by incomplete or superficial knowledge
gained from our past experiences. The practice of meditation
teaches us to be humble about our perceptions and to look more
deeply into things in order to be closer to their reality. If we are too
sure of our perceptions, when things turn out to be different, we
will suffer, and a shock like that can cause us to say that life is illu-
sory.

Many nuns and monks told me that if I practiced diligently, I
could be reborn as a man in my next life. "Then, in another dozen

lives, if you continue to make effort, you can become a bodhisattva, and a long time later, a buddha." They explained to me that a buddha was not a god, that anyone could become enlightened. But their description of enlightenment as a state with miraculous powers sounded irrelevant to me and also discriminatory against women. I did not want to become a man, or even a buddha. I just wanted to help the children whose suffering was so real.

I asked Thây Thanh Tu if he agreed that it was impossible for women to become enlightened, and he smiled, trying not to hurt me. Later he told me that there were more problems in nunneries than in monasteries because women's karma is heavier than men's. For years I thought about that, and now I realize what he meant was that men's and women's psychologies are different. Women may raise difficult issues in an agitated way while men keep their problems to themselves. But we both have problems, and we both have to work steadily to transform our suffering. If this transformation was what the Buddhists meant by enlightenment, I could appreciate its practical value.

CHAPTER THREE

Science and Social Work

My father wanted me to become a pharmacist, because it was a prestigious occupation and a way to earn a good living honestly in our developing country. I did not want to study pharmacology, but as I wanted to please him, I proposed a compromise. I would not become a pharmacist, but I would study science and obtain a university degree. I only did this out of love for my father.

My boyfriend, Nguyen Kha, offered to study pharmacology and become a pharmacist in my place, but I thought that would make sense only if he also shared my interests in Buddhism and social work. He respected these pursuits of mine, but he never joined me in any social work projects or Buddhist discourses. Urged by requests to help those in the slums, I missed two consecutive appointments with Kha, and the following week he did not show up for our date. Slowly our love faded, and I knew it could not be rekindled. Deep inside, I knew I had to follow in the footsteps of the Buddha and leave my dear friend behind.

In September 1958, I enrolled in the Faculty of Science at the University of Saigon. In chemistry, we spent hours mixing chemicals and watching their reactions in beakers—which was not at all engaging for me. In math, we spent weeks learning differential equations and other things that seemed so remote. But in biology, we went into the forest to observe trees and plants, and we sailed to beautiful islands to learn about corals, rocks, fish, and other wonderful living things. So I decided to major in biology.

I did well on my exams and was invited to serve as lab assistant to Professor Pham Hoang Hô, whose specialty was marine algae. Professor Hô was a kind and excellent mentor, and to show my gratitude towards him, I agreed to do research on freshwater algae. Regularly, he would ask, "How is your work? Have you found some new algae?" and I would say, "Yes, I will show it to you tomorrow." Then in the evening, I would go to the lab, stay up late looking into the microscope, draw new algae, and comment on them. I did not have the heart to tell him how little I really cared about algae.

What really inspired me was working in the slums. I found a poor area of Saigon only five blocks from the university, in an abandoned French cemetery behind the Quoc Thanh Theater, and I went there four or five times a week. Each family there built a roof of scrap materials over a tomb, creating a wall-less hut about two meters square. Between the tomb-huts were muddy paths bubbling with microbes that bred tuberculosis. Every noon break, as soon as I finished my lab work, I would run to the slum, spend a few hours with my new friends, and then run back to school. Sometimes my younger sister Thanh would accompany me, and occasionally some other university friends joined as well. But most of the time I went alone. I never felt tired doing this work; it was a joy to be able to help. I continued my university studies only to please my parents and my professor.

My biggest question was always, "How can I bring happiness to these children?" I knew that if I went to the slums as a middle-class young woman, the people there would know I did not belong to their world, and they would not trust me. They might even try to con me. So, I always went wearing a frayed dress, pretending that I had a relative living there: "Do you know my Uncle Ba, the pedicab (bicycle rickshaw) driver?" Then I would sit and listen to people talk about their hardships and think of ways to help them.

Most of the parents in this slum were unemployed and often sick. Some of the women were pregnant by men who had abandoned them. One project I started was giving "rice scholarships" to orphans and children of single parents. Another was setting up a day-care center—I encouraged five young mothers to rotate their childcare so the other four could go to work. I later discovered that this is called "social work," but at the time, I did not know I was a social worker and no one in the slum had any such idea. To them, I was just a helpful student and the niece of a pedicab driver, and this was exactly what I wanted.

The adults played cards, and I suspected that when they got hungry, they would go out pickpocketing. When I asked them, "What kind of work do you do?" they would reply, "I have headaches all the time. I cannot work." When I asked, "How do you have money

Slum in Saigon's fourth district.

to feed your families?" they answered, "We borrow it at a high interest rate." When I asked, "Why don't your children go to school?" they responded, "They don't have birth certificates."

In Vietnam at that time, public schools were free, but in order to enroll, a child had to show his or her birth certificate. I researched how to obtain birth certificates and found out that if you did not apply for one at the time of your child's birth, you had to fill out an application and pay a penalty at the police station. The officer there would ask a number of questions, complete your file, and send it to the District Center, which in turn would send it to the Central Court. Six months later, you would be called into court, and you would have to bring two witnesses who could confirm that your child was born on the day you said. For the poor, this process was far too costly and cumbersome, and few slum residents even considered doing it. So I decided to intervene. A friend of mine invited a young judge to come to the slum and set up a court right there, and on the spot, the judge issued a birth certificate at no charge to anyone who came forward and had two witnesses to confirm the day his or her child was born. My friends and I had already filled in many of their applications in advance, and eventually, hundreds of children were able to go to school.*

But not all of the children in the Quoc Thanh slum received birth certificates, so I began teaching them myself under the shade of a tree. I knew that their parents depended on them to earn a little money selling newspapers or sweets, so I had to find a way for them to have "scholarships" to help out their parents. I began to think of ways to involve people outside the slums. I knew that the well-to-do had little occasion to think of the poor, so I began planting seeds of generosity in them by asking each to give one handful of rice per day for poor children. I started with my own extended family and my colleagues and friends in the university. I gave each of them a box, and said, "Think of me as a small bird. Every day when you cook rice, please take one handful and put it in this box for me, so that I can give it to the poor." In this way, friends and family contributed enough rice to feed many children and adults.

One friend commented, "You are talented in math and science. Why don't you work extra time as a math teacher and buy rice with

---

* The man who did this was among a few young judges of the nationalist government who worked to bring about radical reforms in our legal system. Later, in 1966, another friend of mine, Huynh Trung Chanh, who had graduated from Van Hanh Buddhist University and then law school, became a judge in Kien Giang Province and proved to be an inspiration for my whole generation. According to the law of that time, the police could not keep someone in custody for more than twenty-four hours without the permission of the local judge. But the corrupt Chief of Police in Kien Giang consistently ignored Judge Chanh. He would often arrest people simply because they refused to pay him a bribe, declare them to be communists, and torture them until they agreed to pay him money. Chanh was indignant in the face of this corruption and could not bear seeing the Chief arrest the poorest people for pickpocketing a few dông, while he freely "pickpocketed" millions of dông in bribes. Judge Chanh asked those who had been extorted by the Chief of Police to testify against him, but everyone refused, saying that the Chief was too powerful.

One day Judge Chanh invited the Police Chief to come in for a talk, put his hand on the Chief's shoulder and said, "I am sorry, sir, but I have received an order for your arrest from a very high authority, and I must obey." He instructed two armed guards to lock the Chief in jail. Then the Judge arranged with the Government Information Service of Kien Giang to have a car with a microphone and amplifier, and he announced the Chief's arrest to everyone in the city, inviting victims of his corruption to testify against him. Knowing that their oppressor was behind bars, many victims came forward. Chanh mobilized his staff to work day and night to record the complaints against the Chief. Meanwhile, the bodyguard of the Police Chief went to Saigon to report the news of the Chief's arrest to Nguyen Ngoc Loan, Head of the National Police. After three days of investigation, Loan discovered that the order had not come from the President or the Prime Minister, and he registered a formal complaint against this "unfair act" and issued a warrant for Judge Chanh's arrest. But Chanh already had sixty-six formal complaints with details of the Chief's corruption. When asked by the Minister of Justice who it was who had given him the order to arrest the Police Chief of Kien Giang, Chanh replied, "The spirit of justice that I was taught in law school and find in my own heart." The Chief was eventually convicted, and Chanh continued to arrest corrupt men in powerful positions, inspiring many young people. He also went to remote villages to set up court in order to issue birth certificates to peasant children.

the money you earn?" She didn't understand that for me the work of sowing seeds of generosity in the hearts of friends who rarely thought of the poor was more important. Gradually, with the support of many donors, my friends and I were able to collect 250 kilograms of rice each month to give to the parents of the slum children in exchange for permission to teach their children.

My heart would fill with happiness every time I came into the area and heard the children call to each other, "Big sister Tu (my nickname) has arrived. Let's go to class!" I would sing folk songs and tell the children stories about the Buddha, emphasizing that he was a person, not a god, and that everyone could become enlightened just like him. Slowly, the children came to love me as a big sister, and they began to believe in themselves. The classes were always joyful and engaging, and the children learned to read and write, and sing traditional Vietnamese songs.

One day I realized that I could help unemployed adults start their own small businesses, just as my mother had done years earlier. I knew that it would take some money to get started, and I also knew that if I asked relatives or other friends for help, they would refuse or give just once. So I asked many people to contribute a very small amount—one dông (about ten cents)—each month. They said, "It's so little," but I said, "Giving one dông regularly is a great gift." I approached a wealthy friend of my family's who was usually not generous, and she was pleased to give one dông a month. Then I asked her family members and even her servant to each give one dông a month, and they too were happy to practice generosity so inexpensively. I told them stories about the life in the slums, and they listened with tender hearts. I knew that I was sowing seeds of generosity in their minds and hearts that would one day bear fruit. Others, even children, joined me in the work of collecting funds to help the poor begin small businesses.

I knew that if I just gave the money to the people in the slums, they might squander it on rice wine or gambling, so I set up a system of loans. I went with each "new entrepreneur" to the market to find the equipment to get started, and then I loaned him or her the amount needed to purchase it. For example, I asked one man, "Would you like to sell ice cream?" The man, who usually gambled all day, said, "Ice cream? You need 500 dông ($50) to buy a metal box to carry the ice cream." I told him, "I don't have any money myself, but I can borrow it for you if you promise to pay me back one dông every day from your sales." Together, we went to the wholesale market and bought a big tin container. Every night when he came back from selling ice cream, he put one dông aside to pay me back. One woman obtained the equipment needed to become a street vendor of *banh cuon*, a light, rolled crêpe, and other foods. When I saw that someone was especially enterprising, I would offer a second loan to expand his or her business. In this way, I helped create many jobs. But I never gave anyone money without keeping some control. I knew I had to do that. Whenever someone repaid his debt, I used the money to help someone else start a business. At first, the people I set up in business considered me naive, but after a while they came to love and respect me. I treated each man and woman with both gentleness and firmness, and I finally succeeded in transforming many of them.

I also got involved in caring for the sick. When someone contracted tuberculosis, for example, I would drive him to the hospital on my motorbike. As a biology lab assistant, I had come to know many first-year medical students, so when we arrived at the hospital, I could always find, among the resident medical students, one friend who had agreed to take care of my friends from the slums free of charge.

But when these slum friends returned home, they would often become sick again. I began to realize that life in the slum was one of self-defeat, and I began to think of ways to help slum dwellers move to a healthier environment. At that time in Vietnam, people had the right to clear a plot of land in the rainforest and set up a farm. I thought that I might try to obtain some land for families living in urban slums and help them set up a new life. I knew I could not force anyone to come, but I decided to begin by inviting twenty families. I could raise the money to provide farming tools and a six months' supply of food for each family, and we would set up a small, model community that could inspire other poor people to do the same. But the reality of the war took me elsewhere, and this idea was not to be realized for many years.

CHAPTER FOUR

Meeting Thich Nhat Hanh

In October 1959, I met Thây Man Giac, a prominent Buddhist monk. When I asked him a question about Buddhism, he took out a book by Thây Nhat Hanh and said, "The answer to your question is in this book." I asked him another question, and he showed me another book by the same monk and said, "I am a great friend of his." I was less interested in reading works by some unknown author than I was in having real communication with the monk in front of me, so I persisted in asking questions, but he just continued giving me books. Finally, I told him I would read them when I had time. A month later, Thây Man Giac wrote suggesting that I meet another student from Ben Tre living in Saigon named Thu Ha. When I went to see her, she told me that Thây Nhat Hanh would be teaching a three-month course at the Xa Loi Temple in Saigon beginning in December.

The first lecture I heard by Thây Nhat Hanh impressed me deeply. I had never heard anyone speak so beautifully and profoundly. I used to write down Thây Thanh Tu's talks and give him the transcripts so he could publish them in one of the Buddhist magazines. After Thây Nhat Hanh's talk, I went home and wrote out my notes, thinking that I could offer to do the same for him. I did not realize that he was a writer; I just assumed the books Thây Man Giac had given me were transcriptions of lectures. Many monks published books and articles that way. The following week, I came to him and said, "Thây, I wrote down your last Dharma talk. It was so beautiful. If you like, I can give it to you to edit and use any way you'd like." He looked at me, nodded, and started to speak with the person next to him. He showed no interest at all, and I felt disappointed, so I stopped writing out my notes of his talks.

After his third Dharma talk, to my surprise, he approached me and asked, "Where are the notes you promised to give me?" I said,

"Are you interested? I will bring them next week." A week later, I gave them to him, still not realizing he was an accomplished writer. I attended the entire course, appreciating each Dharma talk more and more.

In February 1960, at the end of the course, I asked Thây Nhat Hanh if he would meet with five of my Catholic friends who regarded Buddhism as a kind of superstition. I wanted to offer them a taste of real Buddhism, and I was pleased that Thây agreed to see us after our March exams. But when I took my friends to the Xa Loi Temple, he was not there. Another monk who happened to be at the temple met with us instead, but I felt hurt that Thây Nhat Hanh had missed our appointment. In July, I saw him at the An Quang Pagoda, and I said, "Venerable Sir, you made an appointment with me in April, but you were not there." His eyes expressed surprise. He had obviously forgotten. Then he said, "Will you write to me? I live in Phuong Boi Monastery, deep in the rainforest. It is beautiful and very far away." He gave me his address, but my studies and my work in the slums took all of my time, and I didn't write.

In September, I received a short note from him: "Fall is coming and it's very cold. In our mountain monastery, we have started to chop wood. Cooking with wet wood is smoky, but it is so nice to cook in the fire's warmth while the cold wind sings outside." His handwriting was beautifully rare and impeccable, and I was moved by his simple words. I regretted that I hadn't written, so I wrote and told him about my work and my dream of social change in Vietnam. I also expressed concern that most Buddhists did not seem to care about poor people. I said that I did not believe that helping poor people was merely merit work. In fact, I did not feel that I needed any merit for my next life. I wanted to help free people from their suffering and be happy in the present moment.

Thây wrote back a kind letter, saying that he appreciated my work and that he would try to visit my project one day. He said that he was sure a person could be enlightened by whatever kind of work he or she liked the most. "We should not be dualistic," he wrote. "We should just be ourselves and live our lives in the most mindful and deepest way we can." Later, he told me a story about a monk who spent much of his time sewing. One day, he was enlightened while mending an old robe. He had been doing it mindfully, with all his heart. If I liked to help poor people, I could be enlightened by this work. I did not have to divide my time between merit work and enlightenment work. He said that I was not alone, that he had seen many efforts by Buddhists to help the sick and the poor in other parts of Vietnam.

Thây believed that Buddhism had much to contribute to real social change. He said he would find ways to support me in a movement for social change according to the Buddhist spirit. He would help bring together many good hearts who wanted to work together. He agreed to write articles about this in national magazines and then start several pioneering development villages to show that social change could be based on love, commitment, and responsibility. Eventually we could start a training center for workers in education, agriculture, and health care, who would then go all over the country. But first he had to finish some important research, and then, he said, he would help my friends and me with these social projects. From that day on, I knew he was the teacher I had been looking for.

In February 1961, Thây and the monks at Phuong Boi Monastery made Earthcakes, traditional New Year's sweet rice cakes in the form of the Earth, and sent them to twenty friends. The cake I received was beautifully wrapped in the traditional way and hand delivered by a young novice. I learned from this novice many details of Thây's life, how he struggled alone against the conservative hierarchy. Every time I read a letter from Thây or saw him, I was inspired. I learned from his other students how he had struggled to renew Buddhism in Vietnam. In time, I read all his books.

One day, I attended a public lecture by Thây Nhat Hanh at the An Quang Pagoda. I was wearing an old gray dress that was much too big for me, and afterwards Thây invited me to the reception room and asked, "Don't you have a better dress?" I was startled and started to cry. I thought he would understand that I wanted to dress like the poor people I worked with in order to be close to them, but Thây seemed to have another idea. Surprised and even a little embarrassed to see me cry, he sweetly explained, "A person's beauty must be seen from the outside as well as from the inside. You don't have to wear fancy or expensive dresses. Very simple ones are fine,

Thây Nhat Hanh in 1964.

but they should be decent and lovely. If you shaved your head, you would wear a beautiful nun's robe. But now your hair is long, and you should wear a simple, beautiful dress like other young people your age. It will encourage those who might like to join you in your work. One's mind, actions, and dress should all communicate one's quality of being. This is the correct way for a bodhisattva."

Inspired by the teaching and encouragement I had received from Thây Nhat Hanh, I attracted seventy friends to join me in my work caring for five slums around Saigon. Each team provided rice for a number of families, scholarships for the children, and, when necessary, transportation to the hospital. On special occasions, such as the Buddha's birthday or Christmas, we really tried to "spoil" the children. We took them to buy clothes, went to the zoo for a whole afternoon, and had dinner in a restaurant. The children thought they were in heaven. I was responsible for the Quoc Thanh slum. Thanh, my sister, was in charge of the Câu Bong slum, not far from

her house. From time to time, I would join her, as when an epi-
demic of dysentery broke out. Tra Mi and ten others took care of
the Hoa Hung slum, where conditions were less desperate. This
slum was near the Ong Ta market, and Tra Mi and her group were
able to find street vendor jobs for many poor families. Phung Thang
and her group cared for the Ban Co slum, and they set up a night
elementary school to educate boys who worked shining shoes during the day. I often gave the lessons in history, telling the boys and
girls about great men and women of Vietnam and encouraging
them to be like those people. In the Gia Dinh slum, people lived in
huts built on sticks constructed over a muddy swamp. We had to
park our motorbikes and walk over a wooden bridge to visit them.
The "toilets" of their houses were small square holes in the floor. At
high tide, the refuse was carried out to sea. Thanh and I took turns
visiting those who had tuberculosis, bringing them medicine, rice,
eggs, and vegetables.

We also had night classes for adults in reading, writing, and
math. One student named Dang, a police secret agent, slowly came
to respect and love me. He often told me secretive things that were
not at all important to me, but which were obviously a great risk for
him to tell. Twice he informed me that there would be a *coup d'état*
within a few days, and he warned me that I should not go out those
days. At first, I did not believe him, but a few days later, there was a
rumor in Saigon that there had been a failed coup, and I knew he
had been right. (To this day, I have no idea if there was any connection between the man "Dang" in the slums giving me information
about coups d'état and the agent at the National Police Center telling me five years later, "We know you have a secret name, 'Dang.'")

In February 1961, Thây Nhat Hanh invited Thây Quang Lien
and Thây Thien Chau to join him in giving a three-month course
on the basic teachings of Buddhism. Every Sunday morning, several
hundred people came to An Quang Pagoda for a lecture by one of
the monks, and in the afternoon, a small group invited by Thây
studied the sutras with him. The first sutra was *The Eight Realiza-
tions of the Great Beings*. In the class, we had real discussions, often
disagreeing with one another. When Thây was not there and one of
the other monks helped, we always felt frustrated because if our
views went in many directions, the monk would take us in yet an-

other direction. But when Thây was there to summarize the discussion, everyone was happy, because his view transcended all of ours and satisfied each of us. An atmosphere of sisterhood and brotherhood began to develop among Thây and the students in the afternoon class. Then, one Sunday in March, Thây was absent and one student told us that Thây had asked him to read us the short story, "The Pine Gate." He said that Thây had gone to Phuong Boi Monastery in the mountains for a rest. Three weeks later, Thây came back quite refreshed and told us that he would be moving to Xa Loi Temple.

In April, Thây Nhat Hanh began another weekly course on Buddhism for twenty of us university students. But within two weeks the authorities in Xa Loi Temple—old fashioned, lay Buddhists who could not understand this young monk who attracted so many students, including young ladies—managed to cancel the course, and Thây moved again, this time to Truc Lam Temple, a one-hour motorbike ride from Saigon, and he taught the course there.

Two years later, I learned that while Thây was in Dalat for a teaching tour, someone at An Quang Pagoda, out of jealousy, erased Thây's name from the records of the *livret de famille* of the temple. This was equivalent to expelling him from the temple "family." Thây had helped found the An Quang Pagoda in the early 1950s. He had been teaching there since 1954 and was the most popular teacher. When it became the Buddhist Institute, he was one of the first teachers. All the young monks were fond of him and wholeheartedly supported his efforts to renew the teachings and practice, but the more conservative elders were not supportive of his innovations, and Thây withdrew to Phuong Boi Monastery until his hurt was transformed. When the authorities of Xa Loi Temple did the same, it did not affect him so deeply, as the lay authorities of Xa Loi were not close friends and Xa Loi was not a temple he had helped build.

From May to September 1961, I went with a dozen friends every Saturday to study with Thây at Truc Lam Temple, and we stayed until late in the evening. Then we rode back to Saigon, singing together under the moonlight. These were wonderful days. We loved and respected each other dearly, like thirteen brothers and sisters.

Learning from Thây, we became the "thirteen cedars" of the Buddhist movement in South Vietnam.*

We thirteen cedars decided to apply our Buddhist understanding
by setting up a night school for poor workers, soldiers, and teenagers who had to work during the day. All were preparing for their
baccalaureate degree. Classes in physics, chemistry, biology, English, and French were held each night from six until eleven o'clock
at the Giac Ngô Temple. It was a great event for the thirteen of us
as we realized we were becoming a happy sangha, a community of
practice, helping others.

In September, Thây Nhat Hanh told us that he had accepted a
fellowship to study Comparative Religion at Princeton University.
He had heard that there were more than one hundred libraries in
the United States with great collections of religious books, including Buddhist texts in Chinese, Sanskrit, and Pali. We helped him
prepare his papers and other things, and he left for the U.S. for two
years. I continued my social work and my university studies.

---

* When Thây Nhat Hanh was a novice in the early 1940s, there had been efforts to
renew Buddhism in Central Vietnam. Thây wanted to continue this work by training a
number of young people to become "like strong cedars to help support the Buddha's
teachings." We thirteen were: Huynh Ba Hue Duong, Nguyen Thu Ha, Do Tuan
Khanh, Le Kim Chi, Truong Thi Nhien, Cao Ngoc Phuong, Cao Ngoc Thanh, Ton
That Chieu, Nguyen Ngoc Diep, Huynh Ba Duong, Nguyen Ngoc Bich, Dang Ngoc
Cuong, and Pham Ngoc Lien.

WORKING FOR SOCIAL CHANGE
1962-1965

CHAPTER FIVE

Nonviolent Resistance

In April 1963, an assistant to Madame Ngo Dinh Nhu, the sister-in-law of South Vietnam's President, contacted me about becoming the head of a branch of her Republican Women's Party, *Phu Nu Cong Hoa*. She wanted every woman in the country to join the party, but I refused, as I did not want to become involved in politics. My refusal was interpreted as the act of a communist, "for only a communist would refuse such a generous offer," and her assistant threatened that Madame Nhu might have me arrested. Working with the poor in the slums was also considered communist activity.

At that time, I was head of the social welfare branch of the Buddhist Student Union started by Thây Nhat Hanh in April 1960 at Xa Loi Temple, which was strengthened and legalized as a branch of the Buddhist congregation by Thây Thiên Minh and Quang Liên in October 1961. We held weekly meetings to study Buddhism, discuss the Dharma, plan projects for the poor, and publish a magazine, *Tin Tuong*, describing our work. The thirteen cedars became eighty, and then over 300 cedars in the Buddhist Student Union. To force me to stop my work in the slums would also mean stopping these 300 students from helping the poor. Friends throughout the country reported similar threats in their provinces—Phan Thiet, Quang Nam, Quang Tri, Quang Ngai, Kontum, Nha Trang, and Qui Nhon. Many had been urged to join the party of Madame Nhu or be converted to Catholicism. As a result, many good people joined the Communist Party, not by their own choice.

There were many other stories of the oppression of Buddhists by the Catholic regime. In Lavang Village in Quang Tri Province, the Buddhists worshipped the silhouette of a woman who had saved a little boy. The child had fallen into a well one night and was floating on the surface of the water when he was rescued barely in time. The boy reported that he had seen a woman who looked exactly like a painting of Avalokitesvara supporting him in the water. On

another occasion in the same province, one group of houses remained untouched during a huge storm that destroyed all the trees
and fields surrounding it. Many people reported seeing the mysteri-
ous woman walking in front of the houses during the storm. At the
beginning of this century, the people erected a small temple to wor-
ship Avalokitesvara, the bodhisattva whom they believed the mys-
terious woman to be. But when Ngo Dinh Diêm came to power, his
brother, Archbishop Ngo Dinh Thuc, ordered that a Catholic cathedral be built, and he declared that the woman had been Mary,
the Virgin Mother of Jesus, and not Avalokitesvara. Government
employees throughout the country were asked to contribute towards
the construction of the Lavang Cathedral.

But in April 1963, the most extreme anti-Buddhist proclamation
was issued by the Diêm regime. They declared that Wesak, the
Buddha's nativity, could no longer be celebrated as a national holiday in Vietnam, and that it was a crime to display the Buddhist
flag.[*] In twelve northern provinces of South Vietnam, Wesak was
the most important holy day. All fish and meat markets and non-
vegetarian restaurants were closed, and anyone could enter a Buddhist temple and receive a vegetarian meal. Buddhist flags were on
display everywhere, and processions of carts made of flowers carrying a statue of the baby Buddha could be seen throughout the cities, towns, and villages. In Hue, the Buddhist stronghold in Central
Vietnam, every household traditionally prepared an altar in the
front yard on the eve of Wesak to welcome the baby Buddha. Imagine what a shock it was for the people to learn that all of these practices were suddenly forbidden.

I later learned that Archbishop Ngo Dinh Thuc intended for all
of Vietnam to "progress" rapidly on the Catholic path, as had happened in one village where everyone was baptized on the same day.
The Archbishop had hoped to be named a cardinal and felt that if
too many Buddhist flags were displayed during Wesak, it would
hinder his chances. For us, the ban on displaying the Buddhist flag
was the last drop in a bucket already filled with the anger of oppression.

---

[*] The multicolored Buddhist flag was designed in 1885 by an American, Henry Steel
Olcott, at the International Buddhist Congress in Sri Lanka.

So, on the eve of Wesak, May 8, 1963, Buddhists in Hue hung their flags and conducted the Wesak ceremony as usual at Tu Dam Pagoda. Everyone in the city waited by their radios to hear the broadcast of the Dharma talk by Thây Tri Quang. But the talk, which had been recorded that morning, was not broadcast, because he spoke about the wish of the Buddhists not to have their flag banned. Thousands of young people came to the radio station, and the authorities ordered tanks to advance on them. Eight young people were crushed to death. On May 10, more than 10,000 people demonstrated, demanding freedom of religion, but President Diêm ignored them, and instead arrested and tortured many of the monks and students he considered to be the instigators.

After long deliberation, our Buddhist Student Union in Saigon joined with the leadership of the National Buddhist Congregation in its struggle for religious liberty, endorsing their open letter and petition to the government: *Oppression*

1. *The presidential decree banning the Buddhist flag must be rescinded.*
2. *Everyone must be granted the same freedoms as those guaranteed the Catholics under the French regime, including freedom to assemble. The National Buddhist Congregation must enjoy the same status as the Catholic Church and not be considered merely an association.*
3. *The arrests of Buddhists must stop.*
4. *Buddhists must be given the freedom to practice the Buddha's teachings.*
5. *The families of those who were crushed by the tanks must be compensated, and those who did the killing must be arrested and brought to trial.*

The High Patriarch of the National Buddhist Congregation, Thây Tinh Khiet, signed the petition and added these five principles:

1. *Buddhists have never aimed at overthrowing any regime. We only wish to change policies that discriminate against us.*
2. *Buddhists have no enemies. Our struggle is not against the Catholics but against discrimination. Buddhists never wish to fight another religion.*

3. The Buddhist struggle for a fair religious policy is part of the struggle for social justice in all of Vietnam.

4. Buddhists vow to follow a nonviolent path, practicing the teachings of the Awakened One during the struggle itself. Because of our commitment to nonviolence, we Buddhists are ready to sacrifice ourselves in the spirit of understanding and love. We want more than just a change of policy. We want the spirit of love and understanding to inspire and transform the hearts and minds of all people, including those in government.

5. Buddhists will not let any political force make use of our struggle.

On May 15, 1963, a Buddhist delegation submitted a forty-five page report of human rights violations to President Diêm, but again there was no response. On May 21, 1,000 monks and nuns gathered at An Quang Pagoda to pray for the young people who died in Hue. Moved by the presence of these peaceful monks and nuns, thousands of laypeople joined them. Police used tear gas, barbed wire, and physical force to break up this and other "demonstrations," and they took many monks and nuns away in large trucks. On May 25, an Interdenominational Committee for Protecting Buddhism,[*] founded in Xa Loi Temple, went to Diêm and asked him to address the demands previously submitted, but still there was no response, and the struggle continued, including demonstrations, collective fasts, noncooperation in the markets, and petitions. Monks and nuns wore their everyday brown or gray robes to these demonstrations, and then, at a pre-appointed time, donned their bright yellow, formal *sanghati* robes. The foreign press was informed of the time to come to photograph these powerful, silent marches for human rights. There was great harmony among the leaders of this committee, led by eloquent and skillful monks from all over Vietnam.[†] Thây Thien Minh was extremely gifted in chairing the meetings and in negotiating with the government.

We students used our underground press to explain to our countrymen and to the world why the Buddhists were demonstrating.

---

[*] *Uy Ban Lien Phai Bao Ve Phat Giao*

[†] Thây Tri Quang and Thây Thien Minh were originally from Central Vietnam; Thây Tâm Châu, Thây Quang Do, Thây Tam Giac, and Thây Duc Nhuan were orginally from the North; and Thây Thiên Hoa, Thây Thiên Hòa, and Thây Hanh Tru were from the South. Thây Tâm Châu was chairman of this committee.

Monks demonstrating.

Censorship in South Vietnam was so severe at this time that residents of Saigon were not informed about the killing of the eight young people in Hue. We printed the news of the Hue demonstrations, including the transcriptions of the BBC and Voice of America reports confirming many human rights violations by the Diêm regime.[*]

In a short time, several hundred students from the Buddhist Student Union in Saigon plus hundreds of other friends joined together to become a group of nearly 1,000 that was challenging the authorities. Huynh Ba Hue Duong was the "brains" behind our publications' distribution network. One group established connections with the public high schools in Saigon, Cho Lon, Gia Dinh, and several nearby provinces. Another group was given responsibility to distribute books to the private high schools, and another to the Buddhist merchants in the dozens of markets of Saigon, Cho Lon, and Gia Dinh. As soon as a new book or pamphlet was printed,

---

[*] We knew that the main support for a nonviolent struggle would be world opinion, so we did our best to bring these issues to the attention of the foreign press. Thây Quang Do spoke French, English, Chinese, Japanese, Laotian, Cambodian, and Thai, and when he addressed the various embassies and reporters, he spoke to them in their own languages.

each unit of our network went to work distributing it to balance the distorted news disseminated by the government. The regime called our work "communist," and we risked arrest and torture.[*]

Our work in the slums helped us. Whenever we were followed by a government agent, we darted into a slum, and it was impossible for the agent to track us down. In prison, police agents were known to torture people until they "admitted" that they were communist infiltrators trying to stir up trouble among the Buddhists. Hue Duong was arrested, beaten, and forced to "admit" that he was communist. Then he had to witness his close partner in the underground work receiving vaginal electric shocks. She fainted several times but persisted in claiming her innocence. Some coworkers were even tortured to death, but the numbers of those supporting our work continued to increase.

On June 11, 1963, Thây Quang Duc immolated himself to call for religious freedom. No one had informed me that he was going to do this, but just at the moment he set himself on fire, I happened to be driving by the corner of Phan Dinh Phung and Le Van Duyet Streets on my motorbike, and I witnessed him sitting bravely and peacefully, enveloped in flames. He was completely still, while those of us around him were crying and prostrating ourselves on the sidewalk. At that moment, a deep vow sprang forth in me: I too would do something for the respect of human rights in as beautiful and gentle a way as Thây Quang Duc.

After the sacrifice of Thây Quang Duc, the inspiration was so great in the country that we could not count all the demonstrations and acts of resistance taking place in every town and province. The press could only report on what was happening in Saigon and Hue. At 2:00 a.m. on June 16, the day of Thây Quang Duc's funeral, the government and the Buddhists reached a five-point peace agreement. The news was broadcast on the radio, but because the atmosphere of the country was so tense, most people did not believe it, and thousands came anyway to demonstrate at Thây Quang Duc's funeral. Thây Tam Giac, a martial arts teacher who had thousands of students in Saigon, stood on the hood of a car announcing through a megaphone that the agreement was true. His car had to

---

[*] The printing was usually at Xa Loi Temple, by Thây Quang Do and Thây Chau Toan.

travel across one-third of the city before the atmosphere was defused. The government postponed the funeral for four days in the hope that the people would calm down. On June 20, after six hours of cremation, all of Thây Quang Duc's body had become ash, except his heart, which was still dark reddish-brown and intact. After a second cremation, at 40,000° C, his heart remained exactly the same shape, although an even darker color.

The office of Ngo Dinh Nhu issued a secret communiqué asking its employees to remain on alert for a new offensive order. When a copy of that communiqué was obtained by the Buddhist leaders, they brought it back to the government and demanded the government honor its peace agreement. On the same day, the government attempted to set up its own Buddhist Congregation by gathering a number of "chanting priests." These priests sent a cable to the World Fellowship of Buddhists (WFB) meeting in Sri Lanka, informing them that the Buddhists in Vietnam were acting improperly and could damage the prestige of the WFB. But the Buddhists in Sri Lanka sent a telegram back supporting the Buddhists' struggle in Vietnam. Then Ngo Dinh Nhu ordered a group of war veterans to demonstrate against the Buddhists, but the veterans instead demonstrated against the regime. Even the military officers in the army of the Republic of Vietnam were pressuring their superiors, saying that they could not fight the communists if the government continued to suppress the religion of their ancestors. Many superiors in the army tried to persuade Diêm to change his policy, to no avail. So a few generals in the South Vietnamese army tried to seek American support to overthrow Diêm, as the communists had the support of the Soviet Union and China. But President Kennedy was not ready to support the generals.

The number of Buddhists who sacrificed themselves increased. Thây Nguyen Huong immolated himself in Phan Thiet on August 4, 1963; the nun Dieu Quang in Nha Trang on the same day; Thây Thanh Tue in Hue on August 13. I know that in the West it is hard to understand why Vietnamese burned themselves. It looked like a violent act. Please try to be in the heart and mind of the person performing such an act of great love and sacrifice. To move the hearts of the hardest men and women, you have to give a gift of great value—even your own life. These people did not die when their bodies turned to ash. When I looked deeply at Thây Quang Duc's sacrifice, I could see his love and deep commitment to human rights born again in me and in thousands of Vietnamese and others all over the world. We received the fire of love and commitment to act from his great sacrifice.

In the early morning hours of August 20, 1963, the army's special forces raided the most important strongholds of the Buddhist movement throughout the country and arrested more than 2,000 monks and nuns in their temples along with active Buddhist laypeople in their homes, including many of my friends. The police in Saigon ransacked Xa Loi Temple, An Quang Pagoda, and several other temples. One monk at Xa Loi, whom they thought was Thây Giac Duc, one of the most eloquent speakers for the Buddhist demonstrations, was beaten to death right on the spot.

That night, twelve policemen circled the house of my elder sister, Nga, where I had been living since 1962. Two climbed on the roof, two stood at the back doors, and two came inside, asking to see the livret de famille. One of them said, "We are here to arrest one communist troublemaker, Mister Cao Ngoc Phuong." My brother-in-law said, "There is no communist troublemaker here and no Mister Cao Ngoc Phuong. There is Miss Cao Ngoc Phuong, my sweet, gentle sister-in-law, who teaches at the Saigon Faculty of Science. Our family is highly respected. I am Nguyen Trung Ngon, the Chief Engineer supervising the Civil Aeronautics Department of the government, and my brother Nguyen Trung Truong, works in the Ministry of Interior as Chief of all the police inspectors of Saigon Cholon stations." The two policemen looked at each other and whispered, "Our Chief!" and they apologized. As my brother walked them to the gate, he saw two men jump from the roof and eight more come from different corners of the house.

Later that day, government agents told my friends that it was I who had denounced them as communist and caused their arrests. Imagine how angry and filled with despair they must have been, being imprisoned and feeling betrayed by their trusted friend Cao Ngoc Phuong. Of course, it was a common technique of the government to use the fact that I was free to divide us and inflict suffering on us. Later, when several friends were released thanks to a bribe to the police, I noticed that they tried to avoid me. Only after the fall of Diêm did I learn of this terrible deceit by the government. One of my closest friends reported to Thây Nhat Hanh that she believed that I was innocent, but she thought that perhaps my sister or brother-in-law had betrayed my friends. This shocked and hurt me greatly. I was quite mindful of my acts and my family members' acts, and if anyone in my family had some sign of fear of being in trouble with the government, I would have known. Everyone in my family wholeheartedly supported my struggle.

Learning of the arrest of so many monks, nuns, and Buddhist friends, I wanted to scream and go to jail, or burn myself in despair. Thây Nhat Hanh was far away, and all my respected teachers and friends were in prison. Tears flooded my eyes as I wandered the streets on my motorbike. Late in the afternoon, I entered my laboratory, saw Professor Hoang Hô, and told him I wanted to tear up my biology thesis and burn myself. Tears streamed down my cheeks, as I asked him, "Why did they imprison so many monks, nuns, and Buddhist friends who worked only for the freedom to practice their beliefs?" He listened carefully, unaware that so many violations of human rights were being perpetrated throughout the country. As a scientist, he was interested in trees, plants, and algae, but he also was interested in truth, and he drafted a petition asking the government to stop all human rights violations. We collected signatures from seventy-nine university professors, all of whom knew that they risked arrest by signing. On August 21, we presented the petition to President Diêm and also to the press. That same day, Vu Van Mau, the Minister of Foreign Affairs, angrily left a cabinet meeting when Ngo Dinh Nhu reported the arrest of "all the communist Buddhists," and three days later, he shaved his head in protest.

Because so many monks and nuns were in jail, university and high school students took charge of the resistance movement, founding the Committee to Work for the Respect of Human Rights in Vietnam. On August 25, when hundreds of high school students gathered at Dien Hong marketplace to demonstrate, the police fired on them and killed one sixteen-year-old girl, Quach Thi Trang. Fear and despair set in, as the people continued to feel suppressed.

On September 9, 1963, thousands more students went into the streets, protesting fearlessly against the Diêm regime in response to the news that Mai Tuyet An, an eighteen-year-old girl, had tried to cut off her left hand on the stairs of Xa Loi Temple to offer to Diêm. She was a tiny, sweet person in the Buddhist youth movement. Her right arm was too weak to manage the large axe she used to chop off her hand, and she bled profusely and then fainted. Her letter to the President, in which she said that her hand was a gift she wanted to offer him to request his understanding of the people's wishes, moved people very much. Mai Tuyet An's act was the utmost sacrifice to wake people up from their ignorance.[*]

After the sacrifice of Mai Tuyet An, Professor Hô looked at me deeply and said, "Would you like to leave the country? You could go to the University of Paris to finish your thesis and present it to the Faculty of Science there. I can introduce you to Professor Bourrelly, a specialist in freshwater algae, and Professor Feldmann, my own teacher, and they can help you complete your work." I thanked him for his kindness and promised I would respond right away. A few hours later, an idea came to me. I would go to Paris and hold a press conference. Like Vu Van Mau, I could shave my head, and then I would offer my long, dark hair to President Diêm in return for his understanding. I could tell the international press about all the cruelties of the Diêm regime. I knew that the authorities intended to arrest everyone in the Buddhist movement, and if I left the country, I could tell people overseas about the extent of the human rights violations at home. When my mother heard my plan to shave my head, she offered to knit me a wool hat to keep me warm through the Paris winter. Because I was an employee of the government, as a lab assistant at Saigon University, I was able to obtain a visa rather easily through diplomatic channels, and I left for France on October 23, 1963.

During all of this time, Thây Nhat Hanh was in New York City, teaching at Columbia University. He translated into English the reports of human rights violations he was receiving from Vietnam and made a document that he presented to the United Nations. On the day of the General Assembly debate on human rights in Vietnam, Thây fasted and prayed for understanding in a temple in New

---

[*] In June 1993, Mai Tuyet An performed another courageous act. She wrote a letter to the communist authorities requesting that they respect the human rights of the people and the right to practice religion freely.

York. The UN agreed to send a delegation to Vietnam to investigate the allegations.

On November 1, a few days before my planned press conference, the Diêm regime fell. Ngo Dinh Diêm and his brother were killed by an angry military officer. I went to a Catholic church in Paris to participate in a service for them organized by their supporters. I had no hatred for these men, even though they had caused so much suffering. I knew they were victims of their own wrong concepts about the reality of Vietnam, and I only wished that from then on, the sacrifices of the nonviolent Buddhists in Vietnam would illuminate the way for those governing the country. The saga of the Diêm brothers is now past, but it remains a vivid lesson, especially for those who have responsibility for millions of lives. We always have to examine our ideas and concepts closely and revise them regularly to stay close to reality. We must never be too certain of our knowledge; we must be humble and open to learning something new every day of our lives.

Later, the *Pentagon Papers* revealed that Washington had given the order to overthrow Diêm. In fact, the nationalist officers who loved their country and had been afraid that the communists would take over if the governing group were too unpopular, needed the support of Washington to balance the Chinese and Soviet blocs' backing of Hanoi. But to claim that it was the U.S. that overthrew the Diêm regime would be simplistic. Ngo Dinh Diêm and his family overthrew themselves with their narrow minds, their lack of understanding, and their inability to listen to the wishes of the nation.

Knowing that the Diêm regime had collapsed, I did not shave my head or hold a press conference. Instead I began to concentrate on my thesis. Then one night I received a telephone call from Thây Nhat Hanh. I had sent him a letter the first day I arrived in Paris, telling him everything that was happening in Vietnam—things I had not been able to tell him while I was still in the country, as all letters were being censored and the security of our friends and families was at risk. I had told him about the press conference I had planned, and the first thing he asked me on the phone was, "Have you shaved your head?" When I said, "No," he seemed pleased. He persuaded me to come to New York, even if just for a week, saying that he needed my advice about whether to return to Vietnam. The

Dean of Columbia University had told Thây that it was not safe for
intellectuals like him to return to Vietnam, and he had invited
Thây to stay and establish a Department of Vietnamese Studies.
Thây did not say this, but I could "hear" the words, "If I stay in New
York, I will not have to struggle with those conservative monks who
give me so much trouble in my efforts to renew Buddhism!" I was a
kind of representative of the younger generation who believed in
him and supported his work, so I promised to come to New York for
two weeks to discuss plans to renew Buddhism and bring about social change in Vietnam. We were both happy with the prospect of
seeing each other again.

   When I arrived in New York, I somehow assumed I would be eating the same mashed potatoes I had found in all French university
cafeterias, and I was quite surprised to see an excellent meal of tofu
and mushrooms prepared by Thây. During my time in New York,
Thây taught me how to cook many vegetarian dishes. Thây, his
housemate Steve, a graduate student at Columbia, and I stayed up
late every night, mostly sitting in silent peace and joy. Sometimes
we sang French or English songs together. During these two weeks
Thây wrote a poem entitled "Butterflies Over the Golden Mustard
Fields" and gave it to me:

> For ten years
> we had a beautiful green garden.
> For twenty years
> the sun always shone on our thatched roofs.
> My mother came out and called me home.
> I came to the front yard
> near the kitchen
> to wash my feet
> and warm my hands over the rosy hearth,
> waiting for our evening meal
> as the curtain of night
> fell slowly on our village.
>
> I will never grow up
> no matter how long I live.
> Just yesterday, I saw a band
> of golden butterflies fluttering above our garden.

The mustard greens were bursting with bright
yellow flowers.

Mother and sister, you are always with me.
The gentle afternoon breeze is your breathing.
I am not dreaming of some distant future.
I just touch the wind and hear your sweet song.
It seems like only yesterday that you told me,
"If one day, you find everything destroyed,
then look for me in the depths of your heart."

I am back. Someone is singing.
My hand touches the old gate,
and I ask, "What can I do to help?"
The wind replies,
"Smile. Life is a miracle.
Be a flower.
Happiness is not built of bricks and stones."

I understand. We don't want to cause each
other pain.
I search for you day and night.
The trees grope for one another in the stormy
night.
The lightning flash reassures them
they are close to one another.

My brother, be a flower standing along the wall.
Be a part of this wondrous being.
I am with you. Please stay.
Our homeland is always within us.
Just as when we were children,
we can still sing together.

This morning, I wake up and discover
that I've been using the sutras as my pillow.
I hear the excited buzzing of the diligent bees
preparing to rebuild the universe.

Dear ones, the work of rebuilding
may take thousands of lifetimes,
but it has also already been completed
just that long ago.
The wheel is turning,
carrying us along.
Hold my hand, brother, and you will see clearly
that we have been together
for thousands of lifetimes.

My mother's hair is fresh and long.
It touches her heels.
The dress my sister hangs out to dry
is still sailing in the wind
over our green yard.

It was an autumn morning
with a light breeze.
I am really standing in our backyard—
the guava trees, the fragrance of ripe mangoes,
the red maple leaves scurrying about
like little children at our feet.

A song drifts from across the river.
Bales of silky, golden hay
traverse the bamboo bridge.
Such fragrance!

As the moon rises above
the bamboo thicket,
we play together
near the front gate.
I am not dreaming.
This is a real day, a beautiful one.
Do we want to return to the past
and play hide-and-seek?
We are here today,
and we will be here tomorrow.

This is true.
Come, you are thirsty.
We can walk together
to the spring of fresh water.

Someone says that God has consented
for mankind to stand up and help Him.
We have walked hand in hand
since time immemorial.
If you have suffered, it is only
because you have forgotten
you are a leaf, a flower.

The chrysanthemum is smiling at you.
Don't dip your hands into cement and sand.
The stars never build prisons for themselves.

Let us sing with the flower and the morning
birds.
Let us be fully present.
I know you are here because I can look into
your eyes.
Your hands are as beautiful as chrysanthemums.
Do not let them be transformed
into gears, hooks, and ropes.

Why speak of the need to love one another?
Just be yourself.
You don't need to become anything else.

Let me add one testimony of my own.
Please listen as if I were
a bubbling spring.

And bring mother. I want to see her.
I shall sing for you, my dear sister,
and your hair will grow as long as mother's.

The day after I arrived, Thây Nhat Hanh received a cable from
Thây Tri Quang, the monk who had started the struggle in Hue
against the Catholic regime, inviting him to come back to Vietnam
to help reorganize Buddhism. In the past, Thây Nhat Hanh had not
received any support from the Buddhist hierarchy in his attempts to
renew Buddhism, especially from Thây Tri Quang. A few days later,
another letter from Thây Tri Quang arrived, saying, "I am too old
now and too old-fashioned to take care of this big responsibility.
Please come back and help." I remember seeing Thây Nhat Hanh,
thoughtful and moved, holding the letter in his hand for a long
time. Later he told me about how wonderful impermanence is, because in the past, Thây Tri Quang was one of the pillars of the con-
servatism he had struggled against. Now, with the support and
understanding of Thây Tri Quang, he might be able to realize the
work he loved so much. I was excited to do the work, too. We
agreed that when Thây returned to Vietnam, I would join him as
soon as possible, but for now, I would go back to Paris to complete
my thesis.

Thây Nhat Hanh cabled Thây Tri Quang agreeing to return to
Vietnam. On his way, he stopped in Paris for a week to visit me and
a number of Buddhist friends. He arrived with a student of his, who
would later be ordained as the nun Thich Nu Tri Hai, and he gave
a public lecture in Paris. On December 16, 1963, he flew to Vietnam.

CHAPTER SIX

Autumn Moon

In January 1964, Thây Nhat Hanh submitted a Three-Point Proposal to the Executive Council of the Unified Buddhist Church (UBC) in Vietnam:

1. The Church should publicly call for cessation of hostilities in Vietnam.

Thây believed that if the Buddhist Church would call for peace immediately, both warring parties would listen, as the prestige of the newly formed UBC was high following the fall of the Diêm regime.

2. The Church should help build an Institute for the Study and Practice of Buddhism to train the country's leaders to practice the tolerant, open-minded spirit taught by the Buddha and sorely needed by the nation.

Thây wished to establish a kind of university to train leaders in the practice of "engaged Buddhism." His vision was based on the experiences of one of the wisest and most peaceful periods in Vietnamese history—the eleventh to fourteenth centuries, a period of peace, stability, tolerance, and a high level of civilization—when everyone in the royal family and their staffs studied Buddhism, Confucianism, and Taoism at Quoc Tu Giam School and served the people well. When there were invasions by China or squabbles with neighbors, the country's leadership directed the nation to be strong and firm when needed and generous peacemakers after the victory. Thây told the UBC that we needed a university not unduly influenced by French or American education, one that would not just produce scholars but would train the leaders of the country how to listen to people and care for their needs without being corrupted by wealth or fame.

3. The Church should develop a center for training social workers to help bring about nonviolent social change based on the Buddha's teachings.

Thây's idea was to go beyond such traditional notions of charity
as giving food, medicine, and money to the poor, by supporting the
peasants in their efforts to improve the quality of their lives. He
wanted to teach social work and rural development as the work of
personal and social transformation. Workers would not consider
themselves "helpers" nor the peasants as "people being helped."
They would cultivate the understanding that they and the poor
peasants were partners in a common task.

The Church elders offered support only for the Buddhist Institute. Calling Thây "an unrealistic poet," they said that without outside financial support, his programs for social change could not be
realized, and that such support would not be forthcoming as long as
Vietnam was caught in a war between the free world and communism. They added that the Buddhists in Sri Lanka, Thailand, and
Burma were too poor to help, and they could imagine no way that
work for peace and social change could succeed on such a large
scale without adequate funding.

Thây responded, "The Buddha taught us to be lamps unto ourselves. We don't need Sri Lankan, Thai, or Burmese money, or the
support of communists or anti-communists. We only need to stand
up and be lamps unto ourselves." But the elders could not understand. I believe that if Thây's proposals had received the UBC's support at that time, we Vietnamese might have been able to solve
many of our problems without such an escalation of the war, and
our country would have suffered much less. In early 1964, the
people's admiration of the Buddhist leadership was high, and the
number of people willing to volunteer or give financial support to
such projects was great. Hundreds of workers in the social welfare
branch of the UBC would have been ready to join such a campaign
for social change. The nationalists were still relatively strong and
had not yet invited so many foreign troops into Vietnam. If peace
negotiations could have started at that time, the Accords would
have been more balanced between North and South, and the North
would not have been able to swallow the South the way it did
eleven years later. Throughout Vietnamese history, every time there
has been a fight between two factions of our people, the one that
received the support of foreign troops has lost. We use expressions
like *cong ran can ga nha* ("carrying snakes to bite our own chick-

ens") or *ruoc voi day ma to* ("inviting elephants to crush our ancestral tombs").

The situation of my brother-in-law, Bui Thanh Thuy, demonstrates the confusion and division that existed in our society at that time. He was an army captain and the chief of the Gia Rai District administration in 1964, greatly admired by the local people. Every time the guerrillas came back from the jungle, their whereabouts were reported to him by local peasants, and he could keep the peace. But after the U.S. troops arrived, he began to receive less and less information, until, in 1966, he was killed in an attack. The peasants apparently lost trust in him when they saw him working with the American soldiers.

Thây's idealism did appeal to university students, and many volunteered to help with all three of his projects. Thây set up an Institute of Higher Buddhist Studies, and he invited many great Vietnamese scholars to teach. He asked the Venerable Thây Tri Thu to be President, Trinh Sam to be General Secretary, and his disciple, Thây Thanh Van, to be head of the office. Students volunteered by the dozens because of the wonderful presence of Thây Nhat Hanh, Trinh Sam, and Thây Thanh Van. With Thây's help, Trinh Sam and Thây Thanh Van prepared the curriculum for a variety of programs leading to bachelor's, master's, and Ph.D. degrees in Buddhist Studies.

The Institute opened in February 1964, and in May, Thây Nhat Hanh invited Thây Minh Chau to be Vice President, Thây Thien An to be Dean of Arts and Human Sciences, and Thây Man Giac to be Dean of Buddhist Studies, and he asked the three of them, who returned from India and Japan when the Institute of Higher Buddhist Studies was already functioning well, to be on the faculty. Young volunteers staffed the office, and the program was fully underway in just fourteen months. The Institute was then renamed The Van Hanh University.

In September 1965, the School of Youth for Social Service was founded as a program of Van Hanh University, although the groundwork for the SYSS began the week Thây returned to Saigon. In February 1964, he set up one pioneeer development village in Cau Kinh, on the outskirts of Saigon. I was still in France, and he wrote to me, "Please come back right away. If you want to work for social change in the ways we spoke about, this is the time. Many people want to help, but you are the one person who can organize this program and make it work."

My thesis, "Freshwater Algae of Vietnam," was submitted to the University of Paris and accepted with honors on June 16, 1964. I was offered a job in the Museum of Natural History in Paris and a scholarship to continue my research, but I could think of nothing except going home to help Thây establish a school for training Buddhist social workers. I returned to Vietnam on June 18. When I arrived, the first "pioneer village" had been underway for four months. It was partially staffed, and the work of meeting the villagers and eliciting their trust was already well under way. To inspire me, Thây had exaggerated and said that I was the only person who could organize the social work, but Thây Dông Bôn and other friends had already done a beautiful job getting things started. Together with the villagers, they had built a three-room schoolhouse, and were using one of the rooms as a medical center. I invited friends to contribute tables and benches for the classroom, and I organized a group of teachers. I also found several young physicians to gather supplies for the medical center.

In addition to helping in Cau Kinh Village, I was asked by Thây to start a second pioneer village, and, with the help of a friend, I chose to do it in Thao Diên. To reach Thao Diên, we had to walk and ride eight kilometers along muddy dikes and on the paths between rice paddies. When we got there, the mud was always caked to our feet and our bicycles. Altogether, we were about thirty persons working in the two villages, including Thây Dông Bôn and many of the friends who had worked in the slums of Saigon. Although the villages were just a few kilometers from Saigon, life there seemed centuries behind. Every week people died from preventable diseases. There were no toilets, no knowledge of science or hygiene, and the defecation of the sick quickly spread bacteria to others. Our goal was to train young people to help peasants establish schools and medical centers, improve sanitation, and develop agriculture and horticulture. Because I had already resumed lecturing in Saigon University, many professional people—medical doctors, agricultural engineers, and others—could identify with this work and they were inspired to join us. Although we were intellectuals, in the countryside we dressed and behaved exactly like the peasants.

In July, one month after my return, we organized a meeting with the peasants of Thao Diên Village to encourage them to set up a school. We had met already with the official in Saigon responsible for that district, and he had told us that it would not be possible for the government to build a schoolhouse for just seventy-seven children; the minimum number needed to receive government funding was 200. So we held a meeting with the villagers and began by saying, "You cannot read or write. Your children are also illiterate, and now your grandchildren have no school. We must do something about it. The government will not build you a school, so let us build one together." To our great happiness, they agreed. One old man donated 2,000 palm leaves for the roof, another gave some bamboo thicket, and many others offered their labor. In a few weeks, we completed the first school in Thao Diên Village! In other villages, the government had to hire guards to protect the schools from vandalism, but in Cau Kinh and Thao Diên, where the villagers built their own schools, the villagers themselves took great pride in caring for the school and protecting it. This work was so much easier than in the Quoc Thanh slum. People here were so cooperative, I was truly inspired. Real change seemed to be coming!

We did our best to improve the quality of health care. Most villagers thought that when a child had a high fever, it was because evil spirits wanted to take the child away. We did not challenge that belief; in fact we joined in prayers to the spirits not to take the child. But we also persuaded the villagers to give the child medicine. When a number of children felt better after taking medicine, the people came to accept our suggestions. Our team members were humble, always acting like sons and daughters of the village, so when we helped the villagers overcome serious diseases, it was especially impressive. Slowly, with the help of the local community, we were able to set up a medical center.

We also helped improve the farming and horticulture. Villagers believed that evil spirits killed their livestock, so we worked to introduce the vaccination of animals. We also taught people to grow mushrooms in wet, rotting straw. With only two bundles of straw, we were able to grow thirty pounds of straw mushrooms every ten

SYSS workers building a bridge.

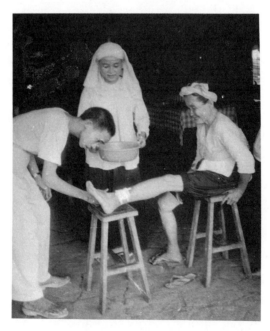

SYSS student examining elderly man's ankle.

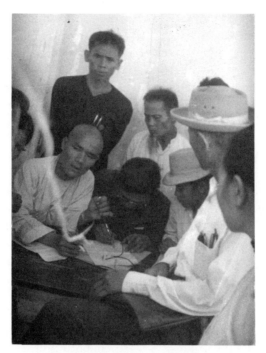

Monk and villagers discussing development.

Outdoor school in Cao Kinh Village.

days. It reminded me of the days when we "thirteen young cedars" of the temple studied with Thây Nhat Hanh outside of Saigon. There was a joy and camaraderie among the young social workers that sustained us, even in the face of adversity.

I was especially impressed by the work of Nhât Tri, a young monk from Quang Nam. Brother Tri had been ordained a novice in 1956 by Thây Nhat Hanh in the Bao Loc Temple in the highlands, and he was Thây's youngest disciple. As an SYSS student and an excellent social worker, he was greatly appreciated by the peasants in both pioneer villages, Cau Kinh and Thao Diên. Even today, I can see so clearly Brother Tri wearing his brown monk's robe and stooping over little Co, whom he cared for like a son. Tri's face was so composed and kind. I also remember him chairing the village meetings with such ease, persuading the better-off villagers to share their resources with those less well-off. I remember the way he helped convince the villagers to build a school and then dig a well.

The children in Thao Diên Village had to go out fishing and crabbing to help feed their families, or they had to watch their younger siblings so their parents could work. Most of the children had never seen the inside of a classroom until Brother Tri appeared. His class in Thao Diên reminded me of the class I had started in the Quoc Thanh slum, where the children loved the chance to attend school. Many of the children in Thao Diên needed to bring their younger brothers and sisters to class, and until the villagers organized childcare for the little ones, the classroom was a real scene!

I remember the day I joined Brother Tri's first grade class. The pupils were twelve and thirteen years old, and many brought their infant brothers and sisters to class with them. Tri clapped his hands loudly and said, "Please be quiet now, children. Look at the words I've written on the blackboard. I'll read them and then you repeat after me." The class grew quiet, except for the muffled sounds of one squirming youngster. Cu was doing his best to keep his younger brother on his lap so he would not crawl on the damp, dirt floor. He looked intently at the board and held his brother tightly, but his baby brother burst out crying. Cu tried to cover his mouth but it was of no use, and he had to carry him out of the classroom.

The quiet did not last long. A moment later, Xiu cried out, "Ba, your sister just shit on the floor! It stinks!" Ba had been so absorbed in the lesson that she hadn't noticed her toddler sister squatting. The lesson came to a halt as Ba cleaned the floor. Tri looked at me helplessly and said, "We must find a way to care for the little ones during school hours! Perhaps the grandparents can help."

That year, 1964, Tri organized an Autumn Moon Festival for the children of Thao Diên. "Can you believe it?" he said to me. "More than 300 families and not one of the children has ever celebrated the Autumn Moon Festival."

A month before the festival, he pointed to the full moon and told the children the stories of Cuoi, who had travelled to the moon, and King Duong Minh Hoang, who dreamed he was welcomed by many goddesses in the moon. He described to the children how autumn looks in a place with four seasons, transporting them with his storytelling and sharing with them the happiness of children who live in peace. Then he said, "Our country is not at peace, but your district is relatively secure, so I want to organize a Moon Festival for you."

Tri asked me to gather donations from the villagers to buy colored paper for lanterns. Then he gave his oldest pupils tasks like rowing across the river to Binh Phu Village to get some bamboo. Palm stems could have been used to make simple pyramid-shaped lanterns, but bamboo was needed if we wanted to make frames for beautiful, star-shaped lanterns. I remember how Tam Thai, from nearby Cau Kinh, showed the children how to make the lanterns. He was planning a Moon Festival for the children in his village, too.

The children from both villages could hardly wait for the festival day to arrive! We told them to watch the moon each night, and as soon as it was full, that would be the festival day. A few days before the eighth-month full moon, we did not know if we would be able to complete the lanterns. There were only twenty left to make, but we had run out of paper, and money too. Nhiu suggested we trim the frames of the star lanterns to have extra paper, and Truong suggested that the last lanterns be pyramid-shaped, since they used less paper. In the end, every child had a lantern.

Tam Thai arranged for the musicians from Cau Kinh to come at three in the afternoon to begin the festivities and a group of students from Saigon to bring presents for the children. But at one o'clock, Brother Tri began to look worried. He said to me, "I'm afraid the students from Saigon won't make it, and we won't have enough presents for all the children." By two o'clock, crowds of students with two gifts each arrived and the musicians came soon after that. Though we held the festival in the largest garden of the village, it was absolutely packed with students and villagers. Everyone was delighted to watch the children do a boat-rowing dance accompanied by the Cau Kinh musicians. A farmer named Bay Ro, who was quite shy, played traditional songs on the flute.

Our pharmacist, Thao, was nominated to be spokesperson for the event. Thuy Uyen and Thanh were in charge of numbering the gifts and helping each child pick a number out of the basket. It was dusk when the last gift was given, and the students prepared to return home. Other friends met the musicians on the main road to take them back to Cau Kinh, where Tam Thai would help the children of his village light lanterns for their procession. Tri and I stayed behind in Thao Diên, as did a few other friends. Evening shadows crept over the garden, and I was thinking about the village farmers who never had the leisure just to gaze at the autumn moon and notice that it is brighter and sweeter than all the other full moons.

Suddenly there was a sound by the gate, and a dozen youngsters carrying red, blue, and yellow lanterns strolled forward, singing, "On Moon Festival night, we carry our lanterns together, and we sing and dance." In the distance, another group of children walked with their lanterns, singing the same song. Tri led another group at the edge of the village, and he looked the same age as the children! The sound of singing filled the air, and the moon peeked over the coconut trees—full, round, and bright. My heart stirred. A simple pleasure like celebrating the Autumn Moon Festival was something all children should know. But without Brother Tri, none of these children would have. As Uncle Hai, the poor farmer stroking his white beard, said, "What joys there are for children! In all my days, I have never seen the children enjoy themselves so much."

Three years later, in 1967, Brother Tri and seven other students were abducted from Binh Phuoc Village, and to this day we do not know what happened. He had returned to the School of Youth for Social Service to study for another two years and was working in

Binh Phuoc when eight social workers were abducted. If I hadn't returned that night to Saigon to visit my mother, I would have shared his fate. If he died that night, I would have died with him. Dying on the path of social service is not unusual. Still, my two greatest sorrows are the loss of Sister Nhat Chi Mai and the loss of Brother Tri. Mai made the choice to immolate herself as a prayer for peace, but Brother Tri wanted to live simply and help build a new society based on love and understanding. He tried to help others lead a better life. His work had barely begun when he disappeared.

My dear brother is gone, but his spirit lives on in my heart and in the hearts of so many of his friends who continue his work. From time to time, I still say "hello" to him when I see myself behaving the way he did. It seems that a part of him has been reborn in me.

CHAPTER SEVEN

Experience

In France, I had written loving letters to my mother each week, telling her how much I missed her. But when I got back, I spent all my days with the poor in the pioneer villages and the slums. Sometimes, Mother would tell me, "You say you love me, but then you spend all your days working for the poor and come to see me only late at night." I gently comforted her, "Please think of me as married—not to a man, but to my ideal of life. If I had married a man, I would have to spend my days and nights with him, bringing happiness only to him. But because I am married to my ideal of life, I can bring joy to many people, and I can also return home at night to be with you." My mother understood, and since that day she has always supported my work.

Among the young professionals who joined our social work in the pioneer villages, one talented and humble physician, Tran Tân Trâm, fell in love with me. I enjoyed working beside him, helping the peasants in Thao Diên and Cau Kinh, but I was devoting all my energy to these projects, and twice I declined to marry him. He waited two years and finally, under pressure from his parents, married another woman. For a Vietnamese woman, her wedding day is supposed to be the most wonderful day of her life, and on the day of Trâm's wedding, I felt very sad. Looking back at my sadness, I can see that it was not because I was losing him to another woman, but because I realized I would never marry. Getting married meant taking special care of one's husband and his family and one's children, and I realized that if I did that, I could not also take care of the "wild" children in the slums and remote areas who desperately needed help, nor could I devote myself to building pioneer villages as models for social change in the country. I had seen many friends who, after getting married, became caught in endless family obligations, and I knew that my life was not for the effort of bringing happiness to one person, but to thousands. Because I was so active during this period, in a short time my sadness was transformed into joy in service, and I felt a great renewal of energy as I came to appreciate more and more the freedom to do the work I cared about most.

In late 1964, there were huge floods in Vietnam. More than 4,000 people were reported dead and thousands of homes washed away. The whole nation was mobilized to help the victims, but the investigation team sent by our Van Hanh Student Committee for Flood Relief reported that victims in villages near the Ho Chi Minh Trail, where the fighting was escalating, were suffering the most. Other relief efforts concentrated on helping victims near big cities like Da Nang and Hôi An, so we decided to go to the most remote areas that no one else dared visit.

Creek bottoms there were filled with rocks, and after many days of heavy rain, these rocky gorges overflowed so quickly that it was impossible for the inhabitants to escape the floods in time. In one hour, water levels in some places increased more than twenty-five meters. (The same kind of flooding occurred again in 1992.) Thây Nhat Hanh joined us on our mission. We took seven boats filled to the brim with food supplies, and we went up the Thu Bôn River, crossing Quang Nam Province and going high up into the mountains, through areas of intense fighting. Many times we saw soldiers shooting at each other across the river.

For five days and nights, we stayed high up in the mountains. We had no mosquito netting or drinkable water. We had to filter and boil river water before cooking or drinking, which was not easy in these conditions. But going with Thây made things easier. Everywhere we went, former students of his, including some high monks trained by him at the An Quang Pagoda in the 1950s, supported us, and on some occasions, it was thanks to the presence of these monks that we experienced some safety and respect from both warring parties. One time we were stopped and searched by nationalist soldiers and then allowed to go. Thây asked them, "What if we are stopped by the other side and given their propaganda literature? We could not refuse." "You may receive it, but when you get to the stream again, throw it into the water," the soldiers responded. Thây asked, "What if we don't have time to throw it in before we are caught again by people like you?" The soldiers did not answer.

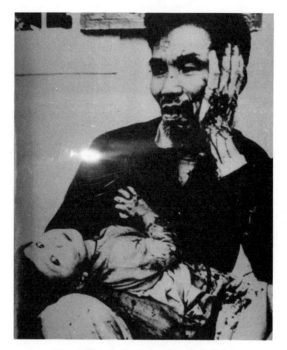

Bloodied man holding wounded child.

When they saw us, old men and women who had been devastated by the floods knelt down in prayer before us, as if they were in the presence of Avalokitesvara. They could not believe that humankind still existed after what they had experienced. Many had lost sons, daughters, grandchildren, homes, livestock, and everything they owned. One old man had lost his entire family and belongings except for one water buffalo, which he floated on as the water rose. Wherever he went, the water buffalo accompanied him like a son.

We stopped at the most devastated villages, distributed gifts, and stayed the day with people. At night, we slept on our boats after a simple meal of plain rice. The smell of dead bodies was everywhere, horribly polluting the air. Although this was a remote mountain area, there was fighting between the nationalists and the guerrillas even up here. When we saw wounded soldiers from either side, we helped them without discrimination.

Seeing such immense suffering, Thây Nhat Hanh cut his finger and let a drop of blood fall into the river: "This is to pray for all who have perished in the war and in the flood." Thây wrote this poem, "Experience," to describe some of the suffering we witnessed during that trip:

I have come to be with you,
to weep with you
for our ravaged land
and broken lives.
We are left with only grief and pain,
but take my hands
and hold them, hold them.
I want to say
only simple words.
Have courage. We must have courage,
if only for the children,
if only for tomorrow.

During the month after the flood,
the young man received only two pounds of rice
from the emergency aid.
Tonight he is eating areca tops and rotten corn.
And he is one of so many children,
jaundiced, with bloated faces.

He had dysentery for a week
with no medicine
and no hope.

The flood carried off
his father,
his mother,
and his brother.
This innocent child's brow
wears no mourning band.

But from the scorched and gutted fields,
a sickly ray of sun
comes to envelop my soul
in its ghoulish sheet.

Please come here
and witness
the ordeal of all the dear ones
who survived the flood of the Year of the
Dragon.

Take this bleeding child in your arms.
She is the only member of her household
whose misfortune was to survive.

A young father
whose wife and four children died
stares, day and night, into empty space.
He sometimes laughs
a tear-choked laugh.

Please come and see
his white-haired elder,
left alone for days on a barren, weedy patch of
land.
He kneels before a startled boy
and offers him some rice.
He is kneeling in love
while the boy weeps,
"O Grandfather, don't kneel in front of me.
I am the age of your grandson."

The message of love has been transmitted.
Again, I put my faith in tomorrow.

Her husband is dead,
her children dead;
her land ruined;

her hearth cold.
There is no spark to light a fire,
for death is here
on a patch of earth sucked dry.

Nothing remains,
not even her resignation,
the last one left.

She curses aloud her existence.
"How fortunate," she says,
"those families who died together."

I tell her, "We are not alone.
There are others,
and we must help still their cries
on this endless road.
Let us walk on with our heads bent."

The villager looks me over.
Agonized yet fearless,
he answers,
"I hate both sides.
I follow neither.
I only want to go
where they will let me live
and help me live."
O life! What misery!

On this high place by the Thu Bôn River,
I cut my finger
and watch the blood drip
and mix with the water.
O be at rest,
you who are lost.
O be at peace!

To you who have drowned, I speak,
and to you who have survived,
and to the river—
having heard all space reverberate
with the infants' screams.
Tonight
I've come to stand midway
between these sheer mountains,
and to watch them bend over the river,
and to listen
to their eternal tales.

Here is the impermanent
and yet continuously flowing world.
Let us stand together for future generations.

Each tiny bodhisattva,
with bowed head and hidden tears,
student's ink still on her hands,
holds a shovel or a mattock
and throws up earth for a bridge
or for burying the bloated dead.

Under palm-leaf hats,
brown-clothed and barefoot,
are they not Quan Yin in all her glory,
her charity, her fearlessness?

The small, bare feet walk over stones,
the sharp stones of pain and grief.
The bare feet enter shacks
built hastily on ash,
that they may approach the living
who have reached the limits of their lives.

While I watch their hands,
as gentle as heavenly silk,

outstretched to infants,
the crying stops,
and the mother's eyes,
staring at cans of milk,
glow like precious stones.

And still I sit
before the Gates of Heaven
tightly shut
with bowed head, waiting.

In the old garden, I wonder,
could one feel the fragrance
of areca blossoms?

O here,
why is there such silence here?—
such silence,
when even the birds of our stricken land
have vanished.
O speak out now,
speak audibly again,
so hearing you in far corners
the birds will return;
our waters be like jewels again;
our land like brocade.

O sing,
sing loud
so True Being may follow the Word.

  This poem inspired many young Buddhists to join our efforts to help victims of the war.

  During the war with the French, Thây had contracted malaria and dysentery, and, during this trip to the remote mountain areas, both diseases recurred. Despite that his presence was very inspiring for our whole team. Thây reminded us to be mindful of every-thing—the way Thây Nhu Van, a high monk who was very popular

with both sides, talked to the officers of both sides; the way Thây
Nhu Hue organized the local Buddhists; and the way the rowers of
our boat ate in mindfulness. We observed the steep canyon of the
Thu Bôn River and were aware of the icy mountain wind and the
homeless victims of the flood on the verge of death. The atmosphere of death permeated our whole trip—not only the death of
flood victims, but our own risk of dying at any moment in the ever-
present cross fire.

As we were leaving the area, many young mothers followed us,
pleading with us to take their babies, because they were not certain
the babies could survive until our next rescue mission. We cried,
but we could not take these babies with us. That image has stayed
with me to this day.

After that, as I went to Hue every two months to lecture on biology, I never failed to organize groups of students, monks, and nuns
to help people suffering in these remote areas. We began with the
daylong journey from Hue to Da Nang, where we would sleep in a
temple and then travel to Quang Nam and Hôi An. In Hôi An, we
rented five midsize boats to carry nearly ten tons of rice, beans,
cooking utensils, used clothing, and medical supplies.

One night, we stopped in Son Khuong, a remote village where
the fighting was especially fierce. As we were about to go to sleep
in our boat, we suddenly heard shooting, then screaming, then
shooting again. The young people in our group were seized with
panic, and a few young men jumped into the river to avoid the bullets. I sat quietly in the boat with two nuns and breathed consciously to calm myself. Seeing us so calm, everyone stopped
panicking, and we quietly chanted the *Heart Sutra*, concentrating
deeply on this powerful chant. For a while, we didn't hear any bullets. I don't know if they actually stopped or not. The day after, I
shared my strong belief with my coworkers, "When we work to help
people, the bullets have to avoid us, because we can never avoid
the bullets. When we have good will and great love, when our only
aim is to help those in distress, I believe that there is a kind of mag-
netism, the energy of goodness, that protects us from being hit by
the bullets. We only need to be serene. Then, even if a bullet hits
us, we can accept it calmly, knowing that everyone has to die one
day. If we die in service, we can die with a smile, without fear."

Two months later, while on another rescue trip, bombs had just fallen as we arrived at a very remote hamlet, about fifteen kilometers from Son Khuong Village. There were dead and wounded people everywhere. We used all the bandages and medicine we had. I remember so vividly carrying a bleeding baby back to the boat in order to clean her wounds and do whatever surgery might be necessary. I cannot describe how painful and desperate it was to carry a baby covered with blood, her sobbing mother walking beside me, both of us unsure if we could save the child.

Two years later, when I went to the United States to explain the suffering of the Vietnamese people and to plead for peace in Vietnam, I saw a woman on television carrying a wounded baby covered with blood, and suddenly, I understood how the American people could continue to support the fighting and bombing. The scene on the television was quite different from the reality of having a bleeding baby in my arms. My despair was intense, but the scene on television looked like a performance. I realized that there was no connection between experiencing the actual event and watching it on the TV screen while sitting at home in peace and safety. People could watch such horrible scenes on TV and still go about their daily business—eating, dancing, playing with children, having conversations. After an encounter with such suffering, desperation filled my every cell. These people were human beings like me; why did they have to suffer so? Questions like these burned inside me and, at the same time, inspired me to continue my work with serene determination. Realizing how fortunate I was compared to those living under the bombs helped dissolve any anger or suffering in me, and I was committed to keep doing my best to help them without fear.

CHAPTER EIGHT

Interbeing

When Thây Nhat Hanh started the pioneer village development projects in 1964, many bright young men and women left their positions of responsibility in the Department of Buddhist Youth of the Unified Buddhist Church to join him. This made some of the conservative elders of the UBC angry at Thây and at those of us associated with his work. They even surmised, somehow, that we had been hired by the communists, or at least that the communists had sent me to influence Thây.

By 1965, our reputation for social development work had become so great among Saigon intellectuals that a number of us thought it might be time to ask the Church elders for their support once again. Thây agreed, and we went to the UBC headquarters, prostrated ourselves in front of those who had criticized us, and said, "By ourselves we can help only a few villages, but with your support, we can bring about social change for the whole country." The key persons in the UBC—Thây Thiên Hoa, Thây Tam Chau, Thây Huyen Quang, and Thây Thiên Minh—agreed to allow us to use the Church's name to launch a nationwide appeal for rural development and social change.*

During this same period of time, Thây Nhat Hanh published a series of articles in the Buddhist weekly newsletter, *Thiên My*, an-

---

* I think this response is the same as elders everywhere towards the younger generation. When you want to do something new and creative, they may not encourage you. But if you take the first steps on your own, they may well support you later. It was the same with my brother Nghiep. When my parents denied his request to become a singer, he pursued his dream without their approval, and when he proved himself, my father expressed real pride and support. I always advise young friends not to be discouraged if their parents or elders do not support their creative ideas. There is no need to be angry at them. We only need to listen to our elders' experiences and arguments without prejudice, and if we are not convinced, we can begin our project silently, with utmost care and with all our heart. Later, when we realize some of our ideals, we can come back gently and request their support.

SYSS office at Tu Nghiêm Pagoda.

nouncing the formation of a School of Youth for Social Service, where young people could train to be social workers and, when they graduated, be sent to remote areas to serve poor people (who comprised nearly 80 percent of the country's population). The response was great—1,000 people applied to be trainees!

The SYSS office and classrooms were set up in the Tu Nghiêm Pagoda, the women's dormitory in Hue Lam Temple, the monks' dormitory in Truc Lam Temple, and the laymen's dormitory on the campus of the future Van Hanh University. We selected 300 of the 1,000 applicants, purchased an old Renault van, and began to transport students from their various dormitory locations to class every day. It took two hours to pick everyone up and two hours to take them home, but despite the difficulty, we were all bursting with joy.

The teaching staff was unpaid. It was my job to coordinate a committee of thirty-five students to visit as many households as possible to describe our program and ask for support. It was similar to the way I had raised funds for the people in the Quoc Thanh slum, but this time, in less than a year, more than 3,000 families became sponsors of our work, even some poor street vendors. We reported our successes and difficulties to each sponsor, and, inspired by our devotion to the work, they became our informal "publicists."

The School of Youth for Social Service was officially founded in September 1965 as a program of Van Hanh University under the auspices of the Unified Buddhist Church. Thây Nhat Hanh served as Director of the Board of Trustees, and Thây Thanh Van was Executive Director. According to the UBC's constitution, only a monk or a nun could be the head of a Church program. Thây Thanh Van was only twenty-four years old, but because he had entered the monastic life and been practicing meditation since the age of seven, he was calm and knew how to think deeply. Fourteen of us worked full-time and shared the staff responsibilities. A few dozen others worked part-time. When anyone was unable to fulfill his or her task, I came to help. I loved to see the work go smoothly, so I took some responsibility in almost every area. Everyone regarded me as a "commander-in-chief." At one meeting, when I sang a traditional Vietnamese love song, people seemed surprised and said, "Phuong, you sing too!"[*]

At the end of 1965, Thây Thanh Van, Trinh Sam, and Thây Luu Phuong found land ten kilometers from Saigon, and we decided to build an SYSS campus there. Rather than divide the space in the traditional way, with separate quarters for nuns, monks, laywomen, and laymen, we decided to have one unified campus. Thây Nhat Hanh designed a small temple of bamboo, mud, and cement, with a palm-leaf roof, and this building served as our spiritual center, where we practiced sitting meditation, reciting the precepts, and sharing tea. Thây wrote a fundraising letter asking for help to build forty dormitory rooms, a dining room, a library, and an auditorium, and we went from house to house explaining our aspirations and projects and soliciting contributions for the construction. In July 1966, we moved in. Thây had a room in one corner of the temple.

In 1964, two students of Thây Nhat Hanh—Thây Thanh Tue and Thây Tu Man—founded La Bôi Press, with a grant from Mrs. Ngo Van Hieu. Two cedars, Thu Ha and my sister Thanh, were the treasurers, and in less than two years, La Bôi printed twelve books

---

[*] My friends would never have believed that, thirteen years later, I would record several tapes of Vietnamese songs to raise funds to feed and educate hungry children.

by Thây on engaged Buddhism and twenty by other authors. On one occasion, Thây Nhat Hanh proposed that we organize a banquet for the artists who had contributed to La Boi Press. I volunteered to be the cook. My sisters in the Dharma were surprised to discover that I could cook also. I selected dishes I had seen my mother prepare, substituting tofu and gluten for fish and pork. It turned out to be a very successful evening. Everyone loved the food, including the dish called "white birds go back to their nest"—a large squash filled with delicious soup and two beaten egg whites (the two birds).

The books of La Boi Press were distributed widely throughout the country, and its work was, at that time, legal. When we published books on peace through our Vanh Hanh University Student Union press, on the other hand, we did so at the risk of going to jail. By 1966, the word "peace" had become equated with communism, so we had to do this work underground. In 1966-1967, we published four books by Thây Nhat Hanh: *Lotus in a Sea of Fire (Hoa Sen Trong Bien Lua)*, *Don't Forget Those Who Suffer (Dung Quen Xin Dung Voi Quen)*, *Dialogue: The Key to Peace in Vietnam (Doi Thoai Canh Cua Hoa Binh)*, and *Let Us Pray for the Dove to Come (Chap Tay Nguyen Cau Cho Bo Cau Trang Hien)*. *Lotus in a Sea of Fire* was a clear assessment of the war, but for the Saigon authorities in 1966, it was communist propaganda. *Don't Forget Those Who Suffer* was written as a letter from Thây Nhat Hanh to city dwellers asking them not to forget the peasants who were suffering so from the war. It was also a report about our work in Quang Nam for war and flood victims, written very beautifully, to awaken people from forgetfulness.

Few printers were willing to print these books. *Lotus in a Sea of Fire* was printed by a Buddhist on Gia Long Street and distributed widely through an informal network. *Don't Forget Those Who Suffer* was printed by Thây Thông Buu's printing house in Quan Am Temple. This temple had been set up by Thây Quang Duc, the first monk who immolated himself for human rights in 1963. Thây Thông Buu was later exiled by the communist government to a remote town, but he escaped and lived in the jungle in Vietnam until 1992, when he finally returned to Saigon.

One day in early September of 1966, I was on my way home from Thây Thông Buu's temple on my motorbike. I had stopped there to pick up 300 copies of *Don't Forget Those Who Suffer*. If I had been driving a car, no one would have paid much attention to me. Wealthy people had private cars, and since they were rarely communist, the authorities never stopped cars to search for guerrillas. But guerrillas did carry grenades on motorbikes, and the police routinely stopped motorbikes. When I drove across Truong Minh Giang Bridge, a policeman stopped and searched me. He saw the books and suspected they might be communist leaflets. When he asked me what they were, I said, "Just some books." But when he started leafing through a copy of *Don't Forget Those Who Suffer*, I became frightened. I invoked the name of Avalokitesvara, the bodhisattva of compassion and fearlessness, and regained my serenity. I saw that my only motivation was to wake people up from forgetfulness and help them realize the suffering of the people in the war zone. Even if I were sent to jail, I knew I was doing what was right, and I was ready to accept full responsibility. With that thought, a big smile came over my face. The policeman smiled back, and read the first line: "Dear *Em*, do you know?" "*Em*" is the familiar greeting from an older brother to his younger sister or from a young man to his beloved, and it communicates intimacy and kindness. Thây always started difficult essays with sweet beginnings. The policeman read the first sentence aloud and said, "This is a love story, isn't it?" I smiled again, and he handed me the book and said, "Okay, you can go." I knew I had barely escaped. I don't know why, but I rarely seem to have problems when my heart is pure with the intention to help others.

In October, I went to Hue to teach as usual, but this time I intended to obtain signatures from students and teachers for a petition asking the warring parties to find a peaceful solution to the war. Unlike most visits to Hue, this time I did not bring any copies of *Lotus in a Sea of Fire*. I carried only a copy of the petition, some school papers, a bag of used toys to distribute to orphan victims of the war, and one beautifully wrapped gift that a friend had asked me to bring to her mother. When I arrived at the Hue Airport, I was surprised to see three policemen standing there, obviously waiting for me. They approached and said, "We have orders to search your luggage." Two officers looked through the bag of toys. The petition was among my papers, and while the young officer was looking carefully at every single sheet, I breathed deeply and evoked the name of Avalokitesvara. I said to myself, "Bodhisattva of Compassion, we are going to jail. There is no way to escape. We must go without fear." The month before, when I had been caught with the carton of *Don't Forget Those Who Suffer*, I had been lucky enough to avoid going to prison, but the policemen at the airport in Hue looked stern, even cruel. Still, invoking the name of Avalokitesvara, I was able to smile serenely at their tense police faces.

Suddenly, the young one discovered the petition. I saw his hand shaking as he glanced at me nervously. I returned his glance with a deep, sad smile, and immediately, he put the petition back among the papers already searched and acted as if he hadn't seen anything. They finished the search, put all the papers aside, and opened my friend's gift for her mother. It was a copy of *Lotus in a Sea of Fire*! Even though my friend's father was the former police chief of Hue, I was arrested on the spot.

On the way to the station, the young policeman sat beside the driver and I sat in back. I knew that if they discovered the petition for peace, I would be sentenced to many years in prison, so I very carefully slipped the petition out of my handbag, folded it five times, put it in my mouth, and swallowed it, bit by bit. It was the only thing I could do! If I tore it up, they would have seen it, and I knew I would be searched again at the police station. When we arrived, I was charged with possessing a banned book and held without bail.

Every day in Hue, my university students went to the Linh Quang Temple to ask the head monk to request my release. When he finally agreed to do so, the Hue police responded by transferring me to a jail in Saigon, where I was held for another eight days in a small cell, two meters by two-and-a-half meters, with eight other prisoners. There was not even enough room for us to lie down, so I practiced sitting meditation day and night, consciously following each breath, and listened to the stories of the other prisoners, including two twelve-year-old girls who said that they had done nothing wrong.

My weeks in jail in Hue and Saigon were important lessons for me. I realized how much I take for granted so many wonderful things in my life. For example, in jail, I dreamed of climbing freely and happily onto my motorbike "like a bird flying in the air," with my long hair flowing, the cloth of my ao dai flapping in the breeze, and two giant bags of rice for those in the slums on top of the back wheel. I realized that having a motorbike and being able to ride on it whenever I wanted was one aspect of living in paradise.

At mealtimes, the prisoners received only old rice and rotten, salted fish. I dreamed of hot, tender, white rice and boiled vegetables dipped in soy sauce with a few drops of fragrant lemon, and slices of green and red peppers. Eating had been something I did only to be of some use to others, but now I realized that if given a chance to go home, I would eat very mindfully, enjoying each taste of tender rice and every morsel of delicious vegetable. One day, when I received a fresh orange from one of the male prisoners who said that he had admired me when I was a student in the Faculty of Science, I vowed to remember the material and moral needs of prisoners. One day in jail is longer than 1,000 years in freedom. In 1978, I started an underground project to send financial aid to political prisoners and their families. Later, in 1982, I helped persuade Amnesty International to send food to prisoners.

When I had been in jail in Saigon for a week, the Head of the National Police, Colonel Nguyen Ngoc Loan, called me into his office and informed me that I would be released, thanks to the intervention of Doctor Tien, a relative of a friend of mine who knew the colonel. I begged Colonel Loan to reconsider the case of the two twelve-year-old girls who had told me that they had not done anything wrong, that they had just happened to be around when the authorities arrested two guerrillas. Jail was not a healthy environment for children. Instead of releasing them, Colonel Loan ordered the guards to be stricter, because "the prisoners had obviously been talking to each other," and the rules specifically forbade that. The other prisoners thought I had denounced them in order to be released. I realized that being Ksitigarbha (Earth Treasure) Bodhisattva, who vows to help those in hell until hell is empty, must be terribly difficult. I'd only wanted to help those two girls, but because of my action, the situation worsened.

Later, from 1984 to 1988, when my beloved sister in the Dharma Thich Nu Tri Hai was jailed by the communists, she practiced much better than I had. She told me that she had received a copy of Thây's book, *A Guide to Walking Meditation*, one week before being arrested, and in jail, she practiced walking five kilometers every day in mindfulness in her cell of four square meters. When she was put into a bigger cell, she gave Dharma talks to the other women prisoners. She even offered the Five Precepts to prisoners in an informal ceremony. To me, she was a real Earth Treasure Bodhisattva. I know there are many Ksitigarbha monks and nuns in the jails of Vietnam today.

The days from 1964 to 1968 were the busiest of my life. I was responsible for many lab workshops in Saigon University. I was also a full-time student in the Bachelor of Buddhist Studies Program at Van Hanh Buddhist University and President of the Student Union there, organizing the book publishing, special seminars, and a group of students who collected food, clothing, and cooking utensils to send to the poor people of Quang Nam and surrounding areas. I was head of the Extension Department of the School of Youth for Social Service, coordinating volunteers to collect donations from families around Saigon and to correspond with the many SYSS supporters throughout the country each month. I worked in the slums of Saigon and in two pioneer villages. As a lecturer in botany at Hue University, 1,000 kilometers from Saigon, I had to fly every two months for four days of teaching and six days of bringing food and supplies to war victims in remote areas of Quang Nam, like Son Khuong and Duc Duc. Although I was doing so many things, I never felt tired. The need in Vietnam was great, and many friends shared and supported my work.

I was not unique. Vietnamese and others around the world were also shouldering great responsibilities to try to help alleviate the suffering in Vietnam, but many of them became exhausted—today we call it "burnout." I never felt that way. I continued to sing and arrange flowers in my room, trying to keep my spirit fresh and happy. One day a cedar friend who had been active for two years before getting married and having children came to visit, and she was amazed at my joyful attitude. "What kind of 'fuel' do you take to be so steady, faithful, and full of joy on this arduous path?" she

The first six members of the Order of Interbeing (left to right):
Cao Ngoc Phuong, Pham Thuy Uyen, Nhat Chi Mai,
Nguyen Van Phuc, Do Van Khon, and Bui Van Thanh.

asked. At her question, I looked back at all my work and was surprised, too, that I was able to take on so many responsibilities with ease. Only later did I realize that my fuel was living simply and practicing one Day of Mindfulness each week.

I have always lived like a nun—eating simple foods, owning just a few changes of clothes, wearing no cosmetics, and having no money of my own in the bank. I even donated the diamond necklace and diamond bracelets my parents gave me to a project for the poor. From the age of twenty, I knew that someday I would shave my head and join an order of Buddhist nuns. In 1960, Thây Thanh Tu, Thây Tri Quang, and Thây Nhat Hanh all advised me to wait before being ordained, but in 1963 Thây Tri Quang encouraged me to become a nun. I asked Thây Nhat Hanh, and he said that the precepts for monks and nuns formulated 2,500 years ago needed to be renewed. He showed me fourteen new precepts he had written that he felt carried the deepest teachings of the Buddha and would be fit for our time. He said he would tell me when he thought was the best time for me to shave my head and become a nun. But for now, he invited six of us, the leaders of the SYSS, to receive the Fourteen Precepts in a formal ceremony.

On the fifth of February in 1966, a full moon day, Thây Nhat Hanh ordained the first six members of the *Tiep Hien* Order, the Order of Interbeing. This Order was created by Thây to help bring Buddhism directly into the arena of social concerns during a time when the war was escalating and the teachings of the Buddha were most sorely needed. Thây proposed that the Order be composed of monks, nuns, laymen, and laywomen, and said that the six of us first ordained were free to choose whether we preferred to live and practice as formal monastics or as laypersons. We three women chose to live celibate lives like nuns, although we didn't shave our heads, while the three men chose to marry and practice as lay Buddhists. Among the three women was Nhat Chi Mai, who immolated herself for peace just a year later.

It was a wonderful celebration! Each of us was given a lamp with a handmade shade on which Thây had calligraphed "Lamp of the World," "Lamp of the Full Moon," "Lamp of Wisdom," etc., in old-style Chinese. During the initiation ceremony, we six ordainees vowed to study, practice, and observe the Fourteen Precepts of the Order of Interbeing. Since that day, I have felt that these precepts are my primary teacher, especially when I have been under stress and do not know the best way to act. These are the Fourteen Precepts:

1. Do not be idolatrous about or bound to any doctrine, theory, or ideology, even Buddhist ones. Buddhist systems of thought are guiding means; they are not absolute truth.

2. Do not think the knowledge you presently possess is changeless, absolute truth. Avoid being narrow-minded and bound to present views. Learn and practice nonattachment from views in order to be open to receive others' viewpoints. Truth is found in life and not merely in conceptual knowledge. Be ready to learn throughout your entire life and to observe reality in yourself and in the world at all times.

3. Do not force others, including children, by any means whatsoever, to adopt your views, whether by authority, threat, money, propaganda, or even education. However, through compassionate dialogue, help others renounce fanaticism and narrowness.

4. *Do not avoid contact with suffering or close your eyes before suffering. Do not lose awareness of the existence of suffering in the life of the world. Find ways to be with those who are suffering, including personal contact, images, and sound. By such means, awaken yourself and others to the reality of suffering in the world.*

5. *Do not accumulate wealth while millions are hungry. Do not take as the aim of your life fame, profit, wealth, or sensual pleasure. Live simply and share time, energy, and material resources with those who are in need.*

6. *Do not maintain anger or hatred. Learn to penetrate and transform them when they are still seeds in your consciousness. As soon as they arise, turn your attention to your breath in order to see and understand the nature of your anger and hatred and the nature of the persons who have caused your anger and hatred.*

7. *Do not lose yourself in dispersion and in your surroundings. Practice mindful breathing to come back to what is happening in the present moment. Be in touch with what is wondrous, refreshing, and healing both inside and around you. Plant seeds of joy, peace, and understanding in yourself in order to facilitate the work of transformation in the depths of your consciousness.*

8. *Do not utter words that can create discord and cause the community to break. Make every effort to reconcile and resolve all conflicts, however small.*

9. *Do not say untruthful things for the sake of personal interest or to impress people. Do not utter words that cause division and hatred. Do not spread news that you do not know to be certain. Do not criticize or condemn things of which you are not sure. Always speak truthfully and constructively. Have the courage to speak out about situations of injustice, even when doing so may threaten your own safety.*

10. *Do not use the Buddhist community for personal gain or profit, or transform your community into a political party. A religious community,*

however, should take a clear stand against oppression and injustice and should strive to change the situation without engaging in partisan conflicts.

11. Do not live with a vocation that is harmful to humans and nature. Do not invest in companies that deprive others of their chance to live. Select a vocation that helps realize your ideal of compassion.

12. Do not kill. Do not let others kill. Find whatever means possible to protect life and prevent war.

13. Possess nothing that should belong to others. Respect the property of others, but prevent others from profiting from human suffering or the suffering of other species on Earth.

14. Do not mistreat your body. Learn to handle it with respect. Preserve vital energies (sexual, breath, spirit) for the realization of the Way. Be fully aware of the responsibility of bringing new lives into the world. Meditate on the world into which you are bringing new beings.

The conditions requested by Thây Nhat Hanh to those of us who formally ordained with him were to practice at least sixty Days of Mindfulness a year and to practice with a community of friends. Even though I continued to be extremely busy, I renewed myself every week with a Day of Mindfulness at our SYSS temple, from Saturday noon until Sunday noon. I would always come laden down with worries about urgent responsibilities, but after a short while I could slowly calm myself and stop even the most anxious thoughts. I tried to dwell mindfully on every act, beginning with putting my overnight bag in my room, boiling some water for washing, and putting on my meditation clothes. Then I practiced walking meditation alone in the woods, picking wildflowers and bamboo branches for arrangements for the meditation hall. After three hours of dwelling steadily in each mindful act and releasing all my worries, I began to feel renewed, and we six members of the Order gathered to recite the precepts and chant the *Heart Sutra* together. Then we shared tea and our experiences of the past week, ate dinner silently together, and practiced sitting meditation before bed. We meditated together again in the early morning. During individual time before and after evening meditation and the next day, I sometimes had to resume my urgent work alone in my room, but I always did it in a mindful way.

One day, Nhat Chi Mai said to me, "We are such a new Order that the Buddhist Church does not accept us as nuns." I comforted her by saying, "Don't worry. We don't need their acceptance. We were ordained by Thây because we wanted to follow the Fourteen Precepts. Others can think of us as laypersons, nuns, or whatever they want. What is important is that we practice the precepts as guidelines lighting our path of service and helping us transform our negative tendencies, like fanaticism, narrow-mindedness, anger, and hatred." In fact, as we continued to practice sincerely, many of the high monks came to appreciate us. Although they didn't call us nuns, they treated us with equal respect.

Today, thousands of friends in Europe, North America, Australia, and Asia have come to know and practice these Fourteen Precepts, although most have not had the opportunity to receive them formally from Thây. I always advise those who wish to practice the precepts to organize a sangha, a community of friends, around them, to recite the precepts every month, and share their experiences of living the precepts. If they do this, already they are members of the extended community of the Order of Interbeing.[*]

---

[*] See Thich Nhat Hanh, *Interbeing: Fourteen Guidelines for Engaged Buddhism* (Berkeley: Parallax Press, 1993).

THE WAR ESCALATES
1966-1968

CHAPTER NINE

Man Is Not Our Enemy

In 1966, thousands of Buddhists demonstrated for the free election of a national assembly and a fully elected government. I remember seeing a photo in the Saigon newspaper of thousands of soldiers joining their palms in front of Thây Tâm Châu and Thây Tri Quang; the caption read: "Soldiers in Danang listen to two monks preaching for an elected government." The officers of Prime Minister Nguyen Cao Ky must have reported to him that his own soldiers of Buddhist background had joined the demonstrations calling for free elections. Under increased pressure from the U.S. and from the leadership of his own Republic of South Vietnam Army, Nguyen Cao Ky agreed to hold elections. The Buddhists were elated. Many who had been demonstrating believed that Buddhists should run their own candidates, but suddenly, Cao Ky sent troops to Central Vietnam and arrested many of the Buddhist candidates. Thousands of Buddhist leaders—among them, senior officers in the National Army—were jailed. It was a most discouraging turn of events.

A grave split in the Buddhist Church occurred. Thây Tâm Châu was a monk who came from North Vietnam and was very afraid of communists. Nguyen Cao Ky also came from the North, and the Buddhist candidates who were from the North or were disciples of Thây Tâm Châu were not arrested. The Buddhist candidates from Central Vietnam—Hue, Danang, Quang Nam, and nine other provinces—all were arrested. Thây Tri Quang cabled Thây Tâm Châu, who was attending a conference in India and asked him to come back to discuss strategies to get the government to keep its promise to hold elections and not arrest those who wanted to participate in a real democracy. But Thây Tâm Châu did not respond. He stayed in India for several more weeks before going to Bangkok. Thây Tri Quang continued trying to contact him, urging him to return to help solve the problem, because the government had arrested all the best Buddhists in Central Vietnam. But Thây Tâm

Châu did not come back, and Thây Tri Quang became so frustrated at the government's repression that he decided to fast until all those detained were released from jail. After seventy-seven days, he began fainting and was hospitalized, but he continued to fast, altogether for more than 100 days.

I was worried that Thây Tri Quang might die. On the ninetieth day of his fast, a Tiep Hien sister, Chan Doan, and I went to Duy Tân Hospital, even though we knew that the police would arrest anyone who approached Thây Tri Quang. Chan Doan asked to have a gynecological problem diagnosed by the physician on duty, and then she slipped past the guards into Thây Tri Quang's room and passed him a letter from Thây Nhat Hanh begging him to stop fasting. But Thây Tri Quang continued his fast. A week later, I put on jeans and a T-shirt, quite different from the traditional Vietnamese dress I usually wore, and coolly, even naturally, walked alongside a nurse right past the police guards into his room. As soon as I entered, I implored Thây Tri Quang not to die, saying, "The entire younger generation of Buddhists is waiting for you to eat again and lead us to peace. Please give your body some food." The nurse chased me away, but in a few days, at the request of Thich Tinh Khiet, the High Patriarch of the UBC, Thây Tri Quang took some food and ended his fast. The effects of his 100-day fast made Thây Tri Quang very weak. He was held under house arrest during the Nguyen Cao Ky/Nguyen Van Thieu regime and is still under house arrest today by the communist regime.

When Thây Tâm Châu returned to Vietnam, some young extremists were so angry at him that they shouted and held up banners that read: "You must pay the debt of so many well-meaning Buddhists who took your advice and were killed or put in jail." The way they acted was too violent—one banner was even painted with blood and bones—and because of their unkind way, they forced Thây Tâm Châu to side with the government. I was too absorbed in my work with the peasants in the countryside, and I did not join the 1966 demonstrations. It was only later that I heard about the attitude of those young people towards Thây Tâm Châu, and I was sorry that I had not been there to propose alternatives to acting out of anger. We might have gone to Thây Tâm Châu, for example, and given him reports of thousands of army officers whom Nguyen Cao

Ky had discharged because they were pro-Buddhist, reports of the names of those who died or were detained in jail, and other information, and then solemnly asked him to act. As a monk for more than forty years and therefore an expert in kindness and compassion, when faced with such betrayal and injustice, surely he would have been moved. Unlike Thây Tri Quang, Thây Tâm Châu was very diplomatic, and he might have been able to skillfully change the situation for the better. But I was not there and my young friends helped polarize the situation with their confrontational demonstrations. As a result, the government hardened its position, and the vast majority of Buddhists began to openly oppose the government.

When A.J. Muste, the General Secretary of the Fellowship of Reconciliation, had come to Vietnam in 1965 to demonstrate against the war, he met Thây Nhat Hanh and liked him very much. In March 1966, Professor Robert Browne, of the Inter-University Committee for the Debate on Foreign Policy, and Professor George McKahin invited Thây to lead a seminar on Vietnam at Cornell University. Alfred Hassler then invited "this frail, young Vietnamese monk" to tour the U.S. following the Cornell conference to explain to the American people the true experience of the Vietnamese people, who were not interested in communism or anticommunism, but who just wanted the bombs to stop falling on them.

By the Spring of 1966, the war had escalated dramatically, and many of our pioneer villages had been bombed, so Thây decided to accept these invitations to go to America, where he felt that so many roots of the war were. By this time, he could see that many of the roots of the war were in the West. I drove him to the Saigon Airport on May 2, 1966, and said good-bye, assuming he would be gone for just a few weeks.

One June 1, Thây held a press conference in Washington, D.C. and released a *Five-Point Peace Proposal*:

1. The United States should issue a clear statement of its desire to help the Vietnamese people have a government genuinely responsive to Vietnamese aspirations.

2. The United States should end all bombing.

3. The United States military should limit its actions to a purely defensive role.

4. The United States should convincingly demonstrate its intention to remove its troops over a specified period of months.

5. The United States should offer reconstruction aid free of ideological and political strings.

That same day, he was denounced on Saigon radio, in the newspapers, and by the Thieu/Ky government as a traitor. From this point on, it was not safe for him to return to Vietnam. He decided to come home after his speaking tour anyway, at his own risk, but we in the SYSS begged him to wait.

During Thây's absence, we had many problems. Tra Loc, a newly developed village in Quang Tri, for instance, was bombed, and the SYSS workers who lived there reported that there was an extremely high level of hatred, suspicion, and fear among the people. So they decided to remain in the village and help the peasants rebuild each house, sharing their difficulties and concerns. In this way, they regained the trust and faith of the local people, and then they also helped them rebuild a day-care center, a school, a medical center, and an agricultural cooperative.

Then the bombs came again, destroying all their efforts. Fear, hatred, and despair were widespread. After several weeks, our friends gathered their courage and helped the villagers rebuild their houses, schools, and medical center again. Then another bombing reduced all their loving efforts to ash. After a fourth bombardment, it was hard for them to maintain their serenity. Everyone felt like picking up a gun and fighting. But by practicing meditation, looking deeply, they could see that using guns would only make things worse, so they did the work of rebuilding yet again in order to demonstrate their support, love, and care for those who suffered so intensely.

Two months before Thây Nhat Hanh had left to attend the forum at Cornell, a general assembly of all the student unions of Van Hanh University had met in the university auditorium to issue a "Call for Peace," which stated, "It is time for North and South Vietnam to find a way to stop the war and help all Vietnamese people live peacefully and with mutual respect." Thây brought that statement with him to Cornell. But a week after Thây left, Thây Minh

Chau, the Dean of the university, issued a statement dissolving the student union and nullifying the university's link with the School of Youth for Social Service. He even sent a copy of his statement to the National Police. Then he told many supporters of the SYSS, "I don't know whether Thây Nhat Hanh is communist or not, but certainly Cao Ngoc Phuong is." In the context of Vietnam at that moment, calling someone communist meant killing him or her even without a weapon.

Thây Minh Chau often said that we must not mix up education with political work. But how could we educate young people to respect life while ignoring the killing of human beings? How could we teach the non-fear of Avalokitesvara in the *Lotus Sutra* if we ourselves were too afraid to use the word "peace"? I told my fellow students that there were two kinds of politics: partisan politics to gain power and fame for ourselves, and the politics of reconciliation to bring peace and happiness to the country. We should avoid the former, but how could we ignore the poor soldiers who had been drafted into the army to kill or be killed? Even at the risk of arrest or torture, we had to work for peace.

Among the three branches of Van Hanh University, the SYSS had the best organized group of students. To allow the SYSS, with me as president of the student union, to remain linked with Van Hanh University, would have meant accepting Thây Nhat Hanh's direction of working for peace, and that was risky for Thây Minh Chau and the university. In my meditations, I came to understand that Thây Minh Chau's motivation was fear of losing the university, and I was able to accept him. Later, when the communists came to power in Saigon, I was not surprised to hear that he was among the first to cooperate with the new regime, ignoring all reports of human rights violations, again because "we should not mix up politics and religion." During the communist regime, Thây Minh Chau and a number of other monks who have cooperated closely with the regime have been able to continue translating sutras from Pali into Vietnamese. I understand their attitude and do not complain about them, but it is easier for me to understand the Buddha when he said, "During forty-five years of teaching, I did not say a word."

Thây Minh Chau's pronouncement left the SYSS with no legal status. I told Thây Thanh Van, our director, "Legality is a matter of how we think. The government of Vietnam was not genuinely elected by the people, so it is not a legal government. And Thây Minh Chau's act toward us proves that his moral values are not worthy of our association with him. So we must continue on our path of service, with or without legal status. When we serve the poor with love and dignity, that is law enough." But Thây Thanh Van was not convinced. He thought we should close the school if we could not obtain legal status. Trying to comfort him, I said, "Do you agree that we can continue without Thây Minh Chau as our spiritual leader? If so, why do we need his legal status? If we have to go to jail, we will go together. But until the police arrest us, we have no choice. We must continue our work." Seeing that I was not afraid, Thây Thanh Van felt more confident, and he agreed. From 1966 to 1973, we operated the SYSS without any legal status from the South Vietnamese government, the UBC, or Van Hanh University. It was not until 1973, when Thây Nhat Hanh met with Thây Huyen Quang and Thây Thien Minh in Bangkok, that the UBC set up the Buddhist Committee for Reconstruction and Social Development and made the SYSS the core of that committee.

Thây Thanh Van and I had many other differences about the SYSS, but we always managed to work through them. For example, I did not want to spend money on new buildings or do anything just for the sake of appearance. I preferred to put all our resources into training workers, even if that meant sending them into the poor areas and the war zones to learn "on the job." I had no interest in doing anything just to give the school some prestige. One staff member, who had trained in rural development in the West, wanted banners and posters about our work to accompany the SYSS workers wherever they went. Such things seemed strange to me. When I worked in the slums, I did not even know I was a "social worker." But the others really wanted banners, so in Binh Phuoc Village, we put them up. I was a little embarrassed, but I did not want to hurt anyone, and I saw that people seemed happy with the banners. Later I wondered if these banners and posters hadn't made the presence of SYSS workers too provocative for those who did not like the Buddhists. I even wondered if such actions might have led to the murder of our friends.

The SYSS staff: Nguyen Van Phuc, my sister Thanh, myself, and Thây Thanh Van.

Under some pressure from outside and from other staff members, Thây Thanh Van wanted to have a large campus, a respectable office, and a good car for the SYSS. He felt that appearance was important in order to get people's support and respect. I often had to remind myself that the realization of the SYSS was the fruit of the efforts of many people, and I had to modify my wishes according to the decisions of the group, even though at times it was not satisfying for me to do so. But this was the collective karma of the community with whom I lived and worked, and I tried my best to forget my individual ego and join with the others.

From June 1964 to May 1966, when I worked under Thây Nhat Hanh's direction, our work proceeded rapidly and thoroughly. Sometimes Thây joined us in Cau Kinh or Thao Diên for the whole day, playing with the peasant children. In the evening, we went back home carrying Thây Nhat Hanh on the luggage rack of our motorbike, the way Vietnamese carry children. Thây did not look very "high-monkish" on the luggage rack!

One day, when I came to Van Hanh University for an appointment, Thây asked if I would give him a lift to Cho Lon to buy a watchband, as his had broken. I said that I would ask one of my friends to get it for him, but he insisted on going himself. So I rescheduled my appointment and drove him. When I parked my car on a small street in Cho Lon under two rows of beautiful, tall trees, Thây suggested that we practice walking meditation under the shade of the trees. We enjoyed the cool air and the quiet afternoon so much, we eventually returned to Van Hanh University without buying anything. When we arrived, a Catholic father was waiting to see Thây. Seeing Thây Nhat Hanh, a monk, sitting alone with a young lady in a car, he looked at us with envy, or perhaps a tinge of disdain, and said, "I wish Catholics could live like that too." That was one of the rare occasions in which I had some private time with Thây Nhat Hanh during the two intense years I worked under his direction. But time like that had been so rewarding that, even when he was far away, just thinking about it made me feel nourished.

By early 1966, we moved all of the classes and dormitories of the SYSS to the new campus in Phu Tho Hoa, just outside of Saigon. One night in June, a group of unknown men threw grenades into the campus temple, and two students, Nguyen Ton and Le Van Vinh, were seriously wounded. Vinh has been paralyzed ever since. One grenade was also thrown into Thây Nhat Hanh's room, but a curtain deflected it. In fact, Thây had left the country a few weeks earlier. In February 1967, grenades were thrown into the SYSS dormitories during the night. A woman student, Le Thi Vui, and a woman teacher, Nguyen Thi Phuong Lien, a supporter of the SYSS from Quang Ngai who had stopped by to spend a few days with us, both died immediately. Another woman, Bui Thi Huong, was hit with more than 600 fragments of grenade. A fourth woman, Ho Thi Dieu, had her liver damaged severely. Altogether, eighteen people were killed or seriously wounded. It was difficult to remain calm with so much hatred and anger directed towards us. We wondered how people could be so cruel. We had no weapons, only love and concern for fellow humans. We cared not only for the poor peasants, but also for many other friends. How could they throw grenades at unarmed young people?

We had to take care of the wounded, and also to organize funerals for our two friends who had died. Thây Thanh Van asked me to write a speech for him to read at the funeral. After one Day of Mindfulness by myself, I wrote this eulogy, which was delivered by Thây Thanh Van: "We cannot hate you, you who have thrown grenades and killed our friends, because we know that men are not our enemies. Our only enemies are the misunderstanding, hatred, jealousy, and ignorance that lead to such acts of violence. Please allow us to remove all misunderstanding so we can work together for the happiness of the Vietnamese people. Our only aim is to help remove ignorance and illiteracy from the countryside of Vietnam. Social change must start in our hearts with the will to transform our own egotism, greed, and lust into understanding, love, commitment, and sharing responsibility for the poverty and injustice in our country." Many important guests—Catholics, Protestants, and Buddhists, conservatives and progressives—were moved by his speech, and after that, Thây Tri Quang and Thây Thiên Hoa, the eldest monks of the UBC, offered their support for our work.

In the U.S., Thây Nhat Hanh's American friends and supporters were presenting him as "the founder of Van Hanh University, an intellectual center of the Buddhist leadership, and the SYSS, a grassroots movement in Vietnam to help the poor." Because Thây spoke so eloquently on behalf of the poor peasants of Vietnam who were under the rain of bombs, those Americans who were in favor of continuing the war wanted to discredit him by challenging his connection with these two key institutions in Vietnam. One U.S. private organization approached Thây Thanh Van in July 1966, when our SYSS was at its lowest ebb financially, and offered us a grant of $100,000. We were at the beginning of the second and final year of training 300 students, who had arrived without knowing that we had only 100 dông ($1) in our bank account. Most of the money that our many supporters had sent us had been used for the construction of the forty-room student dormitory in the new Phu Tho Hoa campus, and the work was only one-fourth done. Confident that we could collect enough donations to complete the work, we had hired a construction team and used all of our money to pay them. But when Thây Nhat Hanh delivered his Five-Point Peace Proposal in May and Van Hanh University severed its relation to the SYSS in June, many well-to-do Vietnamese withdrew their support.

So when the semester started, we ate just rice. Even though we were vegetarian, we could not even afford tofu, mushrooms, bean sprouts, or gluten. We six Tiep Hien members had no place to hold

SYSS campus dining area.

our precious Days of Mindfulness, as the SYSS temple and our Tiep
Hien room needed to be used as dormitories. Two hundred forty-
one young men slept in the meditation hall and on all the verandas
around the hall, and fifty-nine women squeezed into our Tiep Hien
room. In a meeting of the SYSS board, I proposed that we tell the
SYSS students the truth about our financial problems, but Thây
Thanh Van was afraid that panic might spread and we might lose
many of the trainees. So I proposed that we ask our wealthiest and
most generous friends to contribute rice, and we collected thirty-
seven 200-pound sacks! Then our friends from the Cau Ong Lanh
wholesale market brought two truckloads of old cabbages, turnips,
and mustard greens for us to make pickles, and our need for food
was satisfied. But we still did not know how we might raise the
money to complete the construction work.

It was at that time that a U.S. organization offered us $100,000
to complete our dormitories. On principle, we had always refused
help from any of the warring parties, but since this was a private,
cultural organization and not an arm of the government, we were
all delighted when Thây Thanh Van brought us the news. But
months passed, and then a year, and eighteen months later, still no

money had come. Whenever I asked Thây Thanh Van about it, he would smile and say, "No, not yet."

One day in June 1967, I happened to read a notice in an old English-language newsletter of Van Hanh University that, "The Rector of Van Hanh University declares that Thich Nhat Hanh has no responsibilities whatsoever in connection with this university," and it was signed by Thich Minh Chau. Startled by this unkindness—Thây Minh Chau had been invited by Thây to take care of Van Hanh University when the most difficult work had already been completed—I brought the newsletter to Thây Thanh Van. He was also shocked, and then he told me that the private U.S. organization had asked him to sign a similar statement before they would give us the $100,000 grant. He politely replied, "Please wait a few days, and I will bring you the signed statement." Of course he never brought it back to them. He told me that he knew right away that he could never sign it, but he didn't want to cause additional trouble to the SYSS by straightforwardly refusing the grant.

In the same newsletter, Thây Minh Chau thanked that private U.S. organization for their generous donation of $100,000 to build a library at Van Hanh University. Thây Thanh Van and I understood the reason that foundation had offered us a grant—to undermine Thây Nhat Hanh's call for peace. Thây Thanh Van had suspected this from the beginning, but he was afraid that if I had known about it, I would have responded too strongly and created even more problems for the school. He was probably right.

Thây Thanh Van had many gemlike qualities, but I always had the feeling that if Thây Nhat Hanh had been there, the school would have developed more deeply. I did my best under the circumstances to help keep the school on course, and we did all right. I always tried to make my point, not by forcing anyone but by setting an example myself. Still, I cannot deny that we missed Thây Nhat Hanh's presence and wisdom very much.

CHAPTER TEN

Sister Mai

It seems like only yesterday that I stopped by to see my dear friend, Nhat Chi Mai. Mai was a sister in the Dharma, my closest fellow traveller along the Buddha's path of understanding and love. Whenever she spoke, her voice was filled with affection and a unique blend of innocence and wisdom that my friends and I began to call "the special accent of Mai." "Phuong! Where have you been? You're all covered with sweat," she said to me, with her eyebrows knit and her lips pursed, like a mother worrying about her only child.

"Do I look as if I've been working in the rice fields? I've just come from Tan Dinh Market collecting pledge money from our school's supporters." Mai laughed and served me a large glass of cool water—exactly what I needed that hot July day.

Her dress was as simple as a nun's robe, and it made her look especially beautiful. After a moment, I became serious and asked Mai what she thought about Thây's appeal for peace. She sat silently, and then, stroking my hair, she said, "Phuong, you know I love and respect Thây, especially his vision of social service, but his political activities worry me."

I understood. Thây's appeal for a cease-fire and the withdrawal of American troops was still very early. A "nationalist" wouldn't dare demand such a thing, and our government and newspapers condemned him. As the youngest in her family, protected by her parents, Mai had never even seen a bombed village, so how could she not worry when the radio, newspapers, and even the President himself accused Thây of being a communist?

Anxiously, on the verge of tears, I said, "Please consider this, dear sister. The Buddha taught us not to take life, so how can we sit by while our people kill one another? For 4,000 years, our country has defeated every single invader. Why do we need the help of foreign troops now? Mai, do you know that when Thây's 'Prayer for Peace'

was printed in the *Buddhist Weekly,* I asked the Executive Council
of the Buddhist Church to support eight of us in a fast until death
as a prayer for peace? But the Council did not approve, and, without their backing, we knew that our act would be useless."

"Of course they wouldn't approve!" she interrupted. "Who would
care for your aged mother?"

"I know that I would commit the sin of impiety towards my
mother by killing myself, but if my death could help shorten the
war and save lives, I would be willing to pay for the sin of impiety
in another life."

Mai sat still for a long moment, then she took my hands, looked
deeply into my eyes, and said, in a determined voice, "Dear younger
sister, you are right. If there is ever another opportunity to fast for
peace, count on me to join you." The sincerity of her words moved
me so, and I wept.

Three months later Mai joined our work for peace at Van Hanh
University. As the daughter of a well-off family, this kind of "underground" work was new to her, but with copies of Thây Nhat Hanh's
book, *Lotus in a Sea of Fire,* hidden in her white Volkswagen, she
delivered ten to this school, twenty to that, and through her efforts,
Thây's book made its way into the hands of almost every teacher
and student organization in Saigon.

One Saturday, during our weekly Day of Mindfulness, Mai invited me into her room, took my hand in hers and said, "Younger
sister, I have an idea. Remember how the eight of you wanted to
fast for peace? What if I and one other person joined you, and ten
of us left a statement for peace and then disemboweled ourselves?
Our act could reach many people, and it might move them to end
this dreadful war! Fasting and even self-immolation no longer wake
people up. We have to be imaginative!" I was shocked, but I promised Mai I would consider her proposal.

I stayed in my room for four days, weighing the pros and cons,
and finally I told her that I thought we shouldn't do it. The eight of
us had been single when we proposed the fast for peace. Now all the
others were married, and some lived far away. I suspected there
would be only Mai and me. "The peace movement is still quite
weak," I said. "If we sacrifice ourselves, the only thing we can be
sure of is that our brothers and sisters in the peace movement will

be without us. And we promised Thây Nhat Hanh that we would help Thây Thanh Van manage the School of Youth for Social Service, at least until the first students complete their training." Mai knew that the financial crisis of the SYSS was critical after Thây Nhat Hanh's departure. If we two, the main fundraisers for the school, died, who would care for the students? I spoke with all my heart, and she agreed to abandon the idea, although she wanted to wait for the final word from Thây Nhat Hanh. She had sent him a letter but hadn't received a response yet. A week later, she cheerfully told me that Thây had written back forbidding the sacrifice.

Feeling a great sense of responsibility for the School of Youth for Social Service, Mai said to me, "We need to work as much as we can. Phuong, you must make me work harder. You are so good in your work in the slums, the peace movement, and the school. I wish I could be more like you." I held her shoulder tenderly and said, "Dear elder sister Mai, each person is unique, and you are a beautiful flower. There is no need to be like anyone else, especially me!" At the beginning of the second year of the SYSS, we were having a severe financial crisis. When Nga and I collected more sacks of rice than Uyen or Mai, Mai reproached herself, but her disappointment caused her to be even more diligent in starting self-support projects for the school. Each week, she presented a new list of proposals.

Thây Nhat Hanh was far away, and no one had taught us Avalokitesvara's great art of listening or the Buddha's art of sangha building—living in harmony with those around you. So, instead of sitting with Mai, listening deeply, and kindly showing her the strong and weak points of each proposal, we became impatient and ignored her. Many people would have felt frustrated and accumulated internal wounds that might explode at some time, but Mai seemed able to look deeply into herself and heal and transform each wound with ease.

Every week, she would propose something new. In a soft voice, she said to me, "Phuong, if you are free Monday, please come with me to the rice market. We can buy large quantities of rice and then sell it in smaller amounts to raise money." The next week she would suggest, "Phuong, perhaps we can sell soap to the families that support the school." And the following week, she would have yet another plan, and the next week another. Her proposals were not particularly wise, but I did not want to hurt her, so I didn't say anything. Then one day, when too many silent disagreements had accumulated in my mind's "store consciousness," I answered in a very irritated way: "Just go ahead and do it, Mai! But don't force me to do everything with you. I have my own work."

As soon as the words left my mouth, I regretted them, but I could not take them back. At dinnertime, I walked up behind Mai, hugged her, and said, "Where would you like me to go Monday?" She smiled sweetly, and I knew she bore no grudge. The next Monday we went to the soap market together, and on Tuesday we went to the home of a sponsor to sell our soap. On Wednesday we picked up rice, and it was only on Thursday that I got around to my own work. Mai could have done those errands by herself, but she always insisted how much fun it would be to do things together.

To satisfy Mai, Uyen and I would have had to spend two or three days each week just accompanying her. Looking back, I wish we had done so. But at the time, we grumbled to each other, "We spent 1,000 *piasters* on rice, carried it across the city in traffic, and arrived at the home of a sponsor to sell it for a profit of fifteen piasters, while it cost us eight piasters for gas, and took the whole morning! I could earn 300 piasters an hour teaching math." Uyen and I had not yet learned the joy of just being together with a friend, the work, the rice sellers, and the sponsors. Uyen and I did not know how to practice peace with every step, but it seems that Mai did. With or without us, she embarked on many projects just to earn small amounts of money for the school. Then one day, she touched the heart of a wealthy man with her gentle way of being, and he gave the school 20,000 dông that we used to start many self-supporting projects. Little by little, we repaid the construction loans, and the sponsors' pledges were again used to buy food.

One evening after we had recited the Tiep Hien precepts, I suggested that we build a bungalow with six tiny meditation rooms for each Tiep Hien brother and sister to use for a half-day solitary retreat every week. I knew that would be a real treasure. Uyen and the other brothers and sisters were overjoyed by the idea, but Mai opposed it, saying that sharing a room with others was practicing the way also, that it would be too much of a luxury to have our own rooms. I did not want a fancy building, just a palm-leaf and bamboo hut, a place to be alone to calm our emotions after six days of strenuous work.

Mai sat silently and then reminded us that we did not have the money and that if we did, we should use it for the school, not to build a house for ourselves. I was afraid that if we did not build this bungalow, we might lose ourselves and be unable to serve anyone. Seeing my determination, Mai finally agreed. At times, I felt she did not understand my suffering. I suppose that was because she lived on a different level from most of us. She always seemed re-freshed and in touch with her deepest self.

To raise the money, I began by asking my older sister, "Nam, if I get married, how much will you give me as a wedding gift?" My fam-ily had been concerned about me not getting married, so when Nam heard this, she answered right away, "Three thousand pias-ters!" "That's all?" I responded, "How about 5,000?" She said, "Okay, 5,000." I put out my hand and said, "For people who want a family, a wedding is important. But for someone who wants to be a resource for many people, having a special room to quiet her mind is equally important, don't you agree? How about giving it to me right now so we can build a bungalow for a solitary retreat?" Nam laughed and gave me 3,000 piasters.

Mai donated 5,000 piasters of her own money, and with a few other donations, we were able to build a small house. Uyen and I al-ways had a simple arrangement of bamboo or wildflowers in our rooms, while the flowers in Mai's room were always arranged in the formal, traditional way. Every time I entered it, I was struck by the resplendent Buddha on gold paper hanging on her wall—the Bud-dha sat in a full lotus, surrounded by clouds, flowers, and a halo—and a set of eight pictures of Thây Quang Duc. Mai also had a hanging pot with a branch of golden plum flowers and one bright red, plastic rose. It was exactly like entering an old-style nun's room, except that her bed always had many covers and a pink satin pillowcase—appropriate for the favorite daughter of a well-to-do family!

One day Mai entered my room and exclaimed, "Your room is so sad. There are no pictures at all here." When she looked more closely, she noticed a tiny photo of a lake and a forest just above the floor, and near my bed, at eye level, sketches of crying children.

Surprised, she asked, "Phuong, why are the pictures so close to the ground where no one can see them?" I answered, "I did not arrange the room for others. I placed the pictures low so I can see them when I lie down." Mai shook her head and said, "How selfish!" When she accused me of being selfish, I felt angry, but my irritation dissipated quickly when I remembered how different her nature was from mine. We laughed, and everything was fine.

One Saturday in April, when it was Mai's turn to read the Precepts of the Order of Interbeing, her voice faltered as she said, "Do not kill. Do not let others kill. Find whatever means possible to protect life and build peace." From that moment on, she spoke so softly it was nearly impossible to hear her. As we were putting the precept books back on the shelves, Uyen asked, "What happened, Mai?" And I added, "You seemed to lose your concentration during the recitation. Are you all right?" Mai just smiled and returned to her room early that evening.

The following two Saturdays she did not come to our Days of Mindfulness. Because the situation in Saigon was so dangerous—four friends from the school had been murdered—I assumed that her parents had forbidden her from spending the night with us. But when she didn't show up for a third Saturday, I thought that even if her parents wanted her home at night, they would certainly let her recite the precepts with us in the afternoon.

I wondered if something could be wrong, yet, at the same time, I was upset with Mai for not taking our Days of Mindfulness more seriously. At least she could have told us why she had missed the SYSS staff meetings, the Days of Mindfulness, and her work at the university.

Then, on Sunday, May 14, 1967, she came to her last Morning of Mindfulness. I was in my room, looking out the window onto a field of green bamboo, and I didn't hear her car pull up. Uyen knocked gently at my door and said, "Sister Mai is here, wearing a beautiful violet ao dai with gold embroidery!" I stood up and walked slowly from my room, intending to reproach her. But as I entered the hallway, I saw Mai surrounded by friends, all trying to tell her something, and then, like baby chicks with their mother, we all followed her into the dining room.

Mai's hair was arranged beautifully, and her new dress made her look as if she were about to attend a ceremony. Right away, she began slicing the banana cake she had baked especially for us. I smiled and said, teasingly, "First you abandon us for three weeks, and now you dress so beautifully and bring a delicious cake! Are you going to get married?" Others joined in, "Very possible! Mai looks so pretty today!" We all laughed, but Mai just smiled silently.

I felt disappointed that, once again, our dream for peaceful social change was being pushed aside. So many young friends shared our aspiration, but then they married and had children, and always had excuses for not helping with the work. Now Mai was going too. At that moment, her voice pierced my thoughts, "Phuong, please come to Tu Nghiêm Pagoda early on Tuesday morning. It is Wesak, the Buddha's nativity, and something interesting will happen."

Mai was always kind to the old nuns at the pagoda, so I thought she was asking me to help decorate their temple for Wesak. "I respect your wish," I said, somewhat irritably, "but is it really necessary for me to be at the temple so early?" Nhat Chi Mai looked directly at me and said, "If you don't want to come, it's okay, but please don't speak so strongly about it!" When she left, I felt ashamed, and I resolved to go to the pagoda early on Tuesday, just to please her.

◇

On Tuesday morning, Ngoc ran frantically into my family's house and told me that Sister Mai had set herself on fire, right outside the Tu Nghiêm Pagoda! I couldn't believe my ears! I sat perfectly still for a long while, and then I said, "Sister Mai has sacrificed herself for peace." My mother, sitting next to me, burst into tears. "Your friend's act," she said, "will lead her parents to the grave!" She looked at me with each word, preparing herself for the day I might do the same.

Without a word, Ngoc and I went out, knowing that much needed to be done. I went straight to Mai's parents' home, and when I entered the house, they embraced me, sobbing. As we sat together, her mother actually passed out several times. Then I drove them to the pagoda, and they went inside. I don't know why, but I was unable to enter the pagoda and see Mai in death. Instead I ran to the Cau Muoi Market and told our vendor friends of Mai's sacrifice. As I was sharing the news with dear old Aunt Ba, I started to cry and she began to weep with me. Soon everyone in the market was in tears. Aunt Ba walked over to the taxi and pedicab drivers, spoke a few words to each, and immediately the drivers began to carry all the vendors from the market to the pagoda to see Mai for the last time.

The well-known writer, Bac Thieu Son, also came to the pagoda, joined by several other intellectuals. His face was drawn, and when he saw me, he could only manage to say, "Phuong!" and tears rolled down his cheeks. The printer who had refused to print our peace books was also there. He came up to me, sobbing, and said that in the future he would help us in any way we needed. Even government officials and military men came and offered to help our work for peace. It was only then that I realized that my words of advice to Mai against sacrificing ourselves—"We are too few. If we are gone, there will not be enough people to do the work"—were wrong. Her sacrifice had indeed moved the hearts of many people and caused the peace movement to swell like waves in a storm. Even friends who had become guerrillas in the jungle sent back news and asked, "How can we help realize Mai's wish for peace and reconciliation?"

Before she died, Nhat Chi Mai placed two statues in front of her, the Virgin Mary and Avalokitesvara Bodhisattva. In her poems and letters, she asked Catholics and Buddhists to work together for peace so that people might realize the love of Jesus and the compassion of the Buddha.

I never saw Thây Tri Quang more moved. At one o'clock in the morning, he sent a message to Tu Nghiêm Pagoda to ask the nuns to provide a car for me to come to An Quang Pagoda. (He was afraid I would be arrested or kidnapped if I came by myself.) When I arrived at his pagoda, the gate was locked, and I had to climb over it. As I entered his room, he was trying to repair an old tape recorder, and he told me, "This machine hardly works, but I want to have a tape of someone reading the poems and letters of the young woman who sacrificed herself so I can come to know her better. Will you read them? You are also a young woman from the South, so your voice must be close to hers."

The next day, at four o'clock in the morning, Thây Tri Quang disguised himself as a novice and had someone take him to Tu Nghiêm Pagoda. He had been under house arrest for some time, so he could not travel openly. In front of Mai's coffin, he chanted sutras for her. When he finished, he called me into a room of the pagoda and said, "You must find a way to print Mai's letters and distribute them widely. I will pay for the paper and the printing. Ask some of the Buddhist elders to lend you the money, and my younger sister will pay them back."

The following day, Thây Tri Quang called me again, "Mai's prayer was for all religions to work together for peace. I've heard that Father Nguyen Ngoc Lan is a progressive Catholic and close to us. Please ask him to write a preface to Mai's letters." I was very moved. In the past, Thây Tri Quang had been skeptical about working with Catholics. In fact, Father Lan had already offered to print Mai's letters and write a foreword to them. He even agreed to circulate them, a very dangerous thing to do. With each heartfelt act, I thought of Mai's smiling face, and I could hear her saying, "Isn't that wonderful, Phuong?" Just as she had prayed, the elders of the Buddhist Church tried every day to find opportunities to work with the Catholics, and the Catholics also began to have more sympathy for the Buddhists. It all began with everyone's appreciation of Sister Mai.

During the three days her body lay in Tu Nghiêm Pagoda, I tried to keep busy. I went to meet students both inside and outside our movement. I went to all the markets. I visited many organizations and friends. When I saw Hiep and other friends sitting by her body, weeping and clutching the yellow cloth that covered her, I didn't have the courage to come near. I could only think that my body should be there too, or in a pagoda in Hue, Ben Tre, or Can Tho. Hadn't that been Mai's wish? But I was alive, able to stand, walk, eat, drink, and sleep.

Day after day, I met with friends to inform them of Mai's sacrifice for peace. And night after night, I stayed up translating her poems into English and French for newspapers and peace groups around the world. But it was not until Ngoc brought me Mai's final letters and poems that I understood how she had spent her last three weeks: she had stayed with her parents in order to give them those last precious hours of her life. She was "sweet bananas, fragrant rice, and precious honey," a loving child for them, all the while preparing for her sacrifice.

Students came to the pagoda to prevent the police from taking Mai's body away. The police, afraid that the news of her sacrifice would travel to other provinces and inspire others to work for peace, tried to persuade her parents to bury her right away. Mai's father resisted, but his wife's grief was so great that finally, on the third day, he agreed to bring Mai's body to An Duong Dia in Phu Lam for cremation.

On the day after Mai's sacrifice, many newspapers carried blank spaces where the news of her act had been censored. Word of her death travelled only by friends, but even so, on the day of the cremation, a huge crowd came to the ceremony. When the funeral car reached Phu Lam Bridge, the crowd behind it stretched more than five kilometers, all the way back to the Tu Nghiêm Pagoda. Students and teachers, merchants and vendors, politicians and priests were all present. I was surprised to see so many wealthy men and women who, until then, had accused us of being under the control of the communists.

There was a fine, cool rain. The white dresses of young women students, the black shirts of poor workers, the monks' and nuns' robes, the simple rags of our street vendor friends from the markets, and the fine clothes of the well-to-do were all moistened by the gentle rain. My younger sister Thanh, with her gift for lightening even the saddest moments, whispered in my ear, "Sister, do you see Mai? She is sitting on the funeral car looking back at us, her face bright, saying, 'Oh, Phuong and Thanh, I feel very joyful. There really are a lot of people here, aren't there?'" I had been walking in the rain, immersed in my sadness, when I heard Thanh imitate Mai's special accent, and I had to smile. She was right. It was exactly what Mai would have said.

When you want something ordinary, you can just go out and buy it, but when you want something extraordinary, like love, understanding, and peace for a whole nation, you have to pay for it with something much more precious than money. My sister, Nhat Chi Mai, did not commit suicide. She loved life. She had a good education and the conditions to live comfortably, even in the midst of

The funeral of Nhat Chi Mai.

the war. She sacrificed her life because, more than anything, she wanted the killing to stop. She tried to bring peace to Vietnam by paying for it with her life.

I remember Thây's poem, "Recommendation," that she read again and again just before she immolated herself:

> *Promise me,*
> *promise me this day,*
> *promise me now,*
> *while the sun is overhead*
> *exactly at the zenith,*
> *promise me:*
>
> *Even as they*
> *strike you down*
> *with a mountain of hate and violence;*
> *even as they step on you and crush you*
> *like a worm,*
> *even as they dismember and disembowel you,*
> *remember, brother,*
> *remember:*
> *man is not our enemy.*

Banner for peace.

The only act worthy of you is compassion—
invincible, limitless, unconditional.
Hatred will never let you face
the beast in man.

One day, when you face this beast alone,
with your courage intact, your eyes kind,
untroubled,
(even as no one sees them),
out of your smile
will bloom a flower.
And those who love you
will behold you
across ten thousand worlds of birth and dying.

Alone again,
I will go on with bent head,
knowing that love has become eternal.
On the long, rough road,
the sun and the moon
will continue to shine.

After Nhat Chi Mai immolated herself for peace on May 16, 1967, I became ever more determined to find ways to end the suffering of Vietnam.

CHAPTER ELEVEN

In the War Zone

On July 5, 1967, I was on my motorbike en route to Binh Phuoc Village, when another social worker going in the opposite direction waved me down and told me that four SYSS workers—Tuan, Tho, Lanh, and Hy—had been murdered. Their bodies were still lying on the ground near the Binh Phuoc River. Ha Van Dinh, a novice monk, survived the murder attempt and was in the hospital.

My first thought was that someone should guard Ha Van Dinh, because as the only witness, he could be killed in the hospital. So right away I went to see him, and I helped move him to another hospital where he registered under a false name. Dinh told me that the murderers had acted almost friendly as they led the five students to the riverbank. Dinh thought that they were about to get into a boat, when one of the men said rather suddenly, "Are you from the School of Youth for Social Service?" The students all said "Yes," and the man said, "I am sorry, but we have to kill you." Then they shot our five friends, one by one. Dinh fell into the water and survived, but the other four died immediately.

I went to the riverbank and saw the bodies of my beloved younger brothers, and I was close to despair. Thây Thanh Van arrived an hour later, and together we arranged for the bodies to be brought back to the school. We set the date for a funeral, and again, Thây Thanh Van asked me to write a eulogy for him to read.

Pro-communist Vietnamese told us, "You should cry out against the Americans! It was CIA agents who killed your friends!" Pro-American Vietnamese said, "You should speak out against the communists. It was they who killed your friends." Even among Buddhists, there was strong pressure for us to condemn the killers. But we knew that, according to the teaching of the Buddha, humans are not our enemies. Misunderstanding, hatred, jealousy, and confusion are our enemies. Still, it was hard to put that into words when confronted with the corpses of our four dear friends.

For three days and nights, I could hardly sleep. I dwelled in mindfulness, reciting gathas, mindfulness verses, as I did my everyday activities: "Washing my hands, I vow to have clean hands to embrace the path of love. I pray that the thoughts and deeds of those who killed my friends will be cleansed." During the third night, the murderer's words that Dinh had told me, "I am sorry, but we have to kill you," sprang into my mind, and I began to see that the message of understanding and love that Thây Thanh Van had delivered at the last funeral had reached even the killers. It was obvious that these men had been forced to kill our friends, for if they refused, they themselves could have been killed. In the speech I wrote for Thây Thanh Van, I thanked the murderers for saying that they were forced to kill. "That proved that you did not want to kill us, but for your own safety, you had to do it. We hope that one day you will help us in our work for peace." The funeral was held four days after the murders, and from then on, we received support everywhere we went. The number of workers in the SYSS increased quickly, and we had the full cooperation of monks and nuns throughout the country.

In January 1968, eight months after Nhat Chi Mai burned herself to death as a prayer for peace, the fighting continued fiercely. I knew that I had to do something to help my Dharma sister realize her dream of peace, so I drafted a petition calling upon the warring parties to prolong the cease-fire that was already scheduled for Têt, the Vietnamese New Year. I persuaded a number of prominent professors from Saigon University to sign it, and the professors asked their colleagues to sign. Eventually we had seventy-one signatures, more than one-third of the faculty, and we published the petition on January 16, 1968. Students in the peace movement also arranged for a Peace Festival to celebrate Têt and express their wish for a longer cease-fire. The North Vietnamese had declared a three-day cease-fire, but the South Vietnamese had declared only one day.

As it turned out, just a few hours after the cease-fire started, fierce battles broke out in provinces throughout the South. The National Liberation Front forced civilians in the countryside to walk alongside their guerrilla troops, thus forming a sea of people who were screaming, "Advance, advance!" Seeing such huge crowds, the South Vietnamese army panicked and called for the Americans to drop bombs, and hundreds of civilians were killed. Eighty-five percent of the homes in many provinces and cities were destroyed, including those in Ben Tre, my hometown. The guerrillas advanced into Ben Tre City, Hue City, and the Saigon suburbs, infiltrated into crowded slums, and shot at the planes, thus attracting more bombs and destruction.

Following the battle, there were dead bodies all over the streets of Saigon. When the Red Cross workers tried to collect them, they were shot at by the guerrillas. So I suggested to my colleagues at the SYSS that we gather the dead bodies and bury them. I knew that after three or four days, the stench would be unbearable and that diseases could spread. For four years, many Buddhist rescue committees had the experience of going into war zones to rescue the wounded, protected only by the Buddhist flag. In Vietnam the Buddhist flag was safer than the Red Cross flag, because both warring sides respected the Buddhists. But when I told Thây Thanh Van, "We need to go out and pick up dead bodies," he was silent for a while and then reminded me that we were a school for training social workers in rural development, not ambulance drivers or Red Cross workers. I was very disappointed, and silently I decided to do the work alone. I announced this privately to my Tiep Hien friends and a few SYSS coworkers.

Eventually other young monks, nuns, and laypersons joined me in that work. After a few days of gathering up the dead bodies, we went back to the SYSS, deeply touched by the frailty of human bodies. Men and women who were strong and beautiful when they were alive turned to rotten, smelly corpses in just a few days. The images of once joyful, vibrant faces of friends now dead and rotting stayed with me. I shared the experiences of my deep meditation on life and death with Thây Thanh Van, and he was inspired by this and joined us in our efforts to pick up and bury the many corpses.

It was an extraordinarily difficult task. There was an enormous gap between my idealistic perception and the reality of the situation. The bodies smelled horrible! At that time, there were no gloves, work clothes, or chemicals to neutralize the smell, so we put peanut oil on our noses—but that didn't help at all. That stench followed me for months so that the smell of anything organic

Nuns in Hue contemplating those who died under the bombs.

brought back the nauseating smell of rotting corpses, and I could only eat plain, salted rice for several months. Thây Thanh Van may have been right when he said that we could not ask people to do such difficult work.

During the days of the Tết Offensive, when fighting went on in the streets of Saigon, people were asked not to leave their homes unless absolutely necessary. People were glued to their radios listening to the latest news. Suddenly I heard the Minister of Education on the radio calling "the seventy-one university professors who had signed a petition for peace on January 16, 1968" to come to the ministry "for an urgent national matter." Then the speaker read all seventy-one names, including mine, not just once, but every half hour. My family urged me not to go, fearing that I would be shot. We had just seen on television Colonel Nguyen Ngoc Loan shooting a guerrilla he had caught. I was very afraid, but I thought that since the petition had been my idea, I had to take full responsibility and go. If I didn't, it could be all the worse for the others.

Only twenty-one of us came to the Ministry of Education at the time announced on the radio. The minister told us that the National Police suspected we had plotted the Tết Offensive with the communists. He said he wanted to protect us, and that we only needed to retract our peace appeal and sign a new petition condemning the communists. Eighteen professors signed the new petition, hoping to avoid trouble during these tumultuous times. But

Father Nguyen Ngoc Lan, Professor Chau Tam Luan, and I refused. We said that we could not sign the ministry's petition, because our students had heard our names mentioned every half hour on the governmental radio and now the same names on the radio again for signing the new petition. It would be clear that we had succumbed to the government's pressure to sign. We did, however, offer to draft another petition later, outside the ministry, condemning the violation of the Têt cease-fire. By refusing to sign the ministry's petition, I was certain I would go to jail. At that meeting, I told my colleagues, "The most important gift a teacher can give his students is dignity. We have always tried our best to be worthy of our students' trust. If we die under violence, our spirits will blossom in their hearts. But if we sign the petition offered by the government today, it means we have submitted to the government's threats. This is not what we want to teach the younger generation." After that meeting, we were all released, but I suspected the matter was not yet over.

When I returned home, I packed my toothbrush, pajamas, and a light sweater, so I would be ready to go to jail when the police came. But, instead, I received an invitation from the Minister of Education to come to his office. When I arrived, he said, "You have refused to retract your declaration. I am very busy, but the Chief of Police has asked me to settle this matter. If you still refuse to retract, I will have to inform the police, and you will be arrested immediately and relieved of your post at the university."

I breathed deeply and said in a very firm voice, "Sir, I came to you today because I know that you were once a professor, my elder brother in teaching. When you speak in such a threatening way, it is impossible for us to have real communication. So do what you want with me. Please send me to jail. If I allow you to coerce me as you suggest, I would be no better than Colonel Lieu, the cherished comrade of President Thieu, who, as soon as he was arrested by the communists in Ben Tre, called upon all South Vietnamese soldiers to join the side of the North."

With tears in my eyes, I continued more gently, "Sir, I am like a bamboo shoot among university teachers. I am young, but my spirit may grow strong and beautiful. I spoke out frankly about the situation of the country, not for my own sake, but for the sake of the nation, even though prison may await me as a result. I appeal to your conscience as an elder brother to help me grow in this attitude, not to bow before coercion. Don't force me to go against my conscience. If I agree to sign your petition under threat of violence, then tonight if unknown men enter my house with guns and force me to sign a petition saying, 'Long live Mao Tse Tung,' must I not also sign that? If I sign under the threat of guns against my conscience and belief, who will be at fault? Do you really want to teach me that way of coercion?"

He seemed embarrassed and his attitude changed immediately. He said that I had misunderstood him, that he only wanted to protect me. Then he let me go without signing anything, and the police never came to arrest me. Apparently he protected me from the police.

In May 1968, a Japanese Quaker friend, Masako Yamanouchi, came to my home in Saigon to tell me that bombs were dropping around the campus of the SYSS. Masako was a lovely, young woman who came to work voluntarily with us. As an Asian wearing a Vietnamese *ao dai*, she looked just like a Vietnamese woman. She learned and spoke Vietnamese too, so she was a unique foreign social worker who was accepted in our school. We couldn't accept American or European social workers into the SYSS, because we knew we would be labelled by the communists as CIA agents.

Masako said that our water pump motor was out of gasoline and that she was on her way to buy some. "Thousands of people are caught at the school campus," she told me. "The gunfire is very dangerous. The water pump has been working all day and night, and now we are out of water."

I immediately took some medicine and bandages, and I rode on my motorbike to the SYSS headquarters. When I arrived close to the campus, I was terrified to see and hear bombs exploding everywhere. One rocket fell on the field right in front of me, and another landed behind me as I rode along on my motorbike. I realized I could be killed at any moment. There was so much bombing, people did not know where to run. The bombs were destroying homes throughout the area, and thousands of local residents ran to our campus for refuge.

People were ushered into the meditation hall, then the class-rooms, the library, the dining room, the kitchen, and finally the students' dormitory rooms, until all forty rooms of the main building were completely filled with people huddled closely, side by side. People continued to come, and we had to usher them into the bath-rooms and eventually even into the hallways and closets. Nearly 11,000 people squeezed into every nook and cranny of the campus. To try to prevent bombs from being dropped on us, we raised the Buddhist flag from the highest point of the school building.

So many of the people were wounded that we used up our entire supply of bandages in less than two hours, and many girls then tore up their own dresses to make more. Most of us were not trained to be nurses, doctors, or surgeons, but we had to do the work anyway. One young SYSS worker, trained as a nurse, served as doctor, delivering ten babies over the next several days.

At one point, while I was bandaging a wounded man, a small boy started tugging on my dress and saying something to me. His request seemed less serious than the man's wound, so I asked him to wait, but he kept tugging at me. Half an hour later, someone cried, "Look!" and I saw the same little boy pulling the bleeding body of an old woman. The desperate look in his eyes pressed on me like a clamp squeezing my heart. Later, I learned that he was an orphan and the wounded woman was his grandmother. Imagine how desperate he was to save her!

There was so much shooting around the campus that it was impossible for us to go outside and bury the eight dead bodies that had been carried by relatives to our campus. We finally had to ask three male students to go just outside the main building and dig the graves. With bullets flying around their heads, they managed to dig three holes the first day and five the second.

At that time, there were only thirty-seven social workers at the school, organizing the care of almost 11,000 refugees. We invited a few hundred of those able to take responsibility for themselves to help us, and we divided into teams—one team to do the medical work, one for childcare, one to cook, one to distribute food, one to take care of water, one to clear the road, and one to clean the rooms and the bathrooms. In addition, we dug a number of holes outside to use as latrines. We let our water pump run twenty-four hours a day for three days, and when it ran out of fuel, Masako had to go out and find some more. Fortunately, a good mechanic among the refugees was able to fix the pump each time it broke, but during the hours it wasn't working, we had 11,000 people without water. We really came to appreciate such simple things as having water when you need it.

Each night, after the refugees went to sleep, we social workers had a meeting to discuss the problems that had come up that day. We had to figure out many things, such as how to transport the seriously wounded to the hospital. That entailed crossing the fire zone, but we decided to try. We chose the shortest path across the battlefield. The monks and nuns in their yellow robes walked at the head of the line holding Buddhist flags, and behind them, we carried five seriously wounded persons. Crossing the area of the least intense fighting, we arrived at an area where we could hire a van and bring them to the hospital in Saigon.

On the third day of the May offensive, with the sudden influx of refugees on our campus, there was a rumor that the campus would be bombed very soon and that everyone should move out immediately. Some people believed the rumor, some didn't, and an atmosphere of panic ensued. Many people wanted to run away, but outside, the shooting was everywhere. South Vietnamese troops and NLF guerrillas were fighting each other on all four sides of the campus. Thây Thanh Van knew he had to do something.

Four months later, he revealed to us what he had done. He crossed the fire zone by himself, without even a Buddhist flag, just wearing his humble brown monk's robe, and he walked to the largest post of the South Vietnamese army, where he asked to see the commanding officer. When he met the officer in charge, he told him, "I request one thing of you. Please instruct the planes not to bomb our campus. We have 11,000 war victims there who have already lost their homes and their relatives. They have only this refuge in the heart of the war area." I think no one could say "no" to this frail bodhisattva. He also said, "I request your permission to let me go to the communists and ask them also not to attack or enter our campus. Please, don't shoot me en route."

The Saigon officer answered, "I cannot guarantee that there will be no shooting, because if we stop shooting, the other side will

Refugees taking shelter on SYSS campus.

think we have surrendered, and they will advance on us." So Thây Thanh Van suggested, "Please shoot into the sky or at the land, but not at me. If you do that, they will hear the noise of your bullets, and they will think that you are shooting at them. If you refrain from shooting at me, I will have the chance to negotiate for the safety of 11,000 people who suffer so much from the war."

Thây Thanh Van then crossed the fire zone again, and, as he did so, the South Vietnamese troops continued to shoot, but not at him. When he spoke to the communist side, he pleaded in the same way, "Please, do not send troops onto our campus or shoot at our campus. There are 11,000 people who suffer there." And they agreed.

When Thây Thanh Van came back, he didn't tell us what he had done. The few hundred persons who had already left returned when they found so much fighting and bombing right outside the campus. People were panicky, not knowing whether to leave the campus or stay. So Thây Thanh Van took a large megaphone to ask people to stay, but then he thought, What if I ask them to stay and then a bomb drops on the campus and they die? How could I live? So he put the megaphone down.

At that time, a number of villagers who had been assisting us reported that there were some NLF guerrillas posing as refugees, and
they were planning to shoot at the American planes from our campus. We knew that if they did, the campus would probably be
bombed. Because in Vietnam we respect our elders very much, we
decided to ask the oldest persons among the refugees to go around
and say to everyone, "We pray that those who have guns will not
use them. If you know anyone who has a gun, please advise him to
bury it, for the safety of 11,000 people." Finally, there was no
trouble at all.

Everything was going well. We had been able to take the seriously wounded to the hospital, bury eight dead bodies, and deliver
ten babies. The soldiers from both sides, although shooting at each
other at the periphery of the campus, never tried to enter the campus directly. After eight days, when the battle finally ended, the
countryside was in ruins. Thousands of houses had been destroyed,
and thousands of trees were burned to the ground. But our campus
remained intact, fresh, and green. The acacia trees continued to
produce beautiful blossoms, and the thickets of yellow bamboo continued to shine brightly under the delicate green leaves.

That sumptuous, green campus in the midst of a large devastated
area was the fruit of our collective work, but I could see that the
wisdom and fearlessness of Thây Thanh Van played a particularly
important role in its realization.

Those eight days were a turning experience for me. Seeing so
much death and despair, I learned that we must resist war at any
price. Once a war gets started, it has a momentum and intensity
that are very hard to stop.

CHAPTER TWELVE

Leaving Vietnam

In June 1968, Thây Nhat Hanh asked me to come to Hong Kong to bring him a message from the Unified Buddhist Church, give him news from the School of Youth for Social Service, and tell him what we in Vietnam wanted him to do. He needed to know whether he should risk coming back to Vietnam or whether he should stay overseas as a representative of the Buddhist movement. I met privately with most of the leaders of the UBC,* and all of them felt that Thây should not come back. They said that he was the most skillful among the UBC leaders in communicating with the West, recalling the time when he had been instrumental in getting the UN to investigate human rights violations under the Diêm regime. But they asked Thây to be careful about any statements he made, as they were under the scrutiny of the government of Saigon and anything he said, even overseas, would affect them.

At that time, I was vice president of the UBC's Committee to Help the War Victims, and Thây Quang Liên, the committee's president, asked me to try to raise funds from international humanitarian organizations while I was out of the country. In Vietnam, the only food aid for war victims was from the U.S. government, and it was difficult for our social workers to carry U.S. aid to victims who had just been bombed by the same government.

When I left for France in 1963 to submit my thesis, it had been easy to obtain an exit visa as a government employee. Although in 1968 I was still a government employee on the Faculty of Science, since no one in our department had asked me to go on official busi-

---

* Thây Tri Quang, and Thây Thiên Hoa and Thây Thiên Hoà at the An Quang Pagoda, Thây Thien Minh at the youth center, Thây Quang Do at the Thanh Minh Temple, and Thây Duc Nhuan at the Giac Minh Pagoda. Thây Tri Quang was under house arrest at this time, so when I visited him, again I wore jeans, T-shirt, a wig, and dark sunglasses. Even my friends in the An Quang Pagoda did not recognize me. Thây Tri Quang and I both kept silent for a while, and then I said farewell without mentioning my departure.

ness, it was difficult for me to get permission to leave, even for one week. Finally, the head of our department allowed me to go two weeks for family affairs. Rich and powerful people could leave and reenter Vietnam as they pleased, but ordinary people needed to wait six months just to obtain a tourist exit visa. First, an application had to be submitted to the Visa Service of the Central Police Center. Then the application was sent to eight offices of the Police Center, requesting endorsement of the application, identity card verification, taxes, and other references. If the application were declared clean, it would be sent to the Minister of Interior Affairs, who would send it to various other offices before it came back to him for his signature. Then it would be sent back to the Visa Service of the Police Center.

I went to the Visa Service and filled out an application. Then I asked to see the Director, and I showed him a telegram from my brother Nghiep, which read "Brother in Hong Kong seriously ill. Come immediately." I also showed him permission from the university to go to Hong Kong for two weeks. The Director of the Visa Service "kindly" invited me into his personal office. I had no idea that he was asking for a bribe. I waited a week and then went to see him again. This time he told me plainly, "If you want me to be 'kind' to you, you have to be 'kind' to me." I had never been confronted by such corruption before, and I didn't know how to respond. I left his office extremely disappointed, not knowing what to do.

Then I got the idea that my cousin's cousin, Colonel Sat, the Chief of Police in Saigon, might be able to help me. I went to his office and told him about my encounter at the Visa Service, and immediately he picked up the phone, called the Director of Visas and asked him "to help his young cousin." I felt embarrassed returning to the Director's office, and was quite surprised to see the change in his attitude. He told me that to get an exit visa quickly, I had to bring my application personally to each of the eight offices in the Police Center.

Because I was presented as a relative of Colonel Sat, I was allowed to move freely from one office to another. But when it came time to verify my political background, the matter became complicated. The Director of the Political Information Office was very warm, chatting with me while his assistant went to get my file. Still, he interrogated me gently about how it could have been that I, from South Vietnam, was a relative of Colonel Sat, who was from Central Vietnam. I said that the sixth sister of my mother married Prince Ung Le of Central Vietnam, who was the uncle of Colonel Sat's wife.

When the Director's assistant handed him my file, she looked at me suspiciously. Then the Director looked through quite a few papers and finally asked, "Oh, and you have also been the president of the Van Hanh Buddhist University Student Union, yes?" I recalled Thây Minh Chau's statement to the police about my calling for peace, but I smiled back calmly, "You see my file. Yes, that is me. Now can you kindly sign my application for an exit visa?" He said, "Please come back tomorrow." But after that, he refused to see me.

During those days, most of the 11,000 war victims who had taken refuge on the SYSS campus were still living there and were in need of medical help, as the danger of malaria from mosquitoes was serious, and the need for supplies such as rice, cooking oil, and cooking utensils was great. Even though there was a group of friends in charge of each aspect of the work, I had to come to the campus often and arrange for their supplies. I also continued my work on the Faculty of Sciences, preparing exams for my botany students. Along with all that, I stopped by the Police Center every morning to pursue my visa application. One day, a clerk confided in me, "We know that your secret communist name is 'Dang.' You will never be allowed to leave the country." I was shocked. I had never had a secret name. I had only called for peace in a thoughtful way without taking sides, and I always signed in full the only name I ever had, the name my family had given me, Cao Ngoc Phuong. Perhaps it had something to do with Thây Minh Chau denouncing me, but I knew I was not communist, so I decided to speak directly to the Director of Political Information to clear this up.

The next morning, I went to his office. As usual, he refused to see me, but this time I insisted that I had an important matter to discuss with him. He had a clerk tell me that he was sending my file to the Visa Service that very day, and that it was not necessary to see him. He did send my file to the Visa Service, complete with all the information about my peace work: "President of Van Hanh Buddhist University student union. Led assembly to an agreement to call for peace in March 1966. Arrested in Hue and jailed for two weeks for transporting *Lotus in a Sea of Fire*. Close friend of Nhat Chi Mai, who immolated herself for peace. Name appeared in the *New York Times* on May 17, 1967 in a five-column article calling for peace after Mai's immolation. Assistant of Thây Nhat Hanh in his peace work. Secret name: Dang. Relative of Colonel Sat."

The next day, the Visa Service sent my file to the Ministry of the Interior, where no one would talk with me about my case. I knew that if the Ministry of Interior read all that "loaded" information about my working for peace, I would never get a visa. So I tried to intervene, but it was impossible.

Then one day, in a chat with my brother-in-law Nguyen Van Gioi, who was a national tennis champion, I was complaining how difficult it was to get an exit visa, and he told me that I was too naive. He said that to get a visa to Hong Kong, Thailand, or anywhere in Asia, the required bribe was 20,000 dông; for one to Europe or the U.S., 100,000 dông was needed. But he also told me that many of the corrupt officials were friends of his—he had taught them how to play tennis—and that he could get me an exit visa for nothing. It was true! Three days later, my visa was ready at the Ministry of Interior. But when I went there to pick it up, the guard wouldn't let me enter the visa office. He said that I would receive notification when I could pick up my exit visa from the Police Center's Visa Service. I had received permission from my department at the university to be absent from July 15 to July 30, and it was already July 21. I had only nine days left. I told the guard that if I waited for the proper notification to pick up my exit visa from the police, I might not have any days left. While I was arguing with him a ministry official overheard us and asked my name. When I told him my story, he promised to look into it for me. A few minutes later, he came back and said that my file was complete except for one signature, and the next day, he gave me an exit visa for one week only and a document that I had to take to the Visa Service at the Police Center to receive my passport.

That afternoon, with the help of a friend who worked for Air France in Saigon, I was able to buy a ticket to Hong Kong for the next day without having to pay in foreign currency. Then I went to the British Embassy to pick up an entry visa for Hong Kong. I somehow thought I could just pick it up since I had an exit visa from Vietnam and an Air France ticket, but the Embassy official told me that it would take forty-eight hours to process my application. I said that I had only a seven-day exit visa from the Vietnamese government and that I needed to go as soon as possible, but he didn't seem at all interested in helping me.

I stood there, following each breath, evoking the name of Avalokitesvara with my calm mind, and suddenly I remembered meeting the Vice Consul of the British Embassy when he visited the SYSS office along with a representative of Oxfam. I immediately asked if I could see him, and with his intervention, I obtained an entry visa in twenty minutes! However, instead of a seven-day visa, they gave me a five-day one because the rule was that one had to leave Hong Kong forty-eight hours before his Vietnamese exit visa expired. Then I went to get a health certificate, and, finally, I went back home at four o'clock to spend the rest of my time with my mother. When I got home, I received word that my plane for Hong Kong would leave at five o'clock the next evening.

I also received a message that a friend wanted me to come to his house immediately to pick up 500 baby chicks that had been sent from Dalat as a gift for peasants in several villages outside of Saigon. As I was the only one who knew where that friend lived, I had to do it by myself. My car was broken, and the only way I could carry the chicks was on the back of my motorbike, in four boxes. Visualizing myself picking up all those baby chicks if any of the boxes fell, I drove in a very mindful way.

When I arrived at the SYSS office with the baby chicks, it was almost dark. I talked with Thây Thanh Van and other friends, telling them that I was leaving for Hong Kong the next day. Thây Thanh Van said only, "Please tell Thây Nhat Hanh that we have been cut off from the UBC and Van Hanh University, and tell him that we need to reestablish our legal status. If he keeps making statements calling for peace, we will never be legally recognized by this regime. Tell him he has to decide between advocating peace and doing social work." I listened quietly, knowing that only Thây Nhat Hanh could explain to him that it was impossible to divide reality like that.

In those days in Saigon, there was a nine o'clock curfew. By the time I finished my meetings at the SYSS, it was already eight-thirty. As it was a rainy, overcast day with no moon or stars, and the light on my motorbike was broken, I had to drive back in the dark. The words of a woman refugee still living on the SYSS campus came to me as I was riding through the countryside: "Aren't you afraid of ghosts? There are many dead bodies along the five miles of road before the Cau Tre Bridge, especially in the cemetery." Running my fingers through the hair of the skinny boy clutching her arm, I said, "I worry more about hungry fellows like him than I do about ghosts. I have seen so many ghostlike war victims. Why should I be afraid of the disembodied?" Breathing in deeply the fragrant air of my last night in Saigon, my heart was heavy with concern for thousands of these desperate little boys and girls.

Although it was pitch black, I knew that stretch of road like the palm of my hand. I knew every curve and every hole, and I was not afraid. I visualized how beautiful the little houses along the road had been six months before, among the papaya trees, bougainvillea, red hibiscus, and yellow *allamanda* flowers. I saw in my mind's eye the beautiful fields of corn, peanuts, manioc, sweet potatoes, and jasmine. But now, although I couldn't exactly see, I knew I was riding through burned fields, ruined houses, and broken tombs. I hadn't even noticed the cemetery along this road until after the May offensive two months earlier, when dozens of tombs were bombed and corpses in broken coffins were exposed.

As I approached Cau Tre Bridge, my motorbike stopped suddenly, caught in a tangle of barbed wire, and I fell down. Men's voices began shouting, "Raise your hands high!" and lights flashed in my face. Then I heard the sounds of guns cocking for fire, and I raised my hands straight up to the sky and said, "I am a social worker here to help war victims at the Tan Phu refugee camp." In trenches along both sides of the road, soldiers pointed their guns at me. This part of the road was considered "half rice, half beans," controlled by both sides. If these soldiers were from the communist side, they might abduct someone whose identity card was that of a nationalist employee, so I hesitated to show my identity card. Finally I reassured myself that neither side could hate a social worker trying to help war victims.

When he saw my card, the soldier urged me to go home quickly, because the curfew in this area was eight o'clock, not nine. It took five minutes for the soldiers to untangle my motorbike from their barbed wire, and I jumped onto my bike, only to discover that both tires were flat. I asked at a nearby house if I could leave my vehicle there, and I tried to hitchhike home. At that time of night, there were no taxis or pedicabs, and hardly anyone was on the road.

Finally, a soldier on a motorbike picked me up and drove me a few kilometers, and three different drivers took me the rest of the way home. When I arrived at the home of my sister, Diep, where I was living with my mother and four nephews, I was grateful to still be alive. My sister's house was locked tight, and there was no doorbell. I went to the back window and called to my twelve-year-old nephew, Vu, thinking how excited he would be to see me home so late after the curfew. But Vu, knowing nothing about my narrow escape from abduction or death, greeted me at the window casually, asking, "Are you calling me?" I began to laugh uncontrollably, and I was hardly able to say, "Yes, Vu. Please do open the door."

The next day, July 23, 1968, I said farewell to my mother, expecting to be gone for less than a week. As I boarded the Air France flight to Hong Kong at five o'clock in the afternoon, I had no idea this might be the last time I would see Vietnam.

◇

I arrived in Hong Kong at eight o'clock in the evening. In Vietnam, I knew how to avoid being followed by secret police, and I did the same in Hong Kong. Certain that I had not been followed by anyone, I caught a taxi and told the driver the address Thây Nhat Hanh had given me. I walked up to the guest house and knocked on the door. Thây opened the door and when he saw me, his eyes opened very wide. A week earlier, I had told him that it was nearly impossible for me to obtain a visa, so when he saw me, he could only utter, "Oh... oh...," nothing more. I also was quite shocked. Thây was pale and looked ten years older than when he had left Vietnam. I had not imagined that two years in the West would destroy his health so quickly. I wished I could sob in his arms, but, at that time, Thây had not yet taught us hugging meditation.

Tears filled my eyes, and right away I began to tell him about many of the events I had not been able to write about in my letters. Thây listened attentively and served me a cup of oolong tea. Then, considering each word carefully, he said that if the monks wished him to stay in the West, he would desperately need an assistant to help him bring the message of the suffering of the Vietnamese people to the world. He asked me to join him in this work, saying that I could be more effective in bringing the war to a halt outside of the country. Because I had lived the war, he said, I would be able to communicate the innocent message of the poor, illiterate peasants who were under the bombs. I would not need to speak in the sophisticated language of the intellectuals who supported one side or the other, but in the plain, simple talk of the countrypeople who were the victims. Thây invited me to be his assistant in this peace work and also to raise funds to support war victims and orphans, as the high monks in the UBC had asked me to do. I was speechless. I had never imagined not returning home. I couldn't believe the SYSS would survive even one week without me. I smiled sadly and told Thây I could not stay to assist him.

The next day, Thây took me to Po Lin Ch'an Temple, high up in the mountains on Lan Tao Island, near Hong Kong, and we did walking meditation all afternoon. The atmosphere was so serene. That evening, we joined the monks in their meditation, and we stayed at the temple overnight. Thây continued to insist that I consider his request to be his assistant. He said it would be the best way for us to realize our ideal of service at that time.

The next day, my mind was clearer. I remembered Thây Thanh Van asking me to convey to Thây Nhat Hanh how he had to decide between peace work or social work, and I realized that Thây Thanh Van was also telling me the same thing. Since Thây Nhat Hanh had left Vietnam, Thây Thanh Van had silently disapproved of my peace activities, not because he did not want peace, but because for him rural development was already such a great responsibility. When I asked him how we could do rural development without stopping the war, he said that he did not want to think about it.

From time to time, he could not help uttering a few words that had hurt me deeply. When I proposed that our SYSS teaching staff offer to train the UBC monks and nuns in church administration and accounting as a way to show the UBC how capable we were and to help the school attain legal status, Thây Thanh Van had said, "No, we want nothing to do with those high monks. If you wish to help them, I suspect you too." I was surprised by the way he said those words. It seemed he was suspicious that I might want to use the SYSS to influence the UBC leadership for some covert purpose. I wanted to raise the matter with him when my mind was calmer, but we both were so busy that we never took the time to talk about it. Twenty-five years later in Plum Village, Thây Nhat Hanh introduced the "peace treaty" for living peacefully in a community, but we did not yet have this valuable tool, and I regret that many hurts like this were left unaddressed.

Reflecting on my disagreements with Thây Thanh Van, I realized that I had to let him and the SYSS staff work solely at rural development. It would relieve a lot of their difficulties with the Thieu regime if they were, for a time, without me and my peace work. Even though my heart was one hundred percent appreciative of their development work, for the time being, I was more concerned with bringing urgent assistance to the hungry, the orphans, and the victims of war in most desperate areas. At that time Thây Thanh Van and the staff of the SYSS thought that they did not have the time or energy to organize teams to rescue war victims or bring food and relief to the war zones. They only helped war victims when the Phu Tho Hoa area was bombed, and, even then, they only took care of those who were on their own campus. So, from 1964 to 1966, when I organized teams to go to Binh Long, in the military zone, and to Quang Nam, Son Khuong, and Son Tinh, near the Ho Chi Minh Trail, I did so in the name of the Van Hanh University students and, after 1966, under my own name. Many SYSS students did join me, but they did so personally, at their risk.

In my morning meditation at Po Lin Ch'an Temple in Hong Kong, I saw that I could be more effective in obtaining relief supplies for the local Buddhist rescue committees from overseas than I had been in Vietnam, because I could send supplies directly to them without having to obtain the agreement of Thây Thanh Van and the SYSS staff. In Vietnam, I usually raised funds alone to help many Buddhist committees, but the amount was rather small, so

Thây Quang Lien had urged me to go overseas to solicit support
from humanitarian groups.

So I decided to accept Thây Nhat Hanh's invitation to become
his assistant. I knew it would be much more pleasant and inspiring
to work with Thây than with anyone else. He always took seriously
the new ideas that we, the youth, proposed, and looked deeply to
offer us wise advice. He accepted and extolled everyone with appreciation. I believed his statement that he needed my help, because I
had great trust in him and appreciated his wisdom. I also knew that
he would never expect me to follow him blindly. We always discussed our views about each endeavor thoroughly, and he allowed
my view to complete his.

I also knew that peace and social development work were insepa-
rable. If the staff of the SYSS wanted to serve only in the non-war
zones, they could do so without my interference. Here I would be
able to raise funds for both the SYSS and the local Buddhist relief
committees in the forty-two provinces of Vietnam. As the assistant
of Thây Nhat Hanh, representing the Unified Buddhist Church
abroad, I could freely work in all the areas of suffering of Vietnam
by correspondence. By informing those in the West about the real
situation in the country, I would help all of my friends in Vietnam,
including Bac Sieu, the bodhisattva who, after fifty years, continued
to bike to the most remote areas outside of Hue to bring rice and
care to those who were most destitute. And I could help everyone
spiritually by communicating the inspiration and insights of Thây
Nhat Hanh to them. I also would be able to tell Thây the details of
each person's situation so he could prescribe the right "medicine"
for each in his gentle, inspiring, and loving way.

I was able to extend my visa in Hong Kong for only two more
weeks, but I was able to enter Japan after that on a three-month
tourist visa. While I was there, I applied for a visa to go to France.
The French Embassy told me that it would take three to six
months. In the meantime, I worked in a printing house. It was my
wish that as soon as I could return to Vietnam, I would set up a
printing house as a means of self-support for the SYSS. I learned a
lot about four-color printing during those months. My tourist visa
for France was granted on December 29, 1968, and I boarded a jet
for France two weeks later.

WORKING FOR PEACE
1969-1975

CHAPTER THIRTEEN

Buddhist Peace Delegation

In 1968, the superpowers began a peace conference on Vietnam in Paris that, five years later, culminated in the Peace Accords of 1973. There were four main delegations: the Democratic Republic of Vietnam (the communists from the North), the Republic of Vietnam (the nationalists from the South), the National Liberation Front (mostly South Vietnamese dissidents who were in alliance with the communists from Hanoi),* and the United States. The People's Republic of China, the USSR, France, and the UK were co-sponsors and witnesses.

In 1969, students of Thây Nhat Hanh in the Overseas Vietnamese Buddhist Association organized a gathering to present the point of view of the Vietnamese peasants, who were not represented at the superpowers' conference. We asked the French Ministry of Foreign Affairs for permission to convene a four-day conference, but they refused, saying that because France was hosting the official conference, they could be reproached by the four delegations if they allowed us to hold a press conference. We told the Foreign Ministry that we would then hold our conference in another European capital and invite well-known church and peace leaders who would attract the press. If anyone asked us why we were not meeting in Paris, we would tell them that the French government refused to allow it. Realizing that that could harm France's reputation, the Ministry of Foreign Affairs accepted a compromise, which was to allow us to hold a conference, but not a press conference.

We tried to find a location other than Paris to help them avoid embarrassment, and two French diplomats sympathetic to us arranged for us to convene our conference in Fontainebleau, sixty ki-

---

* By assuming that everyone who was not pro-nationalist was a communist, the U.S. forced many who would have preferred a more moderate alternative to join the NLF.

lometers southwest of Paris. They also helped us get entry visas for
Vietnamese Buddhists from eight other countries to join our proceedings.[*]

On June 8, the day before our conference was to begin, 600
friends joined us at the Hotel du Palais du Quai d'Orsay in Paris,
next door to the office of the Foreign Ministry, for a Prayer for
Peace. Since this was neither a conference nor a press conference,
we felt that the authorities could not reproach us. To begin the
gathering, the monks present invited Buddhist temple drums and
bells to sound in the traditional, three-round pattern for announcing the formal ceremony, and then 500 Vietnamese Buddhists
chanted this prayer, written by Thây Nhat Hanh:

Prayer for Peace

In beauty, sitting on a lotus flower,
is the Lord Buddha, quiet and solid.
Your humble disciple,
calm and pure of heart,
forms a lotus flower with his two hands,
faces you with deep respect
and offers this heartfelt prayer:

Homage to all buddhas in the ten directions.
Please have compassion for our suffering.
Our land has been at war for two decades.
Divided, it is a land of tears
and blood and bones of young and old.
Mothers weep till their tears are dry
while their sons on distant fields decay.
Its beauty torn apart,
only blood and tears now flow.

---

[*] The organizers of the conference were Dr. Nguyen Van Huong, Mr. and Mrs. Vo Van
Ai, Dr. Ta Hue Chieu, Mr. Chinh Ba, my brother Nghiep, and myself. Mary Emeny,
Penelope Faulkner, and Raphael Ruiz helped us. Among the monks attending were
Thich Thien Thang, Thich Phap Kien, Thich Thien Qua, Thich The Tinh, Thich
Chon Hoa, Thich Tri Quang, and Thich Minh Tam.

Brothers killing brothers
for promises from outside.

Homage to all buddhas in the ten directions.
Because of your love for all people,
have compassion on us.
Help us remember we are just one family,
North and South.
Help us rekindle our compassion and
brotherhood,
and transform our separate interests
into loving acceptance for all.
May your compassion help us forget our hatred.
May Avalokitesvara Bodhisattva's love
help flowers bloom again in the soil of our
country.
Humbly, we open our hearts to you,
so you may help us transform our deeds
and water the flowers of our spirits.
With your deep understanding, help our hearts
grow light.

Homage to Shakyamuni Buddha
whose great vows and compassion inspire us.
I am determined to cultivate only thoughts
that increase love and trust,
to use my hands to perform only deeds
that build community,
to speak only words
of harmony and aid.

May the merit of this prayer
be transformed into peace in Vietnam.
May each of us realize this, our deep aspiration.

Following the chant, I could see that hundreds in the audience
had tears in their eyes. Among those present were Hannes de Graaf,
the Dutch thelogian; Heinz Kloppenburg, the world-renowned Ger-

My office/bedroom in Paris.

man pacifist; Alfred Hassler, President of the International Committee of Conscience on Vietnam and the Fellowship of Reconciliation; Danilo Dolci, a well-known, nonviolent leader against the Sicilian mafia; Philip Noel Baker, a Nobel Peace Prize winner from the United Kingdom; Jean Goss Mayr, honorary president of the International Fellowship of Reconciliation; and more than 500 Vietnamese Buddhists living in Europe. The French authorities tried to prevent the press from coming to this prayer gathering and to our Fontainebleau conference, but the presence of so many well-known activists drew dozens of reporters, who wrote beautiful stories about the Buddhists who voiced the concerns for the voiceless majority in Vietnam. Out of that conference was born the Vietnamese Buddhist Peace Delegation to the Paris Peace Accords, to which Thây Nhat Hanh was nominated by the Unified Buddhist Church of Vietnam to be the chair.

Starting in May 1970, I assisted Thây with the administrative work of the Vietnamese Buddhist Peace Delegation. We rented a small office in a poor neighborhood in the eighteenth *arrondissement* of Paris, and I lived and worked there. From this humble office, we did our best to keep thousands of people informed of the concerns and wishes of the Vietnamese people. We edited and printed a newsletter in English, French, and Vietnamese, *Le Lotus*, that was reproduced and translated into still other languages by friends throughout Europe. We kept up with correspondence and had many other projects to try to bring peace to Vietnam. In addition, I gave private math lessons one afternoon a week to high school students, and Thây taught a course on "The History of Buddhism in Vietnam" at the Sorbonne Ecole Pratique des Hautes Etudes, to earn enough for us to live.

Many European journalists visited our office, and all of them advised me to find a better location so the public would take the Buddhist Peace Delegation seriously. Nevertheless, they each wrote excellent articles about our work noting that our simple approach had inspired international organizations to support our projects in Vietnam.

Before I arrived in Paris, the French press rarely published news about the Vietnamese Buddhists. They relied on the pro-communist Vietnamese in Paris for their information. I thought that prestigious newspapers like *Le Monde* must have good, honest journalists and that if they only printed news from the communist point of view, it must be because they did not understand us. So one day, despite discouragement from friends, I visited the offices of *Le Monde*. Walking in the door shyly, holding only a copy of an article I had written about my years as a peace worker in Vietnam, I managed to have a brief conversation with the newswriter Jacques de Cornoye. It apparently had a big impact on him, because a week later, he called to tell me that he wished to publish my report in the monthly journal, *Esprit*, and from that day on, everything I sent to *Le Monde* was looked at with care and published whenever possible.

Ethelwyn Best, a dynamic seventy-eight-year-old Englishwoman from Civil Service International joined our work in the Paris office.* I had met her in 1967 when she was travelling between Viet-

---

* Others helped as well. Marthe de Venoge, a wonderful Frenchwoman and professional translator, helped with some of our French editing work. Dr. Cao Thi Dung, an old friend from Marie Curie French High School in Saigon, also helped with the French editing, and Dr. Nguyen Van Huong was in charge of the Overseas Vietnamese Buddhist Association in France. Dr. Ta Hue Chau, who also had been a friend and classmate in Marie Curie French High School, Tran Quang Hai, a talented musician, and his wife, Tran Thi Hang, and my brother Nghiep wholeheartedly helped us translate documents we received from Vietnam about orphans, and they contributed towards our office rent and overhead.

nam and Hong Kong, bringing in medicine for the SYSS pioneer village development projects. Ethelwyn helped me a lot with my English. When she decided to stay and work with us for a year, I rented a larger room in the suburb Maisons Alfort just down the street from where Thây Nhat Hanh lived with Nguyen Hoang Anh, a former novice monk from Vietnam. The four of us cooked and ate together every morning and then drove to our office in the north of Paris. Seeing how tense I was becoming from the news of suffering we were receiving every day from Vietnam and also from the Parisian traffic jams (and bearing in mind how our social work friends in Vietnam had to face far more dangerous events), Thây composed a song to help us stay in touch with the many wonders of life, to help us restore our balance:

Twenty-Four Brand-New Hours

Waking up this morning, I see the blue sky.
I join my hands in thanks
for the many wonders of life;
for having twenty-four brand-new hours before
me.
The sun is rising.
The forest becomes my awareness
bathed in the sunshine.

I walk across a field of sunflowers.
Tens of thousands of flowers are turned toward
the bright east.
My awareness is like the sun.
My hands are sowing seeds for the next harvest.
My ear is filled with the sound of the rising tide.
In the magnificent sky, clouds are approaching
with joy from many directions.
I can see the fragrant lotus ponds of my
homeland.
I can see coconut trees along the rivers.
I can see rice fields stretching, stretching,
laughing at the sun and rain.

Mother Earth gives us coriander, basil, celery,
and mint.
Tomorrow the hills and mountains of the
country
will be green again.
Tomorrow the buds of life will spring up quickly.
Folk poetry will be as sweet as the songs of
children.

One day in 1972, after I gave a talk in Paris about the war and our relief efforts, a shy young Frenchman came over to shake my hand and tell me, "I was very moved by your speech, and I have decided to do something." I invited him to our office, and a few days later he appeared, holding a rose for me. He said his name was Pierre Marchand and that he was seventeen years old. We had a very pleasant talk, and then I showed him photos of orphans and described our work in more detail. He got the idea to organize a concert to raise money for orphans, and right away he wrote down the names of a dozen singers. I didn't think that a concert could bring in much money for orphans, but because I didn't want to hurt him, I said, "Please do what you can. We would be very happy to have your support."

A few weeks later, he came back and said that all of the singers on his list had agreed to perform. He needed 3,000 French *francs* (FF), about $750, to rent a large hall for the concert. Three thousand francs was a lot of money for us. We spent only twenty-five francs a month to feed a hungry child in Vietnam. If we had to spend 3,000 FF just to rent an auditorium, how could we earn enough to cover that expense, let alone raise money for hungry children? But Pierre said, "I'm sure we can. We can make about 5,000 FF ($1,250) profit." So I gave him the names of some friends who might be able to loan him the money. He was able to borrow that amount, and we rented the auditorium.

I was very concerned that we would be in debt and that our cause would lose respect if only a few people came. So Pierre and I printed hundreds of posters, and we went into the streets of Paris every night in the winter rain and snow to hang up the posters. A few days later, we noticed that our posters had been covered by some-

Putting up posters.

one else's posters, and we went out and put up new ones. As the day
of the concert approached, we had to do this almost every night.
Many friends reproached me for wasting my time this way, but I
told them that every kind of work is important if done joyfully,
peacefully, and mindfully. By working together, Pierre and I grew to
be good friends. He knew he could count on my commitment, and
I knew that I could count on his faithful perseverance.

On the day of the concert, I couldn't believe my eyes! Two thousand young French people filled the auditorium, and another 1,000
were outside begging to get in. Pierre didn't have much money, so
he had charged very little for the tickets, and the singers he invited
turned out to be very famous, including Nana Mouskouri, Claude
Nougaro, and Graeme Allwright. We opened the doors and let everyone else in for ten francs each. It was a wonderful evening. We
had to open all the doors and windows for circulation and for the
overload of spectators. And we earned more than $4,000 in profit!
Graeme Allwright became a great friend and supporter. After the
first concert, he continued to raise money for Vietnamese orphans
by giving concerts throughout France. I wrote a letter to Pierre
Marchand's father, praising Pierre for his love, care, and talent in
raising funds for orphans. I had no idea that Pierre's father was a
wealthy industrialist who had expected his son to be a businessman.
His father wrote back, threatening to sue me for abducting a minor.

Pierre was by then eighteen years old, but at that time in France, a young man had to be twenty-one to reach majority. We were all very sad, especially Pierre. Looking at him with tenderness, Thây Nhat Hanh gave him the medal that Pope Paul VI had given him in 1966. Born a Catholic, Pierre was so moved that he said, "With this medal, I have enough strength to cope with any difficulties. From today on, I will not be afraid of anything or anyone, and I will devote my life to service."

And he did. First, he set up a committee to sponsor Vietnamese orphans called the *Comité Pour Les Enfants du Vietnam*. Later, the organization's name was changed to *Partage Avec Les Enfants du Tiers-Monde* (Sharing with the Children of the Third World), and today it is one of the three largest relief organizations in France. In 1992, Partage contributed 60 million francs ($12 million) for hungry children in a dozen countries around the world.

Alfred Hassler was the most faithful supporter of the nonviolent Buddhist struggle in Vietnam. Following Thây's tour of the U.S. in 1966, Alfred arranged for Thây to go to Europe, Asia, Australia, and New Zealand. He proposed that Thây prepare an English edition of *Vietnam: Lotus in a Sea of Fire* to teach people in the West about our culture and the way the war was viewed from inside our country. Eventually, 40,000 copies of the English edition were sold, and it was translated into twelve languages. Many people told us it was the most important book they read during the war. Alfred also wrote *Saigon USA*, recalling his experiences working with the Buddhists in Vietnam. He supported us faithfully for many years, helping us realize many of Thây Nhat Hanh's visions for peace. One of them was *Dai Dong*, a project to protect the environment. At that time, in 1970, very few people spoke about pollution or saving the planet.

The first meeting of Dai Dong was outside of Paris in Thây's tiny room in Maisons Alfort. There were five of us: Thây, Alfred, Alfred's secretary Dorothy Murphy, Ethelwyn Best, and me. We chose the name Dai Dong, "Great Togetherness," to wake people up to the fact that we have only one planet, and that if we do not learn to live on it together, our planet will die, and we will die also. We designed a Dai Dong flag covered with flowers and children's faces.*

The second Dai Dong meeting was held in Menton, near Nice, in 1971. Six well-known biologists, among them Pierre Lepine, drafted an appeal for humankind to care for the planet. I was the youngest one there and the least proficient in biology, but the others appreciated that I was able to describe the ways in which war destroys the environment. Three months after the Menton meeting, branches of Dai Dong were formed in England, France, Germany, Norway, Denmark, Holland, Switzerland, and the U.S. We gathered more than 5,000 signatures from influential scientists around the world to launch an appeal to the governments of the world to care for the planet.

The following year, in June 1972, the United Nations convened a conference on the environment in Stockholm. We convened a parallel conference, also in Stockholm, to give environmentalists and others a forum to say things they might be unable to say at the UN conference. About half of those at our conference also attended the UN conference. Thây Nhat Hanh and I were there, but our joy to support this work was interrupted when we received news that Thây Thanh Van, our dear friend and Director of the SYSS, had been killed by a military truck driven by a drunk American soldier. Thây cried. Thây Thanh Van was one of his most beloved monk disciples.

Alfred's daughter, Laura Hassler, came to work for us in 1971 and stayed until March 1973. For me, she was like an angel in the most difficult situations. She edited my letters to Western friends beautifully, and she taught me about Western culture. She also sang like a songbird and taught me many American folksongs. She and Jim Forest, another young American, listened attentively to everything I told them about Vietnam. Seeing Laura and Jim's eyes as they listened to us with love, care, and deep appreciation, we opened our hearts and shared with them all of our suffering. Jim brought his good friend Father Daniel Berrigan to see us in Paris. In his first

---

* One time, Alfred and Thây went to visit a wealthy donor to ask for help with the Dai Dong project. During the visit, the woman asked Thây a question about reincarnation, expecting that Thây would confirm her ideas about it. Instead, making reference to the Buddhist teaching of interdependence, Thây said, "If there is no self, who is going to be reborn?" His answer apparently caused Alfred to lose a large grant, but the two friends just laughed, not at all regretting Thây's frank response.

book, *Only the Rice Loves You*, Jim reported on his time together with Thây Nhat Hanh and me at the Buddhist Peace Delegation in Paris.

When he returned to the U.S., Jim Forest was an anchor of support for the nonviolent struggle of the Buddhists in Vietnam. At the crucial time of the signing of the Peace Accords, the American "peace movement" attacked Thây's position and the Buddhist monks in Vietnam for not aligning with the "oppressed" side, Hanoi. By then, anger in the anti-war movement was at its peak, and many leaders opposed our demand for an immediate cease-fire. They wanted nothing less than an unconditional withdrawal of American troops, a defeat of the Americans. Every time a delegation of American pacifists went to Vietnam, we had to prepare ourselves for a verbal attack on the Buddhists as being pro-American. Jim sent the news to us; then I explained the true situation to Laura, and she wrote thoughtful and convincing letters back to Jim for him to use.

The day the Accords were signed, Thây Nhat Hanh was in Bangkok, secretly meeting with Thây Thien Minh and Thây Huyen Quang. Laura brought me a large bouquet of flowers and we hugged deeply, our eyes filled with tears. We decided to go to the place on Avenue Kleber where the Accords had been signed to offer flowers to all four delegations. When we arrived, the crowd was so huge it was impossible to approach them. So we went back home, and I, in the name of the Buddhist Peace Delegation, wrote thank-you letters to each of the delegations. Only Tran Van Lam, head of the nationalist Vietnamese delegation, answered my letter. Thây Nhat Hanh sent me a beautiful poem from Bangkok about the newly born peace. In it, he referred to Nhat Chi Mai as "a branch of plum blossom."

Laura and Jim had fallen in love some time before, but because she knew that we needed her, Laura stayed with us as long as she could. With Laura in France and Jim in the U.S., they formed two ends of a silk strand to support us. I was reminded of Nguu Lang, the water buffalo guard in the Kingdom of Heaven, and Chuc Nu, the silk weaver, who, according to Vietnamese folk legend, fell in love and forgot to do their jobs. Because of that, the King of Heaven allowed them to meet only once a year, at the seventh lunar month. Laura and Jim, because of their love for us, had seen each other only a few times a year. Only after the Peace Accords were signed did Laura return to the U.S. to marry Jim.

In March 1973, we moved to the Parisian suburb of Sceaux, and Thây Nhat Hanh, Bui Thi Huong, Mobi Warren, Nguyen Hoang Anh, Pierre Marchand, Neige Achiary, and I all lived and worked together. How sweet were those days! After busy days of typing, translating, making phone calls, and reading letters, we all had a lovely dinner together. After dinner, Thây would invite us to sing. Sometimes he would also read a poem he had written, and Pierre would put it into music. Pierre especially loved the poem "Recommendation," that Nhat Chi Mai had read onto a tape before immolating herself for peace. At around nine in the evening, Graeme and the other singers would join us for sitting meditation, and then some friends would go home while the rest of us would take out our sleeping bags and sleep on the carpet.

The apartment had only three rooms. One was used as an office, dining room, guest room, meditation room, and bedroom for Pierre and Hoang Anh. One bedroom was used to store thousands of files of orphans, projects to relieve war victims, and names of prisoners held by both warring sides. Mobi, Bui Thi, Neige, and I slept there. Thây stayed in the library. After everyone turned off the lights, I would work on correspondence to Vietnam in the bathroom, where we also kept a mimeograph machine. Each morning, we began the day with personal sitting meditation in each corner of the apartment, then tea meditation with Thây, which was always a treat. Students and guests were nourished by Thây's wonderful teachings.

Mobi Warren was an extremely intelligent and devoted twenty-year-old from Texas who had come to work with us. She learned Vietnamese by translating files of orphans, singing songs, and translating short stories by Thây, including *The Miracle of Being Awake*, a letter to the social workers in Vietnam, which later became *The Miracle of Mindfulness*.

In September 1974, Father Daniel Berrigan visited us for a month. Thây let him stay in his room, while he joined Pierre and Hoang Anh in the living room. There is a Vietnamese proverb: "When you think you cannot welcome a friend, it is because your heart is too small; a house is never too small." Sleeping bags and ca-

Translating for Thây Huyen Quang and Thây Thien Minh.

maraderie were enough to house a dozen or more friends in our home/office in Sceaux.

After Laura and Jim's wedding in New York, Laura started a project of the Fellowship of Reconciliation to sponsor orphans in Vietnam, and Jim continued as editor of *Fellowship*. After Mobi had translated *The Miracle of Being Awake*, Jim immediately printed it in *Fellowship* and received hundreds of enthusiastic letters and phone calls about the wisdom in those essays. He had to reprint it several times, and some people who did not want to wait for FOR to mail them a copy drove quite far to pick one up.

In 1974, Thây Thien Minh, President of the UBC, and Thây Huyen Quang, General Secretary, came from Vietnam to a gathering of 300 church leaders in Louvain, Belgium, organized by the World Conference on Religion and Peace (WCRP). Mobi, Thây, and I drove our small Citroën *deux chevaux* to welcome them at the airport. Mobi and I were in front, the three monks in the back, and thirty-seven books and 4,000 orphan files that our friends in Vietnam had asked the two monks to bring us were in the trunk. The rear of the old deux chevaux began to press on the back tires, making a strange screeching noise, and we had to stuff some of the books under Mobi's seat and pile the rest on her lap to continue the journey.

A group of Thây Nhat Hanh's students from Liège, Belgium, came to the WCRP conference to support us, and also a group of Vietnamese musicians and singers. All the delegates seemed to appreciate our presence at the conference, and the two monks from Vietnam were pleased. I did not know that it would be the last time I would see Thây Thien Minh. He was an excellent organizer in the UBC—very calm, clearheaded, and sharp in negotiations during the struggle against the Diêm regime. During the Nguyen Cao Ky regime, in 1966, his car was bombed, and he was unable to walk properly after that. In 1969, Nguyen Van Thieu arrested him without due cause, and he was sentenced to twenty years in prison. Thanks to pressure from inside and outside the country, he was released in 1973, just a few months before joining us at the conference. In April 1977, the communists arrested him and he died in prison on October 17, 1977. There is strong evidence that he was forced to take poison.

Three days after the death of Thây Thien Minh, we issued a press release. The newsmen in Europe were amazed that we were able to know a secret like that so quickly. The French press cabled their correspondents in Hanoi, who inquired of the government themselves. Hanoi acknowledged that he had died, but they said he had suffered a stroke and died of a brain hemorrhage. They also falsified the time and place of his death, saying that he had died in Ham Tan on October 18, not in Ho Chi Minh City on the 17th. They were afraid that people in the city would demonstrate, so they quickly moved his body to Ham Tan, a remote reeducation camp in the jungle. Thây Nhat Hanh wrote this powerful poem the day Thây Thien Minh died:

> *A Free White Cloud*
>
> *I remember*
> *when you were still a white cloud*
> *floating freely*
> *wherever you wanted to.*
>
> *I too was following my own course as a stream,*
> *seeking its way to the immense ocean.*
>
> *You enjoyed listening to the chanting of the pines*
> *on the high peaks.*

I moved up and down,
in and out,
on the white crest
of the infinite waves.

Seeing the world of men suffer so much,
their tears becoming rivers,
you transformed yourself into rain.
Raindrop after raindrop fell each winter night.
White clouds covered the whole sky.
The sun agonized
in such darkness.

You called me back.
You called to me
for us to take each others' hands
and create a powerful storm.

How could we not struggle
when even the flowers of the prairies
and the grass on the mountain
moaned from the pain of injustice?

You lifted up your angelic arms,
determined to dismantle the chains of bondage.

War and darkness enveloped everything.
The dark barrel of the gun—the utmost
violence—
bones heaped up into mountains,
and blood flowing into rivers.

Even after your two hands were crushed,
my dear, the chains were not removed.

I called the thunder back close to your side.
We were determined to confront violence.

You were brave.
During the darkness of the night,
you transformed yourself into a lion king
and let out a powerful roar.
In the foggy night,
tens of thousands of evil spirits,
hearing your roar,
shivered,
filled with fear.

But you, fearlessly,
never took a step backward,
even while in front of us were
so many layers of traps and dangers.
You looked calmly at the violence
as if it weren't there.

What is the nature of life and death?
How could life and death pressure us?

You called my name with a smile.

Not a single moan came from you,
even under chains and torture.

Now you are free.
The chains can no longer confine your true
body.
You return to being a white cloud just like
before—
a white cloud
utterly free
in the immense sky.

Coming and going—
it's up to you.
When you want a glimpse, you just stop.

As for me,
I am still riding on the crest of the waves,
singing for you
this epic song.

The other delegate to the 1974 conference in Belgium, Thây Huyen Quang, was among the UBC's hardest workers. As General Secretary of the Unified Buddhist Church in Vietnam, he received many letters and requests every day, and he answered each one personally, staying up late and waking up early to show all his love and care for people throughout the country. He was arrested in 1977 after sending a letter to Prime Minister Pham Van Dong listing eighty-six cases of human rights violations in Vietnam. Together with Thây Quang Do, he was nominated for the Nobel Peace Prize in 1978. Both of them were released after the death of Thây Thien Minh, due to strong international pressure. In 1982, he was exiled to Quang Ngai. From his place of exile, he continued to write to Thây secretly, and each letter was filled with kind words. I do not know if we will have a chance to see him again.

Admiring our nonviolent response to the many violent acts towards the SYSS, most of the high monks in the Unified Buddhist Church wanted to reestablish the legal connection between the SYSS and the UBC, but they could not think of a way to do it. There was a Department of Youth, but the School of Youth for Social Service did not exactly fit in it. The Church had no department seriously devoted to nonviolent social change, so the high monks were unable to recognize us formally without changing the constitution of the UBC.

We "floated" this way until early 1973, when Thây Nhat Hanh met with the leaders of the UBC in Bangkok on the day the Paris Peace Accords were signed. Together, they determined that the most important project the UBC could put its energy into was caring for the young generation who suffered from the war and working for healing and rebuilding the country. The UBC Committee for Reconstruction and Development (*Uy Ban Tai Thiet Va Phat Trien Xa Hoi*) was born, which included the SYSS and forty-two other Buddhist social welfare committees in South Vietnam. Monks and nuns in every province cooperated with us, and eventually the

Nuns in Hue contemplating the destruction.

Committee for Reconstruction and Development (CRD) engaged 10,000 social workers throughout the country, increased significantly the development work of the SYSS, and coordinated the support of orphans in Vietnam, funded from overseas.

The letter that Thây and the other monks prepared in Bangkok in March 1973 was read by the President of the Buddhist Church. It was a beautiful message to all the monks and nuns throughout the country: "We hope that you can share a few days per week with the young generation that has suffered so much from the war." Before 1973, local Buddhist temples in Vietnam had done only seasonal charity work or urgent relief work for war victims. In March 1973, the entire UBC had only seventeen day-care centers. But after the appeal, many monks and nuns left their temples and began to work with the poor in the villages and slum areas.* By January 1975, more than 300 day-care centers had been set up by the UBC throughout the country without any overseas aid! This was the fulfillment of my dream.

---

* South Vietnam at that time had forty-two provinces, and each province had a Buddhist Committee for Social Welfare, with 100 to 500 monks, nuns, and Buddhist youth. The SYSS sent from four to twelve workers trained in rural development to each province, and these workers skillfully invited the local Buddhist clergy and youth to join them to become a strong team to care for the war victims, orphans, and the hungry, and to set up self-supporting reconstruction projects.

CHAPTER FOURTEEN

Pilgrimage for Peace

I felt very frustrated. When Thây left for the U.S. in 1966 to call for peace, as head of the student union, I was asked about Thây's position and our position by many international journalists. Of course, none of these journalists spoke Vietnamese. My French was good, but most of them only spoke English, so a friend translated for me. Although my understanding of English was poor, I could tell that he was distorting the meaning of what I was saying. When I spoke about the suffering of the people whose only dream was to have the bombs stop dropping on them, he made it sound as if the peasants were asleep and dreaming. So I decided I had to learn English.

I began by reading the textbooks that were available in Vietnam at that time. They had been written for military personnel, and I learned words like "bombing," "machine gun," etc., words that were, in fact, useful for me. Reading the bilingual text, I learned how to make real sentences. Only two months later, my Dharma sister Nhat Chi Mai immolated herself, and I had to explain to the press what had happened. I tried speaking in English, and one *New York Times* reporter politely described my English as "halting."

Because I was teaching myself by reading, I did not learn how to pronounce most of the words. So when I needed to communicate, I tried writing the words down in French or English. Our friend from Japan, Masako Yamanouchi, spoke to me in English to try to help my pronunciation, but it seemed of little use. One day in 1968 in Tokyo I went into a shop to buy some elastic to sew a new waistband into my pants. I printed the word "elastic" on a piece of paper and then I pulled back and forth on my pants' waist to try to make them understand. It was all very frustrating.

In 1969, when I came to the West to help Thây and the Buddhist Peace Delegation, I had to travel throughout Europe and North America to plead on behalf of my countrymen. Thây told me that I

Speaking on Italian television.

would be able to communicate the situation of the war much more clearly and effectively if I spoke to people directly and not through a translator. He said he would teach me English by using the newspaper as a textbook, and that after I had read ten articles, I would be able to give lectures in English. So Thây and I sat down in our small office in the north of Paris, and I began to read aloud from the *International Herald Tribune*. The article was four columns long, and I read in a very loud voice. I pronounced almost every word wrong, and Thây kept correcting me. Then I would write the word down. By the end of the second article, my speaking and writing had become much better.

There was never time to read the third article. I had to leave for Great Britain and Sweden. In the UK, I found that they pronounced English quite differently from the way Thây had taught me, and even from region to region. The sounds varied greatly in Birmingham, Scotland, and Wales. There were so many different kinds of English! The following week I went to Scandinavia, and each country there—Norway, Denmark, Sweden—had yet another kind of English. I just did my best, continuing to pronounce in a more-or-less French way while trying to make it sound like English.

After that, I went to the U.S., and I was on a number of "call-in" radio and TV programs. People's questions were impossible for me to understand. Even when there was a live audience and people asked me questions directly, I could not understand. Everyone spoke so quickly. So the Fellowship of Reconciliation always had someone sit next to me who was able to reword the questions into simple English. Then I could answer. Everywhere I went, I spoke from my heart, and people gave me the benefit of the doubt.

In addition to Britain, Scandinavia, and the U.S., I travelled throughout Italy, Belgium, Holland, Switzerland, Germany and many other countries to plead on behalf of the suffering people of Vietnam. I kept my focus by bearing in mind every day the image of my Dharma sister Nhat Chi Mai. I knew that I could help her dream be realized by travelling everywhere to speak on behalf of peace and reconciliation.

In August 1969, the Italian branch of the Fellowship of Reconciliation invited me to Palermo to attend a seminar with Danilo Dolci for social workers engaged in development work in Sicily. The meeting ended with a large demonstration Danilo had organized against the Mafia. In Palermo, I met Senator Carlo Levi and two journalists, André Romus from Radio Television Belgium and Eliza Calzavara from Radio Television Italy. In Rome, I met the three of them again, as well as André Gillet and Margrit Witwer of the Christian Movement for Peace (CMP). I told them all about the suffering in Vietnam, and because they were so interested, our discussions continued for hours. Carlo Levi, a famous Italian writer and painter, invited me to come to his house so that he could paint a portrait of me. I did visit him, but not to be painted. Later, friends reproached me for not accepting his offer, because, they said, I could have sold a portrait by him for a large sum of money to help hungry children. I appeared on Radio Television Italy on the program, "Each Week, a Figure, a Life," where I was able to tell the Italian people about Vietnam and my own story. Thanks to André Gillet and Margrit Witwer, I was also invited to address the International Conference of the Christian Movement for Peace, at Frascati, Italy, attended by representatives from CMP's twenty-three branches in Europe, Asia, Africa, and Australia. Everywhere I went in Italy, I heard singing, and I shared some folk songs of Vietnam. But the most important part of that trip was meeting the first five "cedars" for me in the West.

In Belgium, André Romus arranged for me to speak on Radio Television and to the press, and André Gillet arranged for me to address the *Comité de Lutte pour l'Amélioration de la Société Belge par des Moyens Nonviolents*, which included 1,000 church people. The Belgian daily newspapers *Le Soir* and *La Cité* printed excellent, lengthy articles. I returned to Belgium many times after that for lectures and meetings.

In November, I was invited by Hebe Kohlbrugge to tour Christian high schools in Holland to raise money for children and war victims in Vietnam. Hebe was head of the Social Welfare Department of the Dutch Reform Church. More than almost anyone else in the West, she was able to understand our situation quickly and deeply. During World War II, as a young woman in her twenties, Hebe had saved thousands of Jews in Germany and Holland from the Nazis. After meeting Thây, she offered her full support to the Buddhists in Vietnam, even against the will of her Church, which wanted to support only the European Protestant social workers in Vietnam. When the Dutch Minister of Foreign Affairs refused to meet us, Hebe gave him back all the medals and certificates she had received from the Dutch government after World War II, saying, "If you refuse to see such wonderful people as Thây Nhat Hanh and Cao Ngoc Phuong, I prefer to return all these."

Meetings with Christians like Jim Forest, who was now General Secretary of the International Fellowship of Reconciliation in Alkmaar, Holland; Hebe Kohlbrugge; and Margrit Witwer opened my heart to Christian charity. In the past, the European Christians I had known were those who converted poor Vietnamese in exchange for rice. Now I could see that within the Christian circles in the West there were more bodhisattvas than in the Buddhist circles. The wonderful reality of a person like Hebe transcended concepts like "Christian" and "Buddhist." In Holland, I gave talks at the Social Academy in Driebergen, the University of Groningen, University of Utrecht, the Council of the County of Zeist, the Theological Institute of Amersfoort, and the University of

Rotterdam, and raised money for children and war victims in Vietnam.

Dutch TV journalists who had come to our Fontainebleau conference in June 1969 to interview Thây and who had been interrupted by the French authorities, filmed my talk in Utrecht and, together with their footage of Thây and images of Thây Quang Duc immolating himself, created a twenty-minute segment for Dutch TV. The prestigious Dutch newspaper *Trouw* published a large article about our work on its front page. Two weekly magazines, *Open Deur Onderweg* and *De Nieuwe Linie*, featured long articles about our work for the poor in Vietnam. On November 19, 1969, I addressed the Dutch Parliament, describing the suffering of the Vietnamese people. Overall, the support and interest of the Dutch people was so great that I returned to Holland at least twice a year after that to keep them informed of the situation in Vietnam and the needs of the war victims.

Margrit Witwer and her Christian Movement for Peace organized a tour for me in Switzerland, and I spoke in Bern, Zurich, Lucerne, Basel, Fribourg, Lausanne, and Geneva, and also on Swiss Radio Television. In Geneva, I met with the President of the World Council of Churches. Wherever I went, everyone seemed to know and respect Thây Nhat Hanh, and they were pleased to listen to my experiences. A number of those from other countries who belonged to the World Council of Churches asked their own radio and television stations to broadcast the tape of my talk, and "the voice of the voiceless peasants in Vietnam" was able to be heard throughout the French-speaking world, including many countries in Africa.

My tour of Switzerland took place just three weeks before Christmas, and the peace, wealth, and luxury of this country at such a beautiful time of year made me feel overwhelmingly sad. How could the world be so unfair? Vietnamese peasants would not need much to be happy—just some moonlight, fresh air, songs, and the smells of a new harvest. Our aspirations were simple, but the bombs continued to drop on our desperate land, while I was travelling in some fairyland.

I spoke to as many groups as I could, and I spoke to each with all my heart. Though the number of people joining our struggle to end the war was growing every day, I knew I had to be patient. I knew

FOR vigil for peace in the UK.

that many days and months would pass before the people of the world were ready to stop the fighting and base their lives on love and understanding. Even as I spoke, the blood and the tears continued to flow. Sometimes I gave seven or eight talks in a day! Those who organized for me were not wealthy people, and sometimes they had to spend a sizable portion of their monthly income to rent a hall. People worried that I might become exhausted, and they wanted to schedule fewer engagements, but I insisted: I was not tired. I was not afraid of being tired. I had to speak. In my pilgrimage for peace, I carried with me only photos of Nhat Chi Mai and of the suffering children of Vietnam. I knew I had to live and die with these images, working for the day when all the children of the world would be able to sing and play in peace.

In 1970, I went to England, and spoke with the Archbishop of Coventry, Lord Philip Noel Baker, and several members of Parliament. I was also on the radio several times. *Peace News*, an excellent pacifist fortnightly founded during the Second World War, wrote extensively about the efforts of the Vietnamese Buddhists; and War Resisters International, another longtime pacifist group, supported us wholeheartedly. I was invited by Devi Prasad to address War Resisters International's triannual conference, and after that, I returned to England every year. All of my trips there were organized by Reverend David Harding of the British FOR.

After that first visit, I helped set up a group called "Third Way for Vietnam" to reprint our newsletter and circulate it among thousands of British friends. The group also found 1,000 sponsors who each gave £2 1/2 a month to support a hungry child in Vietnam. The leaders were generous, devoted high school teachers. I discovered that the UK has a tradition of generosity. In every town and village there seemed to be a humanitarian group set up by an individual like the Huddersfield Famine Committee, or as a branch of a larger organization like Oxfam. In 1968, Oxfam had been the first humanitarian organization to give a large grant to the School of Youth for Social Service. Later, Christian Aid, Save the Children, and Help the Aged all supported projects of the Buddhists in Vietnam. Elizabeth Wilson, founder and President of the Huddersfield Famine Committee, continues to this day to send yearly donations to help hungry children in Vietnam.

During my first year in the West, even as my English was improving, a number of experiences revealed to me how large was the cultural gap between East and West. After one speech in Heidelburg, more than 300 Germans began pounding their fists on the tables, and I became extremely frightened. I learned later that this is a German way of applauding. Another time in Germany, after six back-to-back meetings, I arrived at the house where I would be staying, and my hostess asked if I would like rice for dinner. I said, yes, and all she served me was a bowl of plain rice, while the rest of the family ate ravioli with tomato sauce, salad, and cheese. A meal of just plain rice is equivalent to a meal consisting of just one slice of bread, without butter. In Wales, at five o'clock one afternoon, when my host invited me for tea, I declined, thinking it would be better to wait until dinner and to rest until then. But dinner never came. It turned out that in Wales "tea" means dinner. In Sweden, when I was invited for a meal at two in the afternoon, again I declined, as I had just eaten lunch on the plane. But in Sweden, the mid-afternoon meal is dinner, and that evening, I also went to bed unfed.

One lunchtime at our office in Paris, I cooked a large, beautiful omelette for Thây, Jim Forest, Hoang Anh, and myself. In the Vietnamese way of eating, each person is served a bowl of rice, and throughout the meal, we all share the omelette or whatever else is served by taking bite-sized portions with our chopsticks and eating it with our rice. But Jim didn't know this, so he cut the omelette in four and took his fourth. I thought he must be famished, so I jumped right up and cooked a second big omelette. Only later did I learn that in the West each person takes his whole portion at the beginning of the meal. These were all important lessons for me as I tried to find the best ways to promote and encourage mutual understanding and communication. It was not always easy.

During his 1966 visit to the United States, Thây had had a large impact on the American people. He met with members of the House and Senate and with Secretary of Defense Robert McNamara. He spoke on national television and addressed many large gatherings, including one at the Town Hall in New York City, where he read poetry with Robert Frost and Arthur Miller. He gave many public talks and press conferences. "With the presence of Thây Nhat Hanh," Alfred Hassler reported, "membership of FOR increased tenfold." In 1968, Thây returned to North America and spoke to the Foreign Affairs Committee of the Canadian Senate and with UN Secretary General U Thant to present the Buddhist viewpoint on the Vietnam War. In May 1971, he accepted an invitation from Senators George McGovern, Claiborne Pell, and Birch Baye to speak to a large gathering of congressmen, and then he toured the U.S. for five weeks and met with many religious and political leaders.

From 1966-1968, Thây had cultivated deep friendships with a number of spiritually-based, social activists, including Martin Luther King, Jr., Thomas Merton, Daniel Berrigan, Dorothy Day, Joan Baez, and Jim Forest. But by 1970, we discovered that the American peace movement as a whole was rather young. We could not expect all peace workers to have the spiritual maturity of these great men and women, but by the time I arrived to help Thây, we were surprised to see how many people in the peace movement, frustrated by the prolonged war, were calling for a victory by Hanoi as the only hope. They thought that a victory by North Vietnam and the NLF would end the war quickly. This was extremely painful for us to hear, because we knew how much suffering one bomb or one bullet brings. And from our own experience of the violence perpetrated by the North during the 1968 Têt Offensive, and from

Thây Nhat Hanh and U Thant in 1968.

the book, *The Forest of Reeds*, in which Doan Quoc Sy described how much violence the Hanoi government had already perpetrated against its own people who were not communist, we knew that a victory by the North would not end the suffering. We only wanted an immediate cease-fire, and it was shocking for us to hear so-called peace activists advocating a victory by one side.

In 1970, I met with some peace workers in the U.S. whose intellectual and somewhat distant way of dealing with the painful reality of Vietnam hurt me. With many of them, as with representatives of the State Department, I had the impression I was speaking to a wall. I cried often and felt completely frustrated. Then I remembered the Buddha's teaching that knowledge can be an obstacle to understanding. These people were so sure of their knowledge about Vietnam that they were unwilling to open themselves to any other description of reality. They stuck to the idea that their way of ending the war was the only solution, and they could not listen to alternative approaches that might lead to ending the suffering, even though the recommendations came from someone closer to the situation.

The many leaders of the peace movement who wanted a victory by Hanoi ignored and suppressed our calls for an immediate cease-fire. The organizers of the 1971 Memorial Day March on Washington, for example, refused to allow Thây to speak because they were afraid that people might be moved by his words calling for an immediate stop to the killing. To them, a cease-fire would legalize the presence of American troops in Vietnam. Because of their skillful manipulation, many good-hearted American peace workers did not at all understand the position of the Buddhists in Vietnam. We did not want to start a war in the peace movement, so we kept silent, waiting for an occasion to tell the truth. Whenever we had opportunities to speak, we always made it clear that the innocent people of Vietnam suffered equally from U.S. bombs, bullets used by the Vietnamese nationalists, and Chinese and Soviet weapons deployed by the NLF and Hanoi. The people only wanted an immediate and total cease-fire.

Despite my frustrations with the peace movement and the U.S. government, I came to love many Americans during my visits. While in Vietnam, I never could have imagined that there were so many people in the U.S. working day and night to stop the war—students, workers, homemakers, teachers, and church people. In the past, many of us believed that all Americans were soldiers or CIA agents, so I wrote to my friends to tell them not to be suspicious of all Americans. I met many Americans who suffered as much as we did because of their government's policies.

In the U.S., I told people about the anguish of Vietnamese people in the countryside living under the bombs. I spoke from my own experience of being in touch with the war victims, desperately trying to save lives. During one meeting at Stanford, a group of pro-war students began shouting at me. I told them about the time I was at Thao Diên Village and some American soldiers were about to shoot innocent villagers. Looking into their eyes, I could see the fear in these soldiers, because a bridge nearby the village had been mined. When I had managed to communicate in my limited English that the guerrillas had come the week before and almost burned the common-house of the village, these young American soldiers had listened attentively and then discussed the situation among themselves. Finally, they left. I said to the students, "Look-

ing deeply into the soldiers' faces, I could see that they were good
people, just like you here. But the situation of war had made them
act like barbarous killers. You would do the same, out of fear, if you
were in a situation like that. Please don't send your brothers to
Vietnam. Please only help us Vietnamese resolve our own problems
by ourselves." I could see that they were touched by my words, and
the atmosphere in the room changed completely.

During eight weeks in the U.S. in 1971, I visited New York,
Washington, Philadelphia, Detroit, Indianapolis, Chicago, Denver,
Seattle, Portland, San Francisco, Los Angeles, San Diego, St. Louis,
Ann Arbor, and Atlanta. On a typical day, I would wake up at 5:00
a.m., take an early morning flight, hold a press conference at 10:00,
give an interview with the local TV network affiliate at 11:00 and
another interview with a local TV station at 11:30, eat lunch with
100 or 200 university students at noon, talk to high school students
at 1:00, give a talk at a university auditorium at 3:00, have dinner
with 200 graduate school students at 6:00, give a lecture in a down-
town auditorium at 8:30, go to sleep around 11:00 p.m, and prepare
to leave for another city early the next morning. The day after my
visit, an article with a photo usually appeared in the local newspapers. I never felt tired working like this. I only felt drained after
speaking to State Department officials in Washington, who urged
me to support the Thieu regime, or with certain "peace" leaders
who urged me to support Hanoi.

In 1971, I attended a Christian nonviolence conference in Costa
Rica. After being away from Vietnam for three years, I was happy to
spend a few days in a tropical climate, sitting under mango trees, sa-
voring the sour taste of the young mango fruit, and remembering
how much I enjoyed fruits with salt and chili. In Costa Rica, I met
with forty delegates from Latin American countries, most of whom
were church leaders who thought that armed resistance was the
only solution. I gave a twenty-minute presentation on the positive
achievements of the Buddhists—pioneer development villages, resettlement centers, educational programs for children and adults,
and our efforts for peace, and it seemed to give them some confi-
dence in the way of nonviolence.

After Costa Rica, I went to Europe and met with the Foreign
Ministers of Denmark, Sweden, West Germany, and Belgium, en-

couraging them to use their influence to stop the war. I still felt as if I were in a dream. What was the use of visiting these luxurious offices and meeting with prestigious people while my countrymen continued to suffer under the bombs? I visualized the bodies killed and maimed by the war, and I imagined that even the rice plants must be too afraid to ripen, lest their grains be burned by the hellish bombs.

We decided to start a campaign called "Stop the Killing Now," in cooperation with the International Committee of Conscience on Vietnam (ICCV). The ICCV bought a full-page ad in the *New York Times*, and we gathered 9,000 signatures from government leaders and clergy from twenty-two countries. Five hundred Parliament Members, Congressmen, and Senators signed to support the campaign, among them eighteen members of the Parliament of the Republic of Vietnam! On October 11, 1971, we held a press conference at the Hotel Lutèce in Paris to present to the world and the warring parties the deep wishes of the Vietnamese people. To support us, at the same time as our conference, 300 Catholic priests in Rome each wore a small placard around his neck with the name of one Buddhist monk imprisoned in Vietnam. Following the press conference, a delegation of government and church leaders from the U.S., Germany, France, UK, and other European countries visited the offices of the four adversaries represented at the Paris Peace Talks. The "Stop the Killing Now" delegation invited us, the Vietnamese Buddhist Peace Delegation, to join them in listening carefully to the views of each warring party, and then requested us to express our views. Thây Nhat Hanh, Dr. Nguyen Van Huong, and I confirmed the points upon which we agreed with the warring parties, and we also spoke about their points that were far from the reality and the wishes of Vietnamese people. After that, the Republic of Vietnam proposed eight points, dropping their ideas we had criticized. Then Hanoi and the National Liberation Front proposed ten points, dropping their ideas we had criticized. If only peace could be so easy.

In 1972, Thây Nhat Hanh, Nguyen Van Huong, Thây Huyen Quang, General Secretary of the UBC from Vietnam, and I, attended a conference in Geneva of the World Council of Churches (WCC). At the conference, Reverend Leopold Niilus, the WCC delegate responsible for Vietnam affairs, proposed that the WCC support only the oppressed people. "In the Vietnam War nowadays," he said, "there is only one bandit on the highway raping the young girl. It is obvious that we church people cannot be neutral in this fight. We must support the young girl, who is the Vietnamese people fighting desperately against the American bandit." Reverend Niilus may have belonged to a group called "Theologians for Liberation," and we saw in him his deep love for the oppressed. Thây Nhat Hanh serenely and kindly thanked the representative of WCC and said, "We all agree that we must support the little girl against the bandit, but let me invite you to look deeply at the bandit. Who is the bandit in the Vietnam War? For me, the bandits are those who sit comfortably in the White House, the Kremlin, and the Peking Palace who provide the weapons and ideologies and hide the truth from the public, while giving orders for millions of young men to be drafted and killed. For us, the young women being raped are not only innocent, voiceless peasants, but also the Vietnamese soldiers of both sides and the American soldiers who do not know anything about Vietnamese history or reality. We hope that all of you will look more deeply into the situation in Vietnam."

CHAPTER FIFTEEN

Children Suffer Equally

Traditionally in Vietnam, we did not have orphanages. If your brother died, you adopted his children, and if you were too poor to feed them, you would place them in the home of someone who could, where they would work as a houseboy or housegirl. Our social work programs were designed to help people avoid giving up their children, nieces, or nephews, and we awarded scholarships to support children whose families were too poor to care for them, so the families could stay together.

By 1972, there were day-care centers run by Buddhist nuns all over Vietnam, so we asked the nuns to send us files for every orphan and destitute child, including information about the parents and the child's relatives and a photo. Then, in our office in Paris, we translated the reports into English, French, Dutch, German, and Italian, and we forwarded the translations to committees throughout Europe that were set up to find sponsors for the children.

European families each contributing $6 per month to support one child, were told in detail about the child's life and situation. We sent funds to the Unified Buddhist Church, and they forwarded the money to the nun in charge of the day-care center, who gave it to the child's parents or uncle. Then she would follow up to be sure the money was being used wisely. When the family in Vietnam received the money, they wrote back to us, and we translated their letters for the sponsoring families in Europe. Each of us at the Buddhist Peace Delegation office in Paris set aside one hour per day to translate these documents—the applications for sponsors and the letters. Thây especially loved this work. Each day he translated dozens of applications, and the work helped him be in touch with each child. The whole Buddhist Church cooperated with us on this project, and slowly we built up a beautiful network of human relations between Vietnam and the West.

Orphans in Hue.

The committee in Holland was the most active. In 1972, after helping us raise several hundred thousand *guilders* each year to support Vietnamese war victims through the UBC, Hebe Kohlbrugge had to resign from her position in the Dutch Reformed Church, and, after that, she could no longer help us. I encouraged two other Dutch friends, Kirsten Roep and Hans Lourens to set up a committee to help Vietnam. They agreed, and three times a year I came to Holland to speak to the press, TV, and radio and invite new people to join the work. The committee began by sponsoring twenty-five orphans. Kirsten, an intelligent and wonderful mother of three, taught herself Vietnamese in order to feel close to the orphaned children, and her whole family supported us faithfully. Her husband, a geology professor, listened attentively to everything we shared, and gave me a precious fossil as a gesture of his affection. Their oldest son, Jens, a bright twelve-year-old, would explain the suffering of the Vietnamese people to those who telephoned while his mother was away. Hans Lourens, Secretary of the Dutch FOR, helped us be in touch with members of FOR. My tours in Holland slowly brought other precious friends like Juul and Laura Pauwells and Linda Lijftogt into the group, and by April 1975, the committee was raising $100,000 a month from 14,000 Dutch families for the children in Vietnam.

In 1972, while we were in Sweden for the conference on the environment, Thây met with a number of leaders in the Lutheran Church. When he spoke about the spiritual values of the Vietnamese people, they asked how they could help us, and we told them about our Buddhist relief and development projects. "As Buddhist social workers," I explained, "we take care of children from both sides of the conflict. Children suffer equally whether their wounds are inflicted by South Vietnamese soldiers or by the NLF." In fact, we cared more for the orphans and widows of the guerrillas than the guerrillas themselves did. As guerrillas hiding in the jungle, it was impossible for them to take care of their families or send their children to school.

Until that time, the Swedish government had helped Vietnam only through the National Liberation Front and North Vietnam, and people in Sweden did not seem to know much at all about South Vietnam. They regarded it only as a puppet of the United States. The Lutheran pastors felt it was unfair to help war victims on one side only, and they invited me to meet with them to explain how Sweden could help both sides.

When we met, I did not talk about politics. I only shared my experiences—how I grew up, how the situation in my country became so desperate, how I worked to find support for war victims. I told them how people attacked our school and tried to kill us, but that we tried to understand their suspicion in order to find ways for mutual acceptance. The church leaders felt a strong connection between our Buddhist approach and their Christian ideals, and afterwards, Reverend Karl Exel Elmquist arranged for me to meet with members of the Swedish Parliament to discuss the possibility of Sweden helping Vietnam through the Unified Buddhist Church.

When I met with the first member of Parliament, I tried to tell him all the most important things in just five minutes. I looked into his eyes when I spoke, and then I listened to what he had to say. Understanding what was most important to him, I spoke directly to that, and I could see that what I said touched him. He invited me to speak with five other members of the Parliament, from both the governing party and the opposition parties, and, as a result, in June

1973, the Swedish Parliament agreed to support our Buddhist humanitarian work.

For the measure to become law, it had to be signed by Olaf Palme, the Prime Minister. The Lutheran church leaders said that I had to meet with him to be sure of his support, but it was difficult to obtain an appointment. Then Bo Wirmarck, the head of religious affairs of the ruling Socialist Party, who had attended several of my talks at Lutheran Churches, told me, "Olaf is my friend. I can arrange for you to see him."

My appointment was for just fifteen minutes. Mr. Palme was a fine, attentive man, and I spoke truthfully to him about my experiences as a young person aspiring to create something beautiful for poor people of Vietnam but faced instead with devastation. I described how desperate I'd felt when, with a bleeding baby in my arms, I crossed the fire zone, knowing there was no physician to help; how I tore my dress to make bandages for wounded people; how I volunteered to bury hundreds of dead bodies around Saigon after the 1968 Têt Offensive. He seemed keenly interested in everything I said.

I invited him to be "inside the skin" of a young person growing up in our war-torn country; when she looks around, she cannot seek help from the French, the Americans, or the communists—all those governments are perpetrating the violence. The only people she can trust are the Buddhist monks and nuns. I told him that we had started a movement among monks and nuns to help poor people, without taking money from any warring party. I told him that we now had 5,000 families in Vietnam supporting our work financially, and many more in Europe. Beginning with a small group of people, we now had the trust of the Unified Buddhist Church, and we created a School of Youth for Social Service and a National Buddhist Committee for Reconstruction and Development that had thousands of social workers throughout the country. But as the war continued, many villages were completely destroyed, some several times, and we could not continue to ask for funds only from the Vietnamese people, who were without schools, hospitals, or even houses. Our fifteen-minute meeting was extended to forty-five minutes, and, at the end, Mr. Palme said that he was very pleased to know about our work and to support our projects.

After that, I had to meet with the Swedish International Development Aid, the department of the Foreign Ministry that dealt with support for developing countries. Eight development specialists questioned me about our work. I was joyful and passionate, and I could see that they enjoyed hearing how we got the farmers to plant mustard greens instead of drinking rice liquor and how we set up schools without any money. They were used to large budgets and formal proposals, and I could see that they appreciated our spirit of doing this important work with the limited resources that were available. I told them, "Because the Swedish government has been neutral, we would be grateful to accept your help. If the U.S. government wanted to give us aid, we would have to refuse. We must care for war victims without any money from the warring parties. But even if your government cannot help, we will go on, because for us it is a matter of life and death, and thousands of Vietnamese families are helping us."

Someone asked, "Why don't you support the National Liberation Front or Hanoi?" I said, "If supporting Hanoi would bring happiness to the Vietnamese people, we would do so. But war and violence only bring more destruction. We have witnessed the Vietnamese warring parties violently destroying their own people. We prefer to live simply, helping people control their own fates with their own small means. That is why we refuse to support either side." They seemed to agree with everything I said, but they told me that their rule was to fund programs only through government agencies, and it would be difficult for their government to support a religious group. I hesitated and then said, somewhat presumptuously I suppose, but with a big smile, "Rules are invented by humans to serve humans. If you see that a rule prevents you from serving humans, why don't you break it?" To my delight, they found a way to "break the rule" by supporting us through the Swedish Lutheran Churches. The first grant was for 1,500,000 Swedish *krones* ($300,000) to help us build five resettlement centers for villagers whose homes had been bombed.

All of the money given by the Swedish government to the Swedish Lutheran Church went directly to the Committee for Reconstruction and Development (CRD) of the UBC in Vietnam. Social workers went into the field and planned the projects with the vil-

Distributing 5,000 blankets purchased with Swedish aid.

lagers. They submitted proposals to the CRD and waited for their approval. The high monks had experts review the proposals to judge whether a project was worthy of funding. With the UBC's approval, the social worker would receive the funds and proceed with the work.

Suddenly, many opportunistic politicians in Vietnam claimed to be connected with the CRD, since it was now supported by Sweden, a neutral government. They hoped to be seen as the third element in power in the event a future reconciliation government was formed. But the CRD could not afford to accept opportunists who knew nothing about social development. When they were overlooked, these politicians became angry, and some of them told the Vietnamese press that the high monks in the Buddhist Church were corrupt and had used some of the money from the Swedish government to buy expensive cars for themselves. This was entirely untrue, but when it appeared in the newspapers, these same politicians had the articles translated into Swedish and sent to Stockholm. When our friend, Bo Wirmarck, heard about it, he asked me if the charges were true. I replied, "Why don't you go to Vietnam and investigate for yourself?"

Bo went to Vietnam with a team of people from the Swedish International Development Aid, and they found that the money sent to the Buddhists in Vietnam had been used very carefully. Every dollar was spent with the approval of both the local social workers and the UBC experts. There were receipts for each purchase. The records were so clear that the investigating team dismissed all of the accusations. The Swedish International Development Aid of the Foreign Ministry later revealed to us that when they had given Hanoi and the National Liberation Front large sums of money in the past, they had not received such accurate reporting.

Bo Wirmarck is a very sweet man, but he looks rather serious and businesslike. One Sunday, he arranged for me to speak at three different churches in Uppsala. There was a big fair, and thousands of people had come to the area. The first meeting was crowded, and so was the second, but by the third, people seemed reluctant to come, perhaps because those who were interested had already heard what I had to say. While waiting for people to arrive, I asked Bo whether we could change the subject of the talk. Bo refused, saying, "No, people must hear you speak about the situation because most of them only know the National Liberation Front and Hanoi." So, while gathering in front of the church with some thirty young people, I asked whether they would like to hear Vietnamese folk songs. I explained how people sing while working in the rice fields, rowing small boats along the river, and fishing. The number of listeners increased steadily as I continued singing, and Bo was amazed to see a crowd larger than the one in the morning. I concluded by saying that these songs were no longer sung spontaneously in Vietnam, because of the killing and maiming, the fear and hatred. People artificially performed folk songs on TV, but those were not real folk songs as in times of peace. Tears filled my eyes as I thought about the way the war affects ordinary people, and the people listening were also moved to tears, and they asked many questions. Even Bo recognized the need to sing and not just analyze the war situation.

Most rewarding for the Swedish investigative team was to see the five beautiful resettlement centers built in just six months—in Quang Phuoc, Quang Nam, Quang Ngai, Thua Thien, and Quang Tri. The Quang Phuoc resettlement center, for instance, had 300

beautiful houses for war victims, each with a garden of green vegetables, a school, and a day-care center, while another resettlement
center three miles away, developed by government workers with
U.S. aid was still only half-finished after eighteen months. The
government's Minister of Social Welfare, Phan Quan Dan, com-
plained to our Swedish friends that he had already spent five times
more money than the Buddhists and might not be done for another
eighteen months.

In the Quang Nam resettlement center, Thây Long Tri, the
Chairman of the local Buddhist Committee for Social Welfare,
worked with a team of twelve SYSS workers. When the North
Vietnamese and NLF armies approached the area, Thây Long Tri
asked them to avoid our center, because he knew that all the work
and all the Swedish aid would be reduced to ash if a battle broke
out there. He was a respected high monk of the area who had, for
decades, helped children who suffered from both sides of the war.
When these young people grew up, half joined the NLF guerrillas
and half joined the nationalist army, so those from both sides knew
and respected him. When he asked the communists not to approach, they agreed on one condition: that he remove the police
center and the military post that were located in the Quang Nam
Buddhist resettlement center. Thây Long Tri then approached the
Saigon authorities and arranged to have both the police center and
the military post moved out. The North Vietnamese and NLF
armies went away, and there was no battle.

Hearing about this inspired our Swedish friends, but I told them
I had overheard hundreds of similar negotiations by nameless
bodhisattvas. Because of the jealousy of those who wanted to destroy the prestige of our social workers, our Swedish friends got to
see our work more clearly, and, as a result, they gave us another
10 million Swedish krones ($2,000,000) to build ten more resettle-
ment centers. I used to tell my friends we should not be afraid of
difficulties and misunderstandings. Once we can transform the situation and remove the lack of understanding in people, the fruits
will be great.

Visualize opposite ends of the world: on one end are the poor orphans and on the other are people who are able to support the orphans. The sponsors put a picture of the little child on their desk or

in their living room, and they feel happy to be able to help those in need. In their remote villages, the orphans now feel loved and cared for. Once a sponsor comes to love one child, he or she may also wish to support other projects, such as day-care centers, village wells, or medical centers. By April 1975, the end of the war, we had the support of 14,000 families in Holland; 1,000 in Switzerland; 2,000 in France; 1,000 in the United States; and hundreds in other countries, nearly 20,000 sponsors in all. It was a great linking of the human family.

CHAPTER SIXTEEN

Beginning Anew

W̲e did not have the chance to build another resettlement center, because after the war ended on April 30, 1975, the communist
government took all the money in the bank account of the Committee for Reconstruction and Development of the UBC, including
$175,428, three months' support for 9,746 orphans that had arrived
at the bank just two days before the end of the war, and stopped all
of our work.

In June, Mrs. Duong Quynh Hoa, the new Minister of Social
Welfare, closed down the SYSS and the Buddhist Committee for
Reconstruction and Development, saying that the government
would be solely responsible for social services. In one instant,
10,000 social workers were dismissed. The police arrested SYSS Director Thich Tu Man and held him in jail for more than a year. Le
Nguyen Thieu, the General Secretary, was interrogated by the police every day from 7:00 a.m. until 10:00 p.m. for months, before he
went into hiding and moved his family to another district. He finally escaped in 1980, leaving the country by boat, and spent two
years in a refugee camp. After that, he and his family joined us in
France.

Our friends in the SYSS reported to us that on July 7, 1975, a
group of fourteen communist policemen ransacked the SYSS offices
for two hours and seized all of our property, including typewriters,
books, files, and medicine. The SYSS staff contacted Muoi Anh,
the government's officer for religion, and asked him to come witness the ransacking. He arrived even as the police were still ransacking the offices and took a number of photographs, but when he
reported to his superiors, he said, "I saw SYSS workers destroying
and stealing the property of their own school." We were shocked by
this upside-down report and began to learn some hard lessons about
the new communist authorities.

Thich Tu Man, Le Nguyen Thieu, Pham Dang Phu, an SYSS
worker, and Thanh, my sister, told us that they were summoned by
the police and interrogated about the SYSS. The authorities were
especially suspicious of Thây Nhat Hanh and me. They seemed certain that we were CIA agents. Our friends warned us that it would
be extremely dangerous for us to come back to Vietnam. We could
be put in jail for the rest of our lives or even be killed in an "accident."

How desperate I felt! Since the age of eighteen, I had worked to
bring relief to the poorest people, and thousands of young friends
had become involved in this work. My dreams had been realized—
the bombing had stopped, the Unified Buddhist Church was helping poor peasants, and thousands of hands were reaching to remote
areas of Vietnam to support hungry and orphaned children—and
then, overnight, the fruits of all my efforts vanished completely.

I had no joy or energy to live. Every time I thought of Vietnam, I
wanted to die or to sleep and never wake up. I felt as if my heart
were being squeezed by strong, violent hands. For months, all I
could do was practice going back to my breath, following each in-
breath and out-breath with my mind, because I would sink into
deep despair every time I stopped doing that. Returning to Vietnam
was still impossible. After decades of war, all the country had to
show for it was a dishonest, totalitarian government! I could never
fulfill my dream of real social change in my country.

In November, I went to the Vietnamese embassy in Paris to try to
persuade the new government to allow our project of sponsoring orphans to continue. I had no great hope, but as I entered the room, I
did my best to view the Secretary of the Embassy as a future
buddha. The Buddha taught that everyone has the capacity to become an awakened, enlightened being, so I thought, "I have come
to try to work with this difficult, future buddha."

I had the backing of thousands of Western sponsors of orphans,
and I asked him if his government would allow us to send money to
the orphans we supported. I showed him the names of all the donors, describing how a Mr. van den Berg from Holland or a Mrs.
Rousseau from France could support this child named Le Thi Ngoc
Duong Thi Hoa. I explained that the sponsors sent $6 a month to
the orphans, whom they loved like a relative, and that they often

became interested in supporting other social work projects once they touched the suffering of one child. I knew that with supporters like these, we would be able to rebuild the whole country.

I explained, "If you allow our project to continue, you will not be bound by any government or large organization. Each person gives only $6, but with 10,000 supporters, we raise $60,000 a month. It's a large amount of foreign currency." Until then, I had worked to support orphans in South Vietnam, so I proposed that we would seek sponsors for North Vietnamese orphans exclusively until the number of North and South Vietnamese orphans were equal. Then we could support both.

I continued, "You can take any name or address to see whether it is true that this person gives $6 per month and that this money is not from the CIA. Of the money we receive, we send 100 percent to the child. We do not take one cent for overhead for ourselves." I told him, "If we give this money to your government's social work-ers, they will not be able to locate the children. Our orphans live with their relatives in remote districts, and only the local monks and nuns know where they are. So we must send the money through the Unified Buddhist Church. I can give you $150,000 for the first three months." The Secretary seemed moved by my presen-tation, and he said, "I will contact Hanoi for approval to accept the funds and use them as you request, but I don't dare take your money now."

Many Vietnamese knew about the deception of the communists, and they were shocked that I would even consider giving them so much money. But sponsors throughout Europe were pushing us to send money to the orphans through the government, confident that the new regime would not deceive us. Even after I told them that I doubted the sincerity of the communists, they continued to urge me to send their money to Vietnam directly via the Embassy. So I did my best to follow the wishes of the donors. I also had another rea-son for sending the money this way. Until that time, the communist regime had not allowed any private organizations to operate. We thought that because we were able to raise so much foreign cur-rency, they might be tempted to allow us to become the first private organization they would work with, and we could break their mo-nopoly.

After one month, the Embassy secretary called me and said, "Your project has been approved. Please come to my office, and we can work out the details." I went, and I gave him $150,000. I could see that this man believed in his government and believed the money would be sent to the UBC to help the orphans. But I was skeptical, so when he gave me a receipt stating, "We in the Embassy have received $150,000 from Miss Cao Ngoc Phuong to be transmitted to the children in Vietnam via Thich Tri Thu, the president of the Unified Buddhist Church," I went home and immediately made 300 copies of the receipt and sent a copy to each social worker in Vietnam with a letter: "The project to sponsor orphans has been allowed by the government to continue. Here is the receipt from the Embassy in Paris." The social workers were very excited, and with the receipt in their hands, they were not afraid of the regime. They went to the President of the Unified Buddhist Church, Thich Tri Thu, and asked him to go to the Foreign Ministry to get the money.

But, after one year, we received a telegram from Thich Tri Thu saying that the money still had not been received by the Buddhist Church. He said that the 300 tons of rice that Sulak Sivaraksa and the Thai Red Cross had sent the UBC in early June 1975 on our behalf for the orphans had also never reached him. We sent copies of both documents—the receipt from the Embassy and the telegram from Thich Tri Thu—to 10,000 of our sponsors in the West. Only with this proof could I show them how deceitful the regime really was. After this, the committees in Germany, the UK, Italy, France, Switzerland, Japan, New Zealand, Sweden, the U.S., and Canada that helped orphans agreed to work for orphans in other poor countries like Bangladesh, India, and Ethiopia, but not Vietnam.[*]

Unable to support those in need in Vietnam, I felt like a tree cut at the roots. Day after day, all I could do was meditate, dwelling on my breath. As I sat, walked, gardened, and cooked, I remained aware of each breath. I did not dare think about Vietnam. Every time I did, I felt desperate.

---

[*] In Holland, some members of the committee still wanted to work with the new regime, and they used the list of Dutch sponsors to continue to send funds to Hanoi. A dozen friends, led by Kirsten Roep, refused to cooperate. They supported my silent work to help the hungry children and, even today, continue to support this work.

In July 1971, I had been invited to lead a week-long workshop on nonviolent action in Vietnam at the farm of a peace community in Auvergne, France. I wrote to Thây, telling him how moved I was to see a garden of pumpkins, cucumbers, and lettuce. It reminded me of our SYSS garden in Vietnam. It was sad to see Thây taking care of one pot of mint and one pot of violet leaves on his windowsill in Maisons Alfort, outside of Paris. Every three months, he had to change the soil using the little bags of earth available at the market. One friend in the community at Auvergne told me that in France land was cheap. I knew that a house in Paris with a garden could cost several hundred thousand francs. Because many French farmers were leaving for the city, their land and dilapidated farmhouses were selling for next to nothing. So we decided to try to find an inexpensive house in the countryside.

After looking at many places, we found one tiny, old house that Thây fell in love with, and right away he wanted to buy it. It was on a hill with a panoramic view of the Othe Forest. Behind and all around us were hills with meadows and, further up, fields of wheat and corn. The property was located outside the little town of Fontvannes, 150 kilometers southeast of Paris, and the price was just $3,700, including the house and a small plot of land. The rooms were completely uninhabitable—there was just a roof that also covered a stable and one large room that had recently been divided in half. There were no doors or windows, just a chimney for burning wood and two small holes in the stone walls.

We continued to live in Paris, but every weekend we went to Fontvannes to begin fixing it up. At 5:00 the first evening we stayed there—it was November—I started to understand why people in France love the sunshine so much. The house was like a refrigerator. We burned many logs, but it was impossible to heat the indoors, even after we covered the doors and holes in the walls with nylon sheets. Hoang Anh and I did jumping exercises and went outside running very fast to try to keep warm, but to no avail. The three of us, Thây, Hoang Anh, and I, spent the night on three wooden planks placed right in front of the fireplace. Thây got a terrible cold.

There were no toilets, so we hired professionals to build a bathroom, a septic tank, two windows, and two doors. On weekends, we ourselves insulated each room. Then we transformed the stable into a warm room for Thây. As the stable was separated from the house by a thick, stone wall, Thây had privacy; it was like having his own hut. The big room became our meditation hall and living room. We placed a beautiful piece of wood on the fireplace mantel to make an altar for the Buddha.

Many friends came each weekend to help with the building projects. At night, the men all stayed in the meditation room, and the women stayed in the room behind the living room. When these two rooms were too crowded, some of us slept in the kitchen. Later we added a large room for sitting and tea meditation, because the living room was really too small. Every morning after sitting meditation, we had tea meditation at a table near a large glass door in the kitchen, and then Thây would give a beautiful Dharma talk. Jim Forest took a photo of Thây serving tea at that table that has since been used in many articles and books. For four years, Thây, I, and a number of friends in the Buddhist Peace Delegation went to Fontvannes almost every weekend to build one room, then another, and Thây used the place as a hermitage.

By 1975, the house near Fontvannes had become rather pleasant, with four rooms and a cozy kitchen, and several of us decided to move there. The war had ended, and we were cut off from Vietnam with no way to help. We decided to name the community *Les Patates Douces* (Sweet Potatoes). In Vietnam, when peasants have no rice, they eat dried sweet potatoes. It is the poorest food, and we knew we needed some way to be in touch with the poorest people in our country. Thanks to that house and land, we were able to heal some of our wounds and appreciate the beauties of France. Eleven of us lived there—each with only a sleeping bag as a bed—and Vietnamese friends from Paris joined us many weekends.

Our life in the Sweet Potato Community was meditative and joyful. We did not feel strong enough to sing traditional Vietnamese songs, but we sang songs that arose from our meditations on being in touch with nature—the trees, the birds, the sunshine, the snow. We printed and bound books for refugees and planted vegetables. Thây was the most skillful printer. None of us had expected him to be so adept at manual work. The Fellowship of Reconciliation gave us an old Varityper, and I composed the text of *The Miracle of Mind-*

Cultivating the garden at Sweet Potato Community.

fulness in Vietnamese. Thây did the layout, plate-making, printing, cutting, binding, and cover design. He also wrote *The Sun My Heart*, *The History of Buddhism in Vietnam*, and many short stories— "Giant Pine," "The Lone Pink Fish," about the experience of boat people, "The Moon Bamboo," about the divided love of a refugee for Vietnam and for the new land, and "Peony Blossoms," about the near-death experience of one scientist friend, Ta Hue Chau, and the suffering of Nguyen Van Huong. Thây wrote "Peony Blossoms" to help Nguyen Van Huong overcome his suffering if something happened to his beloved wife, Chau, who was quite ill. (Fortunately, Chau's health returned.) We planted lettuce, carrots, mustard greens, coriander, mint, and many Vietnamese herbs, and we discovered that Thây Nhat Hanh was also an expert gardener. He taught us how to use a hoe, how to dig without bending our backs too much, and how to aerate and cultivate the soil. In that atmosphere, my mind was not disturbed by painful images of Vietnam. We had no photographs of orphans, no telephone to answer, and no visits by those wanting to help Vietnam. At Sweet Potato, I began to feel calm again.

Every week we saw new varieties of wildflowers on the nearby meadows. One week the hill was yellow with dandelions, then white with chamomile flowers. Another week millions of daisies shone on several hills, then the hills were red with poppies, and later we would be astonished to see fields carpeted with violets. The air at Sweet Potato was very fresh, and practicing walking meditation along the hills surrounding the house was a joy. Although we owned only one tiny plot of land, we made no distinctions about property lines. We just walked peacefully on the paths that crossed the many fields and hillsides.

In autumn, the trees in Othe Forest, right in front of us, turned spectacular shades of red, yellow, orange, and brown. When winter arrived with the morning frost, each blade of grass looked like a tiny being covered with angel's silk, and the forest became enchanted, with trees made of tiny gems decorated with fine silk strings. We had never seen anything like this in Vietnam. For my birthday in 1977, Thây gave me this poem:

Always the Same Mind

The stars and moon still look beautiful
on clear nights.
The willow bay is still green,
the thuya tree waving in the breeze
is still gracious.
Although we miss our homeland,
the plum blossoms on the hill
still offer us hospitality.
The luxurious vegetation
brings more vitality to the hills
and strength to the moon.
The squash plants have begun
to put forth flowers,
and children are playing in the sunshine
in the front yard.
We make books and sell them through the mail.

Although we live simply,
each day of our life
is like a festival.

The news from the homeland
is not encouraging.
The temples do not have permission
to ring their bells.
Many children are left without their parents.
Many are in reeducation camps.
Writers and artists remain in dead silence.
So many boat people, including children, perish
in the Gulf of Siam.

Love tries hard to express itself.
What can we do?
We know that our hands are available.
We are ready.
What can we do?
The answer will certainly come
if we know how to remain faithful
and to keep calm in the midst of turbulence.

The sunshine is still calling attention
to the hill above.
Cherry blossoms are still lovely,
moon and stars still beautiful on clear nights,
willows still green,
and the thuya still waves graciously to us.

Life at Sweet Potato Community was beautiful, but I still felt forlorn. I wanted more than anything to help the hungry children of Vietnam. Then, one day in my meditation, I realized that I could go to Thailand, Bangladesh, or another country to work for social change. There was so much suffering in the world, if I could not help the Vietnamese at this time, why not help those in need somewhere else? In less than a month, I flew to Bangkok and immediately started working in the slums there with two Thai friends. But within a few weeks, I realized that my friends did not do things as I did. To support twelve orphans in the slum, I offered to find sponsors if they would only take a photo and start a file, but they were so slow. When I suggested that they rent a hut in a slum to start a day-care center, they hesitated. In Vietnam, when I had an idea, if friends did not agree, I could just start by myself. But in Bangkok, I did not know the language, and it was impossible to work independently. I could not reproach my Thai friends for not following my advice. I knew I was ignorant of their culture and could not impose my plans on them. After three-and-a-half weeks in Bangkok, I decided to return to France. On the way home, I stopped in India and Bangladesh, and I saw the great misery there. Children and adults were so thin they looked like skeletons under the burning sun, as they carried huge bags of rocks and soil. In the mines, the daily salary was less than the price of one kilo of rice. These workers could barely feed themselves, much less their families. I tried to find good local organizations that I could support.

After six weeks, I returned to France, even sadder than before. I had been unable to be of help anywhere. All I could do at Sweet Potato was to immerse myself in sitting meditation, walking meditation, planting-lettuce meditation, doing everything while following my breathing to stay focused and not carried away by my sadness or thoughts. After many months of this, I had an insight: Because I was born in Vietnam, I knew the language, culture, and moral values of Vietnam; I was an expert in that part of the world, and I had to devote all my energies to finding ways to help it!

A few weeks later, during sitting meditation, I remembered a sentence in a letter that I had received from my sister: "The medicine you sent Mother for hypertension was very useful, but she didn't need the other medical supplies you sent, so we sold them in the market, and with that money we were able to buy several hundred kilograms of rice." When I read the letter, I had felt sad, but in my meditation, I realized that this was the solution! If I could not send money to the orphans without the communists stealing it, I *could* send medical supplies for them to sell at the market.

Thây always teaches that when we are in a difficult situation, if we calm ourselves, we may find a solution. But he also says that the first solution that comes into our mind may not be the best; in a few

Wrapping parcels of aid.

days, another solution may arise that is even better. So I continued to practice sitting and walking meditation, sowing fresh, calm seeds of peace in my mind, and after a few days, I remembered another sentence in the letter. My sister had written that she was interrogated at the police station several times because of her relationship with me. I knew that if I wanted to send medicine to hungry children, I could not use my own name. I began sending parcels of medicine to social workers we had worked with in the past. With each package, I gave myself a new name and wrote in a different handwriting. If I used the name Cao Ngoc Phuong, the workers could get into trouble. I enclosed a letter saying that I was a person living abroad who had lived in the same province in Vietnam as that social worker. Sometimes I was a nun, sometimes an old lady, sometimes a little girl. I wrote that I wanted to send medicine to the social worker, but that if she did not need all of it, she might wish to exchange some for food and share it with hungry children. Then I asked her to send me the addresses of some destitute families so that I could send aid to them directly. In this way, I began to accumulate a list of the poorest families.

In just a few months, I had more contacts than I could stay in touch with by myself. I could only send packages to 200 or 300 families by myself, because I was concerned that my address would become suspicious to the communists. So I decided to ask a number of young Vietnamese refugees who came to Sweet Potato to help me.

This made the work even more enjoyable. I was able to get back in touch with our network of sponsors, and I could establish a relationship between the sponsors who contributed the funds, the young refugees who helped me write the letters and pack the medicine, and the children who received the medical supplies. I tried to be deeply in touch with each child, to find out his or her worries and aspirations. In the past, when we were supporting nearly 20,000 orphans, it was impossible to communicate with each one. With this new project, I was able to correspond with each child. In my letters, I taught them how to enjoy the many positive things around them, not just the food and medicine, but their healthy eyes that opened to a world of shapes and colors and many other beauties of their homeland. In some cases, I was also able to help the parents through the child. It is difficult to teach adults when you are giving them money; they might feel offended. So, I tried to teach the children in ways that could also benefit the parents. In just two years, we set up dozens of small groups of young Vietnamese in Europe and America working silently for hungry children.

One day, Bui Thi Huong came to visit us at Sweet Potato. I was quite excited as I told her about our success in sending supplies to the children in Vietnam, and I invited her to join me in the work. Bui Thi Huong had been a dear younger sister in the service for the poor in Vietnam. She joined us in 1965, a few months before the founding of the SYSS; then she joined the SYSS and was one of the best social workers.

During the February 1967 bombing of the SYSS dormitory, when two friends died, Huong received more than 600 pieces of grenade shrapnel in her frail body, and she almost died. Masako Yamanouchi, our Japanese friend working for the SYSS, donated blood to her. Huong was in hospitals in Vietnam and then in Japan for two years, and she lost most of her leg. She learned to walk again using an artificial limb. With the Peace Accords of March 1973, Huong left Japan and joined us in the Buddhist Peace Delegation office in

Paris. Her wonderful presence inspired many friends working for the orphans.

When the war ended abruptly in 1975, the attitude of the new regime was so cruel and ignorant that millions of Vietnamese suffered severe mental wounds. In our Buddhist Peace Delegation, each of us struggled in our own ways. Anh Binh and Anh Anh, for example, both dearly loved their fiancées in Vietnam, but after receiving the news of how desperate things were in Vietnam, they saw no hope of ever going home again, and they became involved with other women. I had always respected these two friends for their loyalty and faithfulness to teachers and friends, and their new relationships shocked me. But I understood that this was a result of their mental wounds. Bui Thi Huong acted also from that mental wound. It started when Thây proposed that we all move to Sweet Potato. Huong said that she preferred to travel around France visiting spiritual communities. She spent a few months here and a few months there. Then, in 1977, after staying six months at the Community of the Ark, she came to Sweet Potato for a visit. I was so happy to see her, and I proposed that she join me in the work for hungry children, as we had done in the past. I was taken aback when she said, almost violently, "No, no. I don't want to hear about social service!" Then she began to talk about a new English translation of the *Upanishads*. I kept silent, feeling hurt by her response.

Only later did I understand. Huong had sacrificed so much for the suffering people in Vietnam, working in the SYSS and the Buddhist Peace Delegation, and she had lost her leg during the service. She always refused to use violence to answer the violence. She made all of these sacrifices so that one day Vietnam would be happy again. Yet, despite all of her sacrifices, Vietnam had become a hateful, arrogant dictatorship where so many cruelties were taking place. Of what use had her kindness been? Why should she bother to help hungry children? What would be the fruit of more sacrifice? She doubted that anything would help. I saw that I had no right to reproach her, because I did not have 600 pieces of grenade in my body, and I had not lost a leg. Tears came to my eyes when I reflected on her wounds, mental and physical. But I had to keep my distance from her, just as she had to keep away from me. I could not discuss philosophy when so many friends in Vietnam were crying for help, and she could not bear to hear their cries. I understood that the only way for us was to keep apart.

My last contact with Huong was in 1988 when she was about to visit Vietnam. She offered to help if I needed her to do something. "But," she wrote, "please don't involve me in anything political." I had to keep silent again. Everything I am involved with in Vietnam is political. If the government knew that I was sending medicine to a family, that family would be in danger. So again I lost an occasion to work with Huong, my beloved young sister in the service.

EXILE
1976-1993

CHAPTER SEVENTEEN

The Boat People

In December 1976, while attending a conference in Singapore of 300 religious leaders sponsored by the World Conference on Religion and Peace (WCRP), Thây was informed by a group of Vietnamese women that there were thousands of Vietnamese in refugee camps in Thailand and Malaysia, with no hope of being accepted into a new country. In Singapore there were fewer refugees, because the government's policy there was to push all refugee boats back to sea, even when that meant leaving the refugees to die. If a Singaporean fishing boat was caught helping a refugee boat, the fishing boat's owner had to post a $4,000 bond for each refugee saved. Only after the refugees were pushed back to sea could he get his money refunded.

The Vietnamese women told Thây that they had tried to save people by paying fishermen to escort "boat people"—a term that has been in use by the United Nations High Commissioner for Refugees (UNHCR) since 1975—to shore at night. They met the refugees and secretly brought them to the French or American Embassy compounds, where, the next day, the diplomats heard their pleas for political asylum. The Embassies turned the boat people over to the police, but they also prepared applications for them to be accepted by French or American authorities. Many lives were saved this way.

The Vietnamese women knew that nine people were about to be pushed out to sea. They invited Thây to witness it. Thây was so moved by what he saw that he wrote a poem about the plight of the boat people and read it to the full assembly of the World Conference on Religion and Peace:

> You stay up late tonight, my brothers.
> This I know,
> because the boat people

on the high seas
never dare go to sleep.
I hear the cry of the winds
around me—
total darkness.

Yesterday they threw the dead bodies
of their babies and children
into the water.
Their tears once again filled
the ocean of suffering.
In what direction are their boats drifting
at this moment?

You stay up very late tonight, brothers,
because the boat people
on the high seas
are not certain at all that mankind exists.
Their loneliness
is so immense.

The darkness has become one with the ocean—
and the ocean, an immense desert.

You stay up all night, brothers,
and the whole universe
clings to your being awake.

Journalists from UPI and *Agence France* reported on Thây's poem over their wire services, and it appeared in newspapers throughout the world the next day. However, the reporters attributed the poem to the Japanese professor to whom it had been addressed, Professor Yoshiaki Iisaka, of the WCRP, who was responsible for the proceedings that day. Thây had asked Professor Iisaka the night before if his plea for the boat people could be included in the program, so he entitled the poem, "To Professor Iisaka: you stay up."

After reading the poem, Thây told the religious leaders at the conference that boat people were drowning because they were not permitted to land in many countries, including Singapore, Thai-land, Malaysia, Indonesia, and Hong Kong. The conference attend-ees were electrified by the news and moved by Thây's poem, and after lengthy discussions, the WCRP asked Thây to conduct a pro-gram on their behalf to rescue boat people. He agreed if I could be allowed to assist him. They sent me a ticket to Singapore, and I ar-rived in less than a week. The project was called *Mau Chay Ruot Mem* ("When blood is shed, we all suffer.") The WCRP convened a meeting of the United Nations High Commissioner for Refugees, the U.S. Ambassador to Singapore, the French Ambassador, and several other Ambassadors, and asked them what they could do for the boat people. The UN High Commissioner said that the United States could only issue 1,000 visas per year, as they had already ac-cepted more than 250,000 Vietnamese people since the end of the war twenty months earlier.

A quota of 1,000 meant that Malaysia, Thailand, Indonesia, the Philippines, and Hong Kong could each have only sixteen visas per month from the United States. Thây asked the U.S. Ambassador to request that his government increase the number of visas. The Am-bassador replied, "We cannot change the quota." Thây tried to ex-plain, "People are drowning on the high seas every day and risking their lives to escape Vietnam. The U.S. is partly responsible for this. If the U.S. will not offer more visas, perhaps we should bring the boat people to your shores without visas and ask the American people to decide what is the correct thing to do."

Thây asked the World Conference on Religion and Peace to rent a large ship to rescue 1,000 boat people and bring them directly to Guam or Australia. Then, if the boat people were not given visas on the spot, we would invite journalists to expose the situation and ask the American and Australian peoples to change their governments' immigration policies.

The WCRP was a relatively very small organization, but several wealthy Japanese church groups promised to contribute $60,000 to-wards this project. The conference nominated Thây Nhat Hanh to be the Director and me to be the Assistant Director. We set up sev-eral small teams of our friends to go up and down the coasts of Singapore, Malaysia, and Thailand to investigate the situation of the boat people. I made a report for friends in Europe who could lend their financial support to the work. A number of committees that had not been able to support Vietnam since 1975 were happy to help, and in a few weeks, each committee contributed from $10,000 to $50,000, and I raised $200,000.

We intended to rescue a few dozen boat people while we were waiting to buy a bigger ship. We had $100,000 to buy a ship and $100,000 for food, supplies, and wages for a crew for twenty days. We were about to buy a ship when we learned we would have to leave it docked for two months while the authorities certified that it was seaworthy. So we rented a cargo ship named *Roland* and an

The Leapdal.   The Roland.

oil tanker named *Leapdal*, and in less than a week, the *Roland* rescued 281 people on the high seas, and the *Leapdal* rescued 285, a total of 566 boat people. Because we were not allowed to go near the shores of Singapore, Malaysia, or Thailand for supplies, we had to rent a small boat named *Black Mark* to transport food and fuel to the rescue ships.

One day, we witnessed a group of sixty boat people sitting in a kind of military barracks of the Malaysian police. Women and children were crying, while the men stared blankly into space. We talked with them, and they told us that they had arrived at the Malaysian coast with two damaged boats—their boat had sixty people; the other had sixty-two—but the Malaysian authorities had hired a carpenter right away to repair both boats and tow them back out to sea. The other boat had not been properly repaired, and it sank. The sixty people aboard this ship had to watch as sixty-two people died right in front of them. They became terrified and decided to return to shore, and now they sat before the police.

On another day, our ship stopped at a remote island to pick up twenty-eight persons we had learned about from a Malaysian fisherman. This angered the UN official, who asked, "Why did you pick up our people? We are taking care of all the refugees in this area." These officials had never come to see those refugees, had never met them or helped them in any way. We answered, "You don't feed, clothe, or do anything for them. How could we have known they were in your care?" The officials said, "We have their names on a list." Thây said, "Even if you have the names of all the stars in the sky, you cannot claim that they are yours."

Thây said that we should wait until we arrived at the shore of Australia or Guam before contacting the press. We did not want anyone to flee Vietnam or the refugee camps to try to join up with us on the sea. Our aim was simply to rescue those who were about to die at sea, not to encourage those on land to escape. We knew that if the press revealed our operation when we were near Vietnam, many Vietnamese would try to join us at great risk to themselves and their families. Everyone at the conference had agreed to keep our project confidential, but the Japanese donors could not resist informing the press about their promised $60,000 contribution to the project.

A number of journalists tried to contact Thây and me, but we refused to see them. They assailed us for information so much that we had to move our office. Then the BBC and the Voice of America began to broadcast news of the project in Vietnamese, and consequently, many boat people in Vietnam and in refugee camps in Thailand and Malaysia did try to go to the sea to meet our ships. A great number of boat people who had left Vietnam in 1975 and had been staying in camps in Thailand and Malaysia for almost eighteen months saw our ships as their salvation, and they wanted desperately to go out to sea to join us.

The High Commissioner on Refugees got angry, and he forbade them from leaving the camps, but they tried anyway. So he came to Thây, and said, "It is because of your project that people are leaving the refugee camps!" I told him, "We are not doing this work to encourage people in refugee camps to go to the sea. Our project is to help you to obtain more visas for refugees. We see ourselves merely as assisting your work of helping refugees who otherwise might have no hope for the future. Please don't be angry with us. You should see the value of this work. Our aim is to expose the situation of the boat people to the citizens of the U.S. and Australia to persuade their governments to allow more people to resettle there. We would never go into a refugee camp to pick anyone up, but we must help those who come to us."

The UNHCR staff in Kuala Lumpur, Malaysia, could not understand, and they wanted to stop our project. They asked, "How can these people go to the United States or Australia without a visa?" We said, "Of course we cannot have visas in advance. But if our project succeeds, we will expose the suffering of these refugees to people in the U.S. and Australia. It is a way to wake people up, and they will do something. We must continue, and we hope you will help us." Thây spoke clearly and kindly, but the staff at UNHCR did not seem to understand or appreciate our position. For years, they had followed the rules in taking care of refugees, obeying without debate the decision of each country, settling for a few visas each month. Thây said, "Our hope is to help the UNHCR obtain more visas. We need your tacit support, as we are helping you indirectly." But, instead, the UNHCR officer in Kuala Lumpur informed the French, American, and Australian ambassadors and the Secretary General of the World Conference on Religion and Peace that "this crazy monk should stop his foolish project."

The WCRP Secretary General, together with the Japanese group who had pledged to contribute to the project, came to Singapore to try to convince us to abandon the project. Thây said, "But we promised the assembly of the World Conference on Religion and Peace that we would do it, so we are responsible to all of them, not just to you. We will continue our work." The Japanese group said, "If you continue a project that is in conflict with the work of the UNHCR and a number of embassies, we will not give you the $60,000 that we promised." I said, "That is all right. We will continue. I have already raised $200,000 on my own."

Then the Secretary General told Thây, "It isn't necessary to take the refugees to Australia without visas. The Australian Ambassador has promised that his government will grant visas and fly any boat people we rescue on the high seas to Australia. We can distribute your $200,000 to the refugees in the camps." Thây said, "They may give us a few visas, or even 600 visas, but what about the 80,000 boat people still in refugee camps and on the high seas? We must bring their plight to the attention of the world." It was not long before we reached an impasse.

A few nights later, a group of boat people arrived at our project office, a small apartment in Singapore. I don't know how they found us; perhaps they were brought to us by the Vietnamese woman who had brought many boat people to the French Embassy. Thây asked them to leave immediately. I was in tears to turn these people away. They had no shelter at all. I thought that Thây was being too cautious, but four hours later, five policemen came to the office, obviously to capture the newly-arrived boat people. They even climbed on the roof, thinking that the boat people might be escaping that way. The police found no one, but they took Thây's travel documents and told him he had to leave Singapore within forty-eight hours. It was two o'clock Saturday morning, and there was only half a work day to try to extend Thây's visa, as all offices closed at noon on Saturdays. With 566 boat people on our ships, we could not just abandon them and leave Singapore.

From two to six in the morning, we did walking and sitting meditation in the office/apartment. At six o'clock, Thây asked me to talk with the French Ambassador, Jacques Gasseau, a good-hearted man who had tried to help many boat people in the past. I visited him at eight o'clock in the morning and explained our situation. He agreed to sign a very strong letter of support that would serve as guarantee for the Singaporean authorities from the government of France.

At nine o'clock, Ambassador Gasseau's secretary typed the letter, and he signed it. Immediately, we went to the Immigration Office and waited until ten o'clock before anyone would see us. Then, an immigration officer read Ambassador Gasseau's letter, and he told us that he did not know what to do. So he sent us to the Ministry of Foreign Affairs. Because Gasseau's letter expressed so strongly the French government's support of Thây Nhat Hanh, a number of ministers of the Singaporean government met and discussed the situation at length. Then, at just ten minutes before noon, they decided to grant Thây a two-week visa extension. In five minutes, we were back at the Immigration Office and obtained the paperwork confirming the extension.

We had only two more weeks, not enough time for the big ship to be deemed seaworthy. So we decided to repair the two smaller ships, *Leapdal* and *Roland*, and sail directly to Australia. Thây was confident that I would be able to lead the expedition to Australia, and he departed for Perth to wait for us. Before he left, he wrote a poem for Jacques Gasseau and another about the boat people which he translated into Vietnamese, French, and English. He gave a copy to each of the refugees on our two boats and asked them to give it to the press when they arrived in Perth:

A Prayer for Land

Lost in the tempests
on the open seas,
our small boats drift.
We seek for land
during endless days and endless nights.

We are the foam,
floating on the vast ocean.
We are the dust,
wandering in endless space.
Our cries are lost
in the howling wind.

Without food or water,
our children lie exhausted
until they can cry no more.

We thirst for land
but are turned back from every shore.
Our distress signals rise and rise again,
but the passing ships do not stop.
How many boats have perished?

How many families lie beneath the waves?

Lord Jesus, do you hear the prayer of our flesh?
Lord Buddha, do you hear our voice?
O fellow humans, do you hear our voice
from the abyss of death?
O solid shore,
we long for you!

We pray for mankind to be present today.
We pray for land to stretch its arms to us.
We pray that hope be given us today,
from this very land.

But the day after Thây left, the WCRP Secretary General fired me. He said, "Sister Phuong, we no longer need your services. Thank you." I said, "I am the Assistant Director of this project, in charge of two ships and 566 people. I will stay in Singapore as long as I wish, and I will complete the project." He said, "From this moment on, I forbid you to be in contact with any boat people or to touch any money in the project's account." I was shocked! I said, "At least please allow me to bring food to the people on our two ships, or they will starve." But he refused. "No, we are in charge," he said. "You *must* leave." I felt as though he were choking me. I was furious, and I lost my calmness. In a trembling voice, I said, "I raised the entire $200,000 for this project, and now you are telling me I cannot continue the work to help these boat people? Well, you can keep that money! I will raise another $200,000, buy another ship, and complete the project myself!"

That night, the Singapore police came to my apartment and seized my passport. They ordered me to book a flight from Singapore the following day and told me that I could pick up my passport at the airport. Because Thây had only a refugee travel document, the Singapore authorities were able to cause him a great deal of difficulty. But I had a French passport, the same as any French citizen, so I should have been able to stay in Singapore as long as I wished. When they seized Thây's passport, I was not harassed. I wondered who had informed the police of my presence. I felt that I would rather die than go on a plane and leave 566 people on the high seas without proper care. Looking back, I see that if I could have remained silent when I was fired from this project, I could have secretly raised funds and been able to transport the 566 boat people to Australia. But when I lost my calm, I did not act in the wisest way. So, this wonderful project was stopped. I called Thây in Perth to tell him what had happened, and he recommended that I leave Singapore.

I began to sob uncontrollably, until I remembered to take refuge in my breath. I knew that if I did not focus on each breath, I would go crazy. I did walking meditation in my apartment all night, and, early the next morning, I went to the travel agency to give back the key to the apartment and book a late afternoon flight for Melbourne.

Thây flew from Perth to Melbourne to greet me, and when I saw him in the airport, I sobbed in his arms for a long time. A Catholic priest friend in Melbourne called a press conference so that I could tell the press about the situation of the boat people. At that time, Australia did not allow refugees to enter. Several newspapers responded favorably to my appeal, and one even ran a large photo of me calling for help for the boat people. Perhaps my plea had an effect, because from then on the Australian government began to accept refugees. We stayed in Melbourne for three days, and then we took a flight back to France.

When we arrived in Paris, we took a taxi to my brother's house, where my car had been parked. In Paris, everything seemed unreal. People walked, sat, ate, and laughed as if the world were normal. "Don't they know that their fellow human beings are dying on the high seas?" I asked myself. "Don't they know that people exactly like them are drowning and starving because they lack one piece of paper, a visa?" The United Nations and the ambassadors had promised to give visas to all 566 people on our boats, but in fact, they issued only thirty-two. As a result, 534 people stayed on the high seas for several months, unable to attain refugee status from any country.

When the *Leapdal* was near the shore of Thailand, nearly 200 refugees from a nearby camp, encouraged by a con man who had entered the camp and sold tickets to board the *Leapdal*, bribed the

Thai police and received their permission to come on board. When these refugees appeared in their small boats and asked Mobi Warren, our young assistant from Texas who was in charge of the *Leapdal*, to save them, she immediately invited them aboard, without asking where they had come from. Later she learned about the tickets and the bribe, and she reported this to the WCRP, naively believing that everyone in the WCRP felt great pity for the refugees.

Later, when only thirty-two of the promised 566 visas were forthcoming, the Secretary of the WCRP was reproached by the WCRP members for discharging Thây in this project. So the secretary held press conferences in Geneva, London, and Washington, D.C. to say that these refugees had paid $800 to be rescued by "an assistant of Thich Nhat Hanh." He made it sound as if Mobi had accepted $800 from each refugee she allowed onto the *Leapdal*. With nearly 300 refugees picked up that way, she would have made a fortune! Some who read the reports even thought that the assistant of Thây who had been mentioned must have been me. Many friends sent us news clippings of these distorted stories of our rescue project, and they urged us to clarify our position and answer the accusations. But Thây told me, "We don't need to start another war," and he never responded.

In my life of service, this was not the first time that my work had been cruelly distorted. Each time it happened, I became furious, and Thây reminded me to take refuge in my breathing and calm down. He always advised me not to use violence and anger to respond to injustice. "The truth will reveal itself, sooner or later," he said.

Fortunately, one *New York Times* reporter, Henry Kamm, did not believe the accusations, and he went to the Gulf of Siam to investigate. He boarded the rescue ship, *Leapdal*, interviewed a number of refugees, and wrote an article that appeared in the *New York Times* on June 16, 1977, explaining the situation. In response to the suggestion that "the unscrupulous assistant to the Vietnamese monk sold places on the ship for $800," he wrote: "Shipboard interviews brought denials and ridicule for the possibility that many of the refugees could have raised such sums. Some said that they had raised what money they could to help to buy supplies and equipment for the voyage. Others, the majority, pointed to their pitiable present condition and their narrow escapes from their countries and asked how people like them could have paid for a place on the *Leapdal*." He did this on his own, with no prompting from Thây, Mobi, or myself.

In March 1977, we went back to the Sweet Potato Community, and after three months of looking deeply into the problem of the boat people, I decided to start another project, with Thây's approval. I flew to Thailand and disguised myself as the owner of a fishing boat. Our project was to "fish" boat people out from the sea. Thây's story, "The Lone Pink Fish," in his collection, *The Moon Bamboo*, is based largely on the experiences of our crew.

One day our boat had a mechanical problem, and we stopped in Trad, a small coastal town in northeast Thailand, to fix it. At that time our crew consisted of six Vietnamese with French passports and three Thais—a young woman, a monk, and a student. A policeman in Trad fell in love with the young woman, and he told her that our boat would be stopped by pirates as soon as we left Trad, and they would rob us, rape the two women, and kill all nine of us. He advised her to abandon us immediately if she wanted to live. The three Thai crew members were terrified. They knew that Thai pirates were capable of exactly what the policeman had reported. They tried to convince me to hire a ship of paid police guards to tow us all the way back to Bangkok.

By that time, I already knew that the police and the pirates in that part of Thailand were linked, so I visited the chief of the province and brought him some French chocolate. I said, "We are French citizens who have stopped in your province to repair our fishing boat. The French Ambassador requests that we must report everything we do to you, and we ask you to safeguard our journey back." He asked, "How long will you stay?" and I answered, "We will need at least two weeks to repair our boat, and then we can return to sea." He said, "All right. I will cable the police in Trad to protect you during your entire stay in this area." Rumor spread that we were going to be docked for two more weeks before leaving. The pirates were not prepared when we went out to sea to test the repairs and just kept going, escaping from both the police and the pirates!

My brother Nghiep and I on our "fishing boat."

Many times on our rescue boat, I learned that following each breath mindfully was the best way to avoid getting seasick. One time we were caught in a storm. Everyone was vomiting, but I held tightly to one beam on the roof of the boat, sat cross-legged, followed my breathing, and I recovered my equilibrium.

Every time we saw a refugee boat, we gave them food, fuel, and directions to the nearest camp. At that time, if boat people reached the shore of a Thai province where there was a refugee camp, they would be accepted. But if they reached other provinces, they would be pushed back to sea.

Our work to help boat people from Singapore had been difficult, but much less dangerous. It was mostly making policy decisions and contacts, encountering the local police, and bringing food to boat people on remote islands. Working on our "fishing boat," on the other hand, was extremely dangerous. The violence on the high seas was so great that our Thai friends quit as soon as the Thai police warned us about the sea pirates. Eventually, there were only my brother Nghiep, the four Vietnamese crew members, myself, and Avalokitesvara Bodhisattva. We did this silently for almost a year. During that time, the number of boat people increased so dramatically that the French government convened a conference in Geneva on boat people. When we saw the plight of the boat people being called to the world's attention, we knew that our aim had been fulfilled, and we drew our project to a close.

Looking back, even though we failed to bring all of the 566 boat people to Australia and Guam, we did help in bringing the cries of the boat people to the world's ears. In 1977, President Jimmy Carter increased the U.S. quota of Vietnamese refugees to 7,000 per year, and just a few months later to 15,000. That generous increase came after President Carter read the *New York Times* article correcting the misinformation of the WCRP. Then, Australia opened its doors to more refugees, and other governments followed. In 1979, the U.S. raised its quota to 100,000. Despite these gains, hundreds of thousands of Vietnamese boat people continue to this day to die on the high seas or languish in the refugee camps of Southeast Asia, now with the added fear of being repatriated to Vietnam.

When we closed our project on the Gulf of Siam and returned to France, my work sending financial help to refugees in camps in Thailand, Malaysia, Indonesia, the Philippines, and Hong Kong increased. We tried to offer a few dollars to each victim of sea pirates, along with a loving and caring letter. Orphans and families with young children were given ten or fifteen dollars and some advice on how to prepare for the new land. In time, we were overwhelmed with hundreds of letters each week calling for help.

To be able to continue writing 200 to 300 personal letters to refugees each week, I developed a new method. I handwrote one letter sharing the fruit of our listening to the suffering of many refugees on the high seas, communicating all our love, concern, and care, and each week, I photocopied more than 300 copies of this letter, adding a short personal note to each person. In this way, each person felt they had received a long personal letter from someone who really cared about their situation.

CHAPTER EIGHTEEN

Rare Flowers of the Country

One day in 1980, I was at Sweet Potato thinking about the sixty million Vietnamese people who were suffering under the totalitarian regime, and I knew that my work and the work of all the committees worldwide to help relieve the hunger of a few thousand families was not enough. I knew I had to do more to help people in that part of the Earth so dear to me.

After practicing sitting and walking meditation for several days, an idea came to me. I saw that artists, writers, painters, and musicians are the rare flowers of a culture, and each one blooms only once. There is only one Beethoven, one Van Gogh, one Shakespeare, one Nguyen Du. The lives of each of these flowers is unique in the garden of humanity. In the past, North Vietnam had been known for its rich heritage of poetry, but for decades since the communists came to power, none of the many excellent poets in North Vietnam had produced a single poem. I said to myself, "I must help the rare flowers of this country bloom."

I began by sending money to one friend in Vietnam and asking her to share some of it with writers and artists she knew who were in trouble with the government. She wrote back two months later and told me that she had helped the families of a dozen novelists, poets, journalists, playwrights, and artists, and she gave me their names and addresses. I began to read their writing and listen to their music, and then I sent each of them a gift and a letter of appreciation and encouragement.

A group of young Vietnamese in Europe, students of Thây Nhat Hanh, joined me in forming a group to study the work of these artists and to try to understand deeply their art. When we could not understand, we asked Thây. An artist himself, Thây could see more deeply than we could, sometimes even more deeply than the artist himself, and he shared his insights with us. We came to really love the writings, paintings, and music of the various artists.

When I wrote to one poet and sent him some gifts, I wrote with the understanding of Thây and the freshness of a young woman, commenting on his poetry and appreciating it. The poet was surprised and deeply moved. He wrote back that he had never met a young person who understood his poetry so deeply. He said that for the first time in many years he was inspired to write. For more than ten years, my friends and I have continued this work, and we have helped many flowers of Vietnam bloom again.

Here is one letter that I sent to the young daughter of a painter in North Vietnam:

Dear Hoang,

Today I have a special gift for you. It is more precious than medicine or money. But first, I want to tell you a story. It is about a friend who lost his eyesight in a car accident. His world is entirely one of darkness, all the time. Do you know what he told me? He said that if he could see again, he would be in paradise. How I wish I could fulfill his wish. If I cannot help him, at least I can share his insight with you: Do not wait until you lose your eyesight before knowing how happy you can be just by opening your eyes. You have excellent eyes, and each time you open them a marvelous paradise of forms and colors appears.

My gift for you is this exercise: Look very deeply at your mother. Her face may be pale, and her hands reveal much hard work. She has worked hard because of her love for you, your seven brothers and sisters, and your father. Look deeply into her beautiful eyes, and really hug her before you go to sleep tonight. Be aware of her precious presence in your arms. As you hold her, breathe in and out and say, silently, "Breathing in, I am aware how wonderful it is to hold my mother in my arms. Breathing out, I know that she is a treasure for all of us." Don't wait until your dear mother has passed away before you decide to really appreciate her. We have so many treasures—our eyes, our mother, and our health. We only need to be aware of them, and we can tap a fountain of great joy. From that joy, it is easy to express and share our happiness and our insight.

Your father is also a precious gift. I know he sometimes looks unhappy, but that is because he is unusually gifted. Look at his delicate fingers. There are many secrets hidden in them. Have you ever seen your father paint? His hands, with a brush and paint, can transform a blank sheet of paper into a magical world of birds singing and wind laughing, of clouds, trees, and houses dancing. You can see love and sacrifice come forth from his hands, creating scenes in which understanding opens her arms wide, embracing all of humanity.

She wrote me back a beautiful letter:

Dear Aunt,

All of us gathered together around the box of medicine you sent, and we read the beautiful letter you taped inside. We cut it free and hung it on the wall of our small home, so that all of us could see it and be mindful. Mommy cried sweetly when I hugged her the way you taught me. But Daddy was silent for many days. Then, yesterday, he left home for a whole day and came back with a brush and some paint! Guess what happened next?

Most of the artists did not know our real identities, especially that Cao Ngoc Phuong was involved in this. We have collected many treasured works of art, but we know that if we publish them, the artists may be in trouble with the regime. So, we will keep them until the country is free. The plays and sonnets of Shakespeare, even after 400 years, are still precious flowers of English culture and the culture of humanity. We will wait until the time is right, and then we will share these beautiful works with the world.

◇

In June 1976, I met with a number of Vietnamese in Paris who told me that many former officers of the South Vietnamese army, many former high employees of the South Vietnamese regime, and many engineers, writers, artists, and physicians who happened to be drafted into the army during the war had been arrested by the hundreds of thousands and were in reeducation camps! I was deeply shocked and could not understand why the leaders of our nation would behave in such a way to our own people. Vietnam was finally at peace. Wasn't this the moment for engineers, physicians, artists, and writers to rebuild the country? Why would the authorities put all these intelligent people in jail? Vietnamese nationals all over Europe and the U.S. tried to publicize the situation, calling for the release of these prisoners. But no Western news agencies, press, or organizations printed this news except for a few extreme, right-wing papers. Many refugees whose relatives had been arrested came to Amnesty International for help, but without ironclad proof, AI could not do anything about it.

By that time, I had already learned the art of calming my feelings. So I did not try to act or write or do anything about the situation right away. I just tried to stay mindful of my breathing as I drove back to Sweet Potato. But when I got back and reported to Thây and other friends about these injustices, I burst into tears. The entire group of us went out on the hills for long walking meditations, sometimes for several hours, and we continued to do this every day for weeks. We tried to be in touch with the beautiful pine trees, the fields of wheat, the clouds, and the sparkling sunshine.

Days passed before I felt strong enough to look deeply into the hearts of the leaders of Vietnam. How would I act if I had been born in the North and spent more than fifteen years fighting to save the nation from the "imperialist" Americans? I would be proud to be part of the victorious side, and I would probably condemn all the South Vietnamese as puppets. If I had been trained for many years to believe that everything the Communist Party did was right and everything the "American side" did was wrong, I would probably believe that any order coming from the party was only for the benefit of the people. I was able to see from the point of view of a North Vietnamese leader. I knew I could not trust anyone from the South. They might try to trick me or even to overthrow our government. Filled with fear, suspicion, and also arrogance from having won the war and being one of the rulers of Vietnam now, I could see myself behaving in the same way as those who were raised in that atmosphere. Because I had the impression that I was beginning to understand them a little, without hatred or anger, I started to write a letter describing the situation of human rights violations in Vietnam. In the letter, I tried to explain why the rulers of Vietnam might be acting in such a way, out of fear and ignorance, and I sent the letter to Amnesty International and PEN International.

We began to receive firsthand accounts of many of the arrests. We learned that the people arrested had been asked to be "reeducated for one month," and were then moved to unknown destinations. Even after a year, their wives and children did not know where they were, and requests to be in touch with the prisoners were suppressed. We also learned that the government had seized the bank accounts of many families and limited their income and their spending. For instance, in order to spend more than ten dollars on their daughter's wedding or brother's funeral, people had to obtain permission from local authorities, and they could not be sure the authorities would consent. We also learned that to go from one location to another just ten or twelve kilometers away, citizens had to apply for a "circulation permit," and they could be arrested for staying overnight at friends' or relatives' houses if they did not have such a permit.

Large businesses were, of course, nationalized by the communists. But we were shocked to learn that all private houses, cars, television sets, motorbikes, and other belongings of members of the immediate families of those formerly in the South Vietnamese regime, could be confiscated for the use of the communist government's high party members. All drugstores were closed, and no Western medicines available in the markets. I know that herbs can be of great help, but the banning of all Western medicine surprised me. Why did we have to regress to the last century, curing ourselves only with herbs while many infectious diseases and other maladies needed Western medicine?

Everything I learned from the Vietnamese who emigrated to France after 1976 brought tears to my eyes. After thirty years of war, the country desperately needed the help of those precious hands and minds that they were putting into jail. Refugee groups in Paris, London, Amsterdam, Hanover, Washington, D.C., Los Angeles, and elsewhere tried their best to make these atrocities known, but the majority of people in the West, so tired after thirty years of war, did not want to hear more bad news about Vietnam.

I wanted to do something to help the prisoners, but every time I thought about Vietnam I felt powerless. Despite the joy of many warm cups of tea taken mindfully every morning with Thây and friends in the Sweet Potato Community, I cried each time my mind went back to the way the rulers of Vietnam treated our own people, those they claimed to have liberated. I tried to stay with my breath while gardening, cooking, washing dishes, and binding books.

"Breathing in, I calm myself. Breathing out, I am aware that I am cutting this carrot (or binding this book)," I said silently, immersing myself in mindfulness verses, while tears flooded down my cheeks. Sunny or foggy, the mornings on the hills or in the forest helped ease my pain. In the past, when there was news from Vietnam, I immediately shared it with friends like Kirsten Roep, Laura Hassler, or Jim Forest, but now it seemed pointless. I knew they would believe me, but the rest of the world was not ready.

One day in Paris, a woman who had just left Vietnam told me that twelve monks and nuns had immolated themselves on November 2, 1975, in Phung Hiep district near Can Tho, to protest the human rights violations of the new regime, especially the prohibitions against the free practice of religion. Thây Quang Do had given her a full set of the letters and photos that Thây Hue Hien and eleven others had left behind, but she had not dared bring such dangerous documents with her. By now, I was not surprised to learn such news, but I knew that for Amnesty International or the Western press to accept a report like this, I needed proof. Since the woman in Paris had told me that there were photos and twelve letters left behind by the monks and nuns, I knew I had to obtain copies of them. A few days later, I received a copy of Ho Chi Minh's biography in the mail from a friend in the SYSS. I was so angry at Ho Chi Minh and anything that had to do with the ruling communists in Vietnam that I threw the book in the trash can, never imagining, as I found out later, that copies of the twelve letters and photos of the immolated monks and nuns had been sewn into the spine and jacket of the book.

I thought that Thanh, my younger sister, might be able to help me obtain the documents, so I wrote to her using indirect language. She understood and tried her best to obtain the full set of documents. When my older sister, Tho, and her husband emigrated to France (he had graduated from medical school in Paris and was already a French citizen), Thanh proposed that she bring my brother-in-law's belongings to the customs office for inspection. After the inspection, Thanh skillfully inserted the set of photos and letters of the monks and nuns who had immolated themselves into two boxes containing precious glassware, and alone she took those boxes to the air freight office to be flown two days after my sister's family left.

Then she cabled me, saying "Take good care of the precious glassware." I immediately understood. My elder sister did not know anything about the secret box, so she did not encounter any risk if the documents were discovered. Thanh was the one at risk for "disseminating news against the regime," an act punishable by life imprisonment. Although she took full responsibility, she still keeps silent about her brave act.

When I received the documents, Thây Nhat Hanh and all of us thought about how the documents would be most helpful for human rights and for those who had given their life for human dignity. Thây asked me to call the Vietnamese Embassy to tell them that we had received documents about the immolation of the twelve monks and nuns in Vietnam, and we wished to invite the Ambassador to our office in Paris to see Thây and discuss ways that we could be helpful both for the dignity of human beings living in Vietnam and for the reputation of a nation just restoring its peace. But the man I spoke with at the Embassy rejected outright the possibility that there had been any immolations or any human rights abuses in Vietnam. I said that we had all the documents with us, but he continued to deny the accusations. Finally, he said, "We have an Embassy. If you want to talk to us, why don't you come here?"

I was afraid that if Thây Nhat Hanh entered the Vietnam Embassy, legally the territory of Vietnam, he could be arrested. So I told the man at the Embassy, "Uncle Ho Chi Minh said that under the light of communism, the government is the servant of the people. Now the people are inviting the government to come visit, but the government is refusing to come. Your government no longer serves the people, as Uncle Ho Chi Minh said it should." I continued gently, "Please understand that our teacher, Thây Nhat Hanh, is a humble monk. He rarely comes to any governmental office to beg for any privilege. We feel uncomfortable visiting a victorious government office. Please come to our office to discuss these matters to help relieve the suffering of our fellow countrymen and women."

But they never came. One month later, on September 9, 1976, Thây Nhat Hanh allowed me to issue a press release from our Sweet Potato Community. I made many copies of it and sent it to newspapers and news agencies all over Europe, listing our telephone at Sweet Potato as the contact number.

Many jounalists called and asked why, if the immolations had occurred in November 1975, were we only revealing the news a year later. I said that we needed time to obtain proof, that several persons who had left Vietnam had agreed to bring the documents, but, in the end, had refused to do so out of fear of being caught and condemned to life in prison. I also told them that we had tried to negotiate with the Hanoi authorities in Paris a month earlier. We had hoped the regime would have issued a declaration, acknowledging human rights abuses due to mistakes and a lack of understanding on the part of local cadres. If the government had been willing to condemn these past mistakes in the Vietnamese press and to request all its employees to respect human rights in Vietnam, as stated in the Constitution of the Socialist Republic of Vietnam, then we would not have revealed the news of the immolations to the international press. But the government stubbornly refused to discuss this with us, and we had to reveal the news.

The *International Herald Tribune* of September 9, 1976, had a three-column front-page headline—"Buddhists Report 12 Immolated in Vietnam"—and in the article stated that they had asked the Vietnamese Embassy to confirm my declaration about having tried to contact them for negotiations and that the Embassy had declined to comment. *Le Monde, France Soir, Le Figaro,* and many papers and news agencies carried my first press release on human rights, and this made the Embassy furious towards Thây Nhat Hanh and me. We later found out that Vietnam was applying for admission into the UN at that time, and because of our press release, the General Assembly discussion about the acceptance was postponed.

Jim Forest and Laura Hassler immediately launched a campaign for human rights in Vietnam. Some American "peace activists" who were clearly "pro-Hanoi," told Jim, "There are no reeducation camps in Vietnam. There are only 'students' who need to learn more about the policies of the new regime." Jim replied that he preferred plain truth to embellished language. At gunpoint, humans put humans in jail, force them not to exit at the risk of being shot, and then they used beautiful words like "reeducation." Jim called it "arrest and imprisonment." The first appeal for human rights in

Vietnam made by Jim Forest was published in *Fellowship*, the magazine of the FOR, where Jim was editor-in-chief. He had the support of hundreds of peace workers, including the Berrigan brothers, Joan Baez, and Daniel Ellsberg.

Many of the "peace workers" who had suppressed our voice in the past, tried to get the signers to withdraw their names. They phoned each person who had signed and said, "You are destroying all chance for reconstruction for Vietnam. With your signature, you are killing sixty million Vietnamese trying to rebuild their country." They harassed Jim by phone, day and night. Jim felt guilty and exhausted after each conversation. He called me, and I did not know how to comfort him except to cry with him. But Joan Baez was more skillful. She too was under pressure to withdraw her signature, and she comforted herself and Jim by singing a few songs to him over the phone.

After the appeal by Jim Forest, Amnesty International, who until then had been reluctant to adopt any prisoners of conscience in Vietnam, started to consider some requests. So I contacted them. They had been sympathetic to us during the war. In 1973, I submitted to AI a long list of prisoners arrested by both Saigon and the NLF, and they helped us work for the release of many on that list. However, by 1976, those who had been in charge of AI in 1973 were no longer there, and friends in London told me that the new people were rather bureaucratic and could not be counted on to help.

One day I felt calm and refreshed, so I wrote a letter to AI, trying to show my understanding of why the rulers in Vietnam were acting as they were—their fears, suspicions, and overconfidence from having won the war. I said that I believed the country still needed the many intelligent people who were being arrested, and I wished that AI, with its worldwide prestige, could kindly explain to the authorities of Vietnam its concern for these prisoners of conscience. I did not give a figure of 500,000 detainees or 300,000, as some groups had done. I said I did not know the exact figure, but I did know physicians, writers, engineers, and people who had been lowly officers of the South Vietnamese army who were in jail, and I could extrapolate from that that there were great numbers of other detainees as well.

A week later, I called AI and asked to speak with the person responsible for Asia. My voice was calm, but very sad. The woman with whom I spoke seemed interested in my letter. Then, several months later, two events helped me succeed in encouraging AI to work for Vietnamese detainees. In August 1977, one Vietnamese friend who had been an employee of several newspapers and literary magazines in South Vietnam in the past, described to us an event he had witnessed in Vietnam in April 1976. The authorities had invited many well-known writers, journalists, and artists to attend a conference, including this friend. After a lecture given by a government official, all of the writers and artists present were arrested, including him. He was released after a short detention, because he belonged to a "patriotic" family, but many of the others were still being held. He remembered most of their names and wrote them down for us.

I was invited to London to ~~speak at the Friends House~~, and I asked those responsible for the Asia Desk of AI to attend. I shared with everyone the way I usually worked, trying to be "in the skin" of the other person to understand why they acted as they did. I also told them the way I acted when I received news from Vietnam. I listened to the source persons, tried to understand through the words to see whether there was anger, hatred, or exaggeration behind their words. When I was informed that a well-known person was killed or arrested, I tried to find several other sources in Vietnam to be sure of the news before I passed it on to the press or to AI.

After meeting me face-to-face, the people from AI wanted to cooperate with us in launching the first campaign for Vietnam. I also sent the AI Asia Desk a list of thirty-four well-known monks and forty-eight writers and artists who were prisoners of conscience. One week later, they wrote and agreed to work for their release. I knew that others had invited AI to work for prisoners in Vietnam, but this was the first list AI had accepted. Most of the AI people in London were wonderful, but I was especially impressed by two young men, David McAree and Udo Janz. I had met Udo when I gave the talk in London, and after that he called me regularly to share his concerns about the fate of prisoners of conscience. Udo told me that he would try to go to the refugee camps in Asia to be in touch with the suffering people—to listen to them and under-

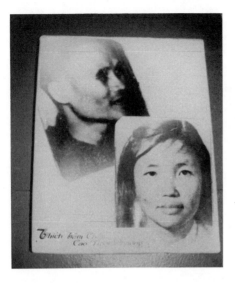

Photo in War Crimes Museum, Hanoi, 1993.

stand them. One day, I met him in a camp in the Philippines. Udo was very moved by seeing so much suffering, and he told me that he felt that if he only sat at a desk and made decisions, it would be dangerous. I admired him for this effort to be in touch with reality.

David McAree had graduated from Oxford University and spoke Vietnamese fluently. Many of his friends were diplomats, but he preferred to work for Amnesty International, making a small salary, because he wanted to be in touch with those needing help urgently.

He knew the Vietnamese expression, "One day in jail is equal to a thousand autumns in freedom." Thanks to the presence of David in AI, the work to press for the release of prisoners in Vietnam as well as in other countries went well. In the past, whenever a prisoner was adopted, AI would choose one group in one country to adopt him or her, and then only this group would be responsible for writing letters on the prisoner's behalf. But David proposed that up to twelve groups adopt one prisoner and that the different groups be in touch with each other to receive encouragement from news that any group received.

David also proposed that each local Amnesty group support a prisoner not only by writing letters but also by sending food to his or her family. David got many of these ideas from his Vietnamese "sister" in France. Thanks to him, we were able to work for the release of the novelist Duyen Anh, the writers Thanh Tam Tuyen and Doan Quoc Sy, Hoang Hai Thuy, and Nguyen Sy Te, the poet Hoang Cam, and several important monks and nuns—Thây Tam Quang, Vinh Hien, Phan Nhat Nam, Duy Lam, Tri Hai, and

Nguyen Thi Nghia. When Duyen Anh escaped by boat and arrived in France with his family, David married his daughter.

Later David left Amnesty International and began working for the Committee Against Famine. He felt that in AI he would spend from two to ten years to bring happiness to just a dozen prisoners, while in CAF he could bring immediate relief to thousands of people. His joy in helping hungry people was very like my own, and we felt very close. When we learned that Thanh Hoa, Nghe An, and Ha Tinh, the three poorest provinces in North Vietnam, were beginning to experience a famine, I asked David if he would consider going to Vietnam as a representative of a donor organization, and, to my surprise, he said that he was already going very soon with his wife, Thien Huong.

I was happy that Thien Huong was going to be in Vietnam, as she could offer love and care to the children in the famine areas on my behalf. I asked her to make an accurate report of the situation for me. Then I would see how I could silently help. Thien Huong promised to do this for me, but she and David never came back to France.

The plane that carried them from Ho Chi Minh City to Bangkok crashed. When I learned the news, it shocked me deeply. I felt as though she and her husband had died on my behalf. *"Dear David and Thien Huong, I loved you. Please know that I am living for you." Your work will continue in me.* Looking deeply, I can see that David and Thien Huong will never die. David's work for prisoners is continuing beautifully by his colleagues everywhere in the world, and his work for hungry children is continuing too. I can see him smiling gently to me even as I write these lines. These days, there are many wonderful, devoted persons like David in Amnesty International.

Our work for human rights intensified when Thây Man Giac escaped from Vietnam in March 1977, bringing with him an important letter written by the UBC Executive Council, prepared by Thây Thien Minh, pleading for human rights and including photos of statues of the Buddha that had been dynamited by communist cadres and papers specifying eighty-six cases of violations of religious freedom, with the dates of the violations, the names of the arrested persons, and the names of the communist cadres. This document had been compiled by Thây Huyen Quang, who was arrested immediately after sending it to Prime Minister Pham Van Dong. We helped Thây Man Giac translate the documents into English and held a press conference for him in Paris. Then I brought him to the U.S., and we held a press conference in Washington, D.C.

After this trip to the U.S. with Thây Man Giac, I helped Nguyen Cong Hoan, a member of the communist parliament who had escaped by boat, and together we travelled in many European countries calling for the respect of human rights in Vietnam. The voice of Hoan was especially powerful, because he had been well-situated in the new regime as a member of Parliament. He told many people of his great disappointment in the government and that finally he had fled the country because of the abuses of human rights.

After several months, during which letters from the AI London office and from local groups that had adopted a prisoner were sent to Vietnam, there was still no news. So I also approached the *Ligue des Droits de l'Homme* (League of Human Rights) in Paris and Brussels, and they promised to write letters to Vietnam. Despite all of these efforts, many years have passed and there are still very few results. My deep desire to transform the situation of human rights in Vietnam continues, and I keep trying to find ways to help. We have printed thousands of postcards with lists of selected prisoners, their camp numbers, and a few lines addressing the authorities requesting their release, and everywhere I go, I invite people to sign these cards and send them to Vietnam. Although spectacular improvements have been few, we believe that this international pressure has influenced the authorities, and, over time, will bear fruit. One campaign to the Vietnamese authorities to release eight prisoners on our list took six months, and another asking the Thai authorities not to repatriate refugees in camps was accepted in only six weeks. Thai authorities held a press conference and said they would not send refugees back to Vietnam if other countries would help them resettle these refugees.

Our efforts have not brought spectacular results, but we have never risked a single life in our work. It is much safer and ultimately more true to our aims to work this way. As soon as we have the name and address of any prisoner of conscience, we get in touch with his family and send medicine for the prisoner and for the family. We also praise the family for having such a gem as their beloved, imprisoned relative.

Duyen Anh, a writer who was held in the Ham Tam jungle re-education camp, sent me a tiny Buddha carved in black hardwood with these words: "The day I heard that you sent your love and care for my children and wife, I saw a Buddha being born in this dark, cruel forest. May I offer you this tiny statue that I carved." Kha Nang, a comedian, sent me a beautiful comb made from a piece of metal broken off from a bomb. It was beautifully hand-carved with my name "Nguyen Thi Phuong Huong"—one of my many "reborn names," written with the tip of a needle and sent in a delicately hand-carved box made of precious hardwood. When I look at that handwork, tears of gratitude spring forth in me. My assistance is nothing compared with the long months Kha Nang spent in a dark room, secretly carving at night, knowing that he could be caught by a guard and punished because of this small act. I know that the news "someone is taking care of you and your beloved ones" brings some peace during many dark days in prison. This gift sent to "Nguyen Thi Phuong Huong" is for all of the dear friends who have faithfully joined and supported me during my efforts to be with those who suffer in jail, in slums, and everywhere.

Every time I received news of a new arrest, I became angry, and I knew that I had to do walking meditation. Sometimes I would walk several hours in order to regain my calm. Sometimes I needed several days or even weeks to relax my heartbeat, knowing how unfairly the authorities have acted in arresting such a lovely monk, nun, or artist. I always waited until I felt serene before beginning any campaign. Thanks to this serenity, my words were gentle but firm, and people found it easier to cooperate. I succeeded in persuading PEN International to work for the release of some writers and artists, and I worked closely with Ligue des Droits de l'Homme, Fellowship of Reconciliation, Humanitas International, and other organizations.

When I received news of the arrest of a well-known person, I first checked several sources to confirm that it was true. After that, I usually sent out a press release, and then followed it up with a phone call to each journalist. In this way, I was able to publicize the

Thây Quang Do in internal exile.

arrest without going to Paris and renting a room for a press conference. I could stay at the Sweet Potato Community. The arrests of
five leaders of the UBC, of Thây Thien Minh and his subsequent
death in prison, of poet Hoang Cam, of Thây Quang Do and Thây
Huyen Quang, of Doan Quoc Sy and dozens of other writers and
artists, of twelve scholars, monks, and nuns, and the death of Thây
Tri Thu, the president of the UBC, in the hospital after being interrogated by the police, all appeared in the press this way.

When all efforts by the press and various human rights organizations had had no effect, I did not know what to do. After weeks and
months of dwelling on my breath to calm myself, during one sitting
meditation, I realized that I had met many parliamentarians, congressmen, and even heads of State. So I contacted Olaf Palme, the
former Prime Minister of Sweden, and thanks to his intervention,
the authorities in Vietnam released Thây Huyen Quang, Thây
Quang Do, Thây Thong Buu, and seven other monks in 1979. Un-
fortunately, as soon as they were released, Thây Huyen Quang and
Thây Quang Do began once again to work for human rights, and
both of them were sentenced to internal exile in 1984.

To work for the release of my old friend, Nguyen Kha, who had tuberculosis and was confined in a re-education camp in a far northern province, and the writer, Thanh Tam Tuyen, I asked Fritz Siegathalen, the secretary of the Christian Movement for Peace in Switzerland, who was on his way to Vietnam to bring hearing aids to deaf children, to request their release. Then, whenever I met a journalist, a Senator, or a Member of Parliament, I immediately asked him to write a letter to the Vietnamese authorities on behalf of the families of several specific prisoners.

One day in April 1985, I felt desperate. Ly Dai Nguyen, a writer and a good friend, had been jailed in the Kontum Gia Lai camp for more than nine years, having been arrested in April 1976, together with many other writers and artists. Efforts by Amnesty International and others sending thousands of letters to the Vietnamese authorities had had no effect at all. Suddenly I thought of Laurent Schwartz. He was Dean of the Polytechnic School in Paris and President of the French Vietnam Association, a group that had worked exclusively with Hanoi since the time Ho Chi Minh was still alive. I had just seen his name, among others, on a letter asking for the release of Andrei Sakharov. Friends discouraged me from going to see "this communist," but deep inside, I believed that he was a good man. I looked up his name in the Paris telephone book. There were many Schwartzes, and I called them all. Finally, I reached him and we arranged to meet each other. I brought all the documents about Ly Dai Nguyen and other writers and artists who had been persecuted. Later I sent him reports about hungry children in Vietnam. He agreed to work for the release of the prisoners, and he contributed to support hungry children. Since that day, he has sent a donation of $100 every time I send documents about needy children, and whenever I tell him about a prisoner of conscience, he works hard for his or her release. Ly Dai Nguyen was released just one month later, and several other prisoners as well, thanks, I believe, to Professor Schwartz's help.

In 1985, Thây Nhat Hanh and I toured the U.S., leading retreats on mindfulness meditation. In northern California, I met a young American, Stephen Denney, whose name had been familiar to me since the early 1980s, when I read the *Indochina Journal* (now called *Vietnam Journal*), which he published. The *Journal* was the only consistent source of news about human rights violations in Vietnam. From France, I had thought that this magazine must be published by a large group, so I was quite surprised to meet this shy, young man who worked mostly by himself to print whatever news he could obtain. He printed the *Journal* with his own money and sold it for only $1 a copy.

From that day on, we became friends, and Steve is still my American bodhisattva on human rights. Every time there is news about human rights violations, he always makes initiatives to help me work effectively for the release of our friends. Every two years now, when Thây Nhat Hanh tours the U.S., Steve helps me draft letters to the authorities in Vietnam and the U.S., and after every public lecture, Thây invites me to speak about violations of human rights in Vietnam and to ask the audience for support by signing the letters and petitions. In 1985, we obtained 2,200 signatures on a petition requesting the release of monks, nuns, artists, and writers in Vietnam. A friend in New York delivered the petition to the office of the Vietnamese Delegation to the UN, and a few of the people on the list were released. During our tour in 1987, we drafted individual letters and obtained more than 3,700 letters which were sent separately from various cities to the authorities in Vietnam and to the President of the United States.

While in the U.S. in 1989, I was introduced to Congressman Tom Lantos, of California, who is the cochairman of the Congressional Human Rights Caucus, and to several of his key assistants. I presented the plea of the imprisoned intellectuals of Vietnam, and thanks to the help of two wonderful women, Annette Lantos and Margery Farrar, Congressman Lantos gave a speech about human rights violations in Vietnam on the floor of the House of Representatives, and another about the suffering of the boat people.

I was also able to meet with the person in charge of the Vietnam desk at the State Department. He was about to leave for Geneva for a UNHCR conference on boat people, where the outcome was likely to be forced repatriation. I tried my best to let him see that even "buffalo boys" or "fishermen" (his terms) were deserving of human rights. In Vietnam, the fruits of their fishing were confiscated, and every one of their activities was under the control of the government. They had no liberty. Their presence in the West could

help American industry. We cannot say that we only accept intellectuals who are suppressed politically. We also need to care for
simple people like buffalo boys and fishermen. I was moved to learn
that in Geneva a week after our meeting, he was one of the few delegates who supported the boat people. My negative impression of
the State Department dating from the Vietnam War was alleviated
a little, thanks to him. After our 1989 trip to the U.S., a number of
prisoners—Thich Nu Tri Hai, Nguyen Thi Nghia, and Hoang Hai
Thuy—were released.

During our Spring 1991 tour of the U.S., thanks to the help
of Steve Denney and the well-organized assistance of Therese
Fitzgerald, 14,120 individual letters were signed and sent to Vietnamese authorities to press for the release of prisoners. After that
trip, Doan Quoc Sy was released, then Thây Quang Do, and a few
other monks who had been condemned for life. Even though they
were few in number, they were the prisoners the communist government was most reluctant to release. Doan Quoc Sy is a living
bodhisattva of fearlessness. The day twelve policemen ransacked his
house and arrested him for the second time, he sat serenely in the
lotus position for six hours while he was terrorized by the police. In
jail, he was asked several times to write a short confession so that he
could be released, but he kindly and firmly refused.

Thây Quang Do is one of the bravest monks I ever met. His non-
fear and kindness have impressed everyone living near him in exile.
He was the soul of the Buddhist underground press and demonstrations on the streets of Saigon during the struggle against Ngo Dinh
Diêm in 1963. It was he who listened to the radio, wrote reports,
sent them to overseas radio stations, and phoned the embassies of
many countries every time we were about to have a demonstration.
He spoke Japanese to the Japanese reporters, Thai to Thai reporters, and so on, so the secret police did not know how to prevent the
demonstrations. Every time we the thirteen "cedars" came to Xa Loi
Temple, he always gave us many documents to be distributed. Thây
Chau Toan, his assistant (the second director of SYSS after Thây
Thanh Van died), duplicated thousands of documents on their mimeograph machine. Ngo Dinh Diêm arrested Thây Quang Do on
August 20, 1963, together with thousands of monks and almost tortured him to death. Diêm's agents tried to get him to say that he

was a high cadre of the communists. As that was not true, he was tortured until he lost consciousness.

At the liberation day, Thây Quang Do coughed blood, had tuberculosis, pneumonia, and pleurisy, and finally had to have one lung removed. It was reported that under torture, he was the bravest monk and the most fearless. For many years he was in internal exile in a remote village in North Vietnam. He works hard, writing poetry to send to Thây Nhat Hanh, including one poem addressed to Andrei Sakharov. All the local communist cadres love and admire him, but the higher-ups fear that he will inspire demonstrations that could lead to the overthrow of the regime. Under international pressure, he was recently released to Saigon, where he is still under strict house arrest.

We do not have an organization on human rights and never claim to work for human rights, but many human rights organizations in the West know, trust, and rely on us for information. Most of this work has been done thanks to the wise advice of Thây Nhat Hanh. He smiles, offers tea, and it looks as if he does not do anything, but without him, I know we could not have made any progress with these difficult projects. At the beginning of the fall of Saigon, Thây started to write personal letters to all Vietnamese monks living abroad, giving them information about human rights violations in the country and suggesting how to respond. He did that steadily for two years, until Thây Man Giac arrived in the West. Since that time, Thây Man Giac has assumed this work of coordination. From his temple in Los Angeles, Thây Man Giac always does his best to help those detained in jails in Vietnam as soon as we pass the news on to him. Now Thây Quang Ba, Thây Minh Dung, and Thây Vien Ly also continue this work. Thây Man Giac has also been extremely generous with boat people, including monks and nuns in refugee camps in Asia, generously sending them sponsorship papers and then feeding and sheltering them when they arrive in the U.S.

Thây Nhat Hanh also continues to help and support all the monks and nuns in jail in his quiet way. The work for human rights is huge. There is still so much to do.

CHAPTER NINETEEN

Plum Village

By 1982, our Sweet Potato Community had become too small. Even with tents, we could accommodate only thirty guests, and in the summer, we often had to ask one group of thirty people to leave after a week to allow thirty more to come. As more and more people wanted to visit, we began to look for a new place.

Thây had heard that farmland in the south of France was cheap, and he liked the idea of living in the south, where it was warmer and sunnier than Sweet Potato. I loved the idea of being able to grow bitter melons and all kinds of Vietnamese fragrant herbs that could not withstand the cold in Fontvannes. Our first destination was Provence. But on our way to Aix-en-Provence, we stopped at a gasoline station to ask for directions, and we were nearly lifted off the ground by a *mistral*, the high velocity wind common to that area. Within a day, we both came down with terrible colds, and we decided to head west, to the area near Toulouse and Bordeaux. We knew there would be less sunshine, but at least the winds wouldn't be so strong.

We looked in local newspapers and found listings for twelve abandoned farms. Thây particularly liked one twenty-acre property that was surrounded by beautiful, rocky slopes covered with green forest, near Thenac, in the Dordogne region. The land was only one franc (20¢) per meter, and the three old farm buildings—200-year-old stone buildings that had been used for cattle, pigs, and sheep—were included at no additional charge. Thây was happy walking through the forest there; it was easy for him to envision a beautiful meditation path. But when a hailstorm destroyed the owner's vineyard and thereby his income for the year, the price of the property rose from one to four francs per meter. So we visited another dozen farms. But the farm near Thenac was the one Thây liked the most, so we decided to buy it despite the price increase.

Our old friend, Le Nguyen Thieu, the last General Secretary of the School of Youth for Social Service, had just arrived in France, and he expressed an interest in joining with us on this land project. The property near Thenac was not arable, and Brother Le and his family knew that they would need to farm to support themselves. So we located a fifty-acre farm with five old stone buildings, just three kilometers away, and Le Nguyen Thieu, on our behalf, bought both farms and moved there with his family and a half dozen other recently arrived refugees. We named the properties "Upper Hamlet" (the Thenac property) and "Lower Hamlet" (the farm in Loubès-Bernac), and we called both hamlets together "*Làng Hông*," literally "Persimmon Village." It was named after the retreat center we had planned to build in Vietnam that was never realized.

In 1973, a beautiful parcel of land in the forested highlands of Vietnam was acquired for us in the hopes that we could return to Vietnam and start a retreat center for social workers. This land had been chosen by Thây Chau Toan, the second director of SYSS. Chau Toan was an artist and the best flower arranger I have ever known. He was a dear younger brother in the Dharma who loved, cherished, and cared for Thây Nhat Hanh. When my friends and I—the thirteen cedars—first studied Buddhism with Thây Nhat Hanh in Truc Lam Temple in 1961, Thây Chau Toan and Thây Dong Bôn built Thây a hut there. Whenever Thây was sick, Thây Dong Bon, an excellent traditional physician, gave him massage, acupuncture, and delicious porridge. Thây Chau Toan took care of him, washing his clothes, tidying up his hut, and preparing flower arrangements. Behind Thây's hut was a tall green bamboo thicket, and around the hut were beautiful honeysuckle, plumeria, and yellow plum blossoms. From 1964 to 1966, it was Thây Chau Toan who hosted us so warmly for the weekly Days of Mindfulness that Thây led at Truc Lam Temple.

Thây Chau Toan was Thây Nhat Hanh's editorial assistant for the weekly Buddhist magazine, *Hai Trieu Am* (*Sound of the Rising Tide*). Thây was editor-in-chief, and Thây Chau Toan did much of the work—contacting the best Buddhist writers, bringing each issue to the printing house, correcting the proofs, and overseeing the magazine's distribution. In 1966, when Thây's call for peace was printed as an editorial in *Hai Trieu Am*, Thây Tam Chau, the UBC president, rescinded UBC's funding for the magazine, and Thây Chau Toan suffered a great loss. I saw him walking alone through the streets of Saigon as if he had just lost a loved one. Slowly, he recovered his peace and became his former joyful self.

When Thây Thanh Van died in an automobile accident in 1971, Thây Chau Toan was chosen to be director of SYSS. As director, he had a very different style of working, and he was greatly admired by the students. Even while directing thousands of workers and organizing so many details—he was a skilled administrator and an expert in accounting—he was always very humble, driving himself back to Truc Lam Temple on his old motorbike each night to sleep. By that time, the SYSS had become quite large, with several campuses and cars, and it was thanks to the harmony maintained between Thây Chau Toan and the senior monks of the UBC (even though he still had many "internal formations" with the older generation from the time they stopped funding *Hai Trieu Am*) that the merging of the SYSS with the forty-two provincial UBC Committees for Welfare and Social Service to form the Buddhist Committee for Reconstruction and Development went so smoothly.

In 1973, Thây Chau Toan wrote to us describing the beautiful parcel of land he had found. There were tall trees, huge boulders, and a lovely, winding creek. His plans for the center were like a huge flower arrangement: "There are three giant oaks near the creek, where we can sit for tea meditation. There is a wonderful corner with *sim* flowers and small pine trees where we can hang hammocks and make a playground for children. And there is much fertile land near the creek, where we can build housing for families." We wanted to plant persimmon trees and sell the fruit to support the center, so we named this retreat center for SYSS workers Làng Hông, "Persimmon Village." But Thây Chau Toan never realized his wonderful "flower arrangement." He died of a heart attack in June 1974.

In southwestern France, where we found these two parcels of land, the varieties of plums that are grown for drying are among the most delicious in the world, so we decided to "translate" Làng Hông into French as *"Village des Pruniers"* and into English as "Plum Village." In the Lower Hamlet, adults and children planted 1,250 plum trees, including 750 that were purchased from donations by children who knew that the money raised from the sale of the plums would go to hungry children in Vietnam and other Third World countries. It has been a lot of work caring for these trees, but by 1990, they were already beginning to bear fruit, and the harvest in 1992 was six tons!

In October 1982, we left Sweet Potato and moved to Plum Village. At first there were only Thây, myself, Brother Le, his family, and the other recently arrived refugees. That first year, we discovered what an extraordinary place it is. Each February, when the oak, linden, and poplar trees are still bare, millions of green buds spring out from the cold, rocky soil in the forest in the Upper Hamlet, and, a few weeks later, in early March, fragile, yellow buds and petals of thousands (yes, thousands) of daffodils open their delicate wings and wave at us. Because of their enchanting beauty, Thây named that hillside *Dharmakaya Store*, "the store of the Dharma body." We don't know why, but the other farms in the area do not have such hidden treasures of daffodils. Thây proposed that we organize a Daffodil Festival to welcome these little angel bodhisattvas. Each year, people from Bordeaux, Toulouse, and other nearby cities come and spend a day with us walking in the sea of yellow daffodils, listen to a Dharma talk by Thây, and enjoy tea meditation and songs and dancing by the children. What a special gift from Heaven and Earth!

We knew we wanted to open Plum Village to social workers and others needing a retreat, so as soon as we moved there, we began clearing out the old buildings and putting in wooden floors. Then we made beds by placing plywood boards and foam pads on top of red French clay "cinderblocks." In the summer of 1982, we received 100 people; in 1983, 200 people; and since 1991, more than 1,000 people have come each summer from all over the world. During the July 15 to August 15 summer opening, anyone who signs up in advance can stay at least one week sharing with us the practice of mindfulness under the guidance of Thây Nhat Hanh and his sangha. Together, we practice sitting meditation, walking meditation, tea meditation, work meditation, and Dharma discussion. It is not an intensive course. Families and friends practice joyfully together, and every day Thây gives a talk in Vietnamese, English, or French, with simultaneous translation into those languages plus

Stone Building in the Upper Hamlet.

German and Italian. We have many cultural activities for Vietnamese children—the older children teach the younger ones about their homeland, and there is a lot of singing. We also have beautiful programs for Western children. Every week, we organize a festival, such as "Welcoming the Full Moon," "Happy Continuation of Our Ancestors," "Staying in Touch with the Suffering of the Boat People and the Victims of the Atomic Bombs," and "Thanksgiving."

The teachings of Thây Nhat Hanh during the summer retreat are for children and adults to create peace in themselves and in the world. The unique aspect of Plum Village as a retreat center is the focus on children. We don't force them, but the children are invited to join us for the short periods of sitting meditation, walking meditation, tea meditation (the children have "lemonade meditation"), and eating meals quietly, with awareness and appreciation. It turns out that many children practice mindfulness better than their parents, and when they return home, they remind their parents to come back to the present moment and enjoy the many wonders that are all around them. The Summer Retreat is one of the great joys of Plum Village.

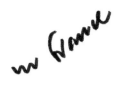

After four years of farming in the French way, Brother Le Nguyen Thieu and the other refugees realized that they could not earn enough to support themselves and their families, and in 1987, they all moved out. At about the same time, a number of Vietnamese monks, nuns, and laypersons, and several Westerners asked if they could stay year-round to study Buddhism and practice mindfulness with Thây. As a result, a residential practice community of about fifty members has formed. Due to the lack of year-round facilities, we can only accept about this number of trainees. More than half the residents are monks and nuns. Thây has developed a four-year Dharma teacher training program to produce "agents of transformation" for Vietnam and the West. Trainees first learn to transform their own "internal knots" and become "solid as a mountain and fresh as a flower," so they can share the Dharma through their own insight and their own "being," not just from books. (But we also study books.)

Annabel Laity, Sister True Virtue, is an Englishwoman, well-suited for the responsibility of teaching the Dharma and also helping with the administrative work of Plum Village. Thanks to her care, we have been able to accept new trainees, as well as negotiate with the French authorities and keep up with the administrative work. We now grow much of our food organically, including vegetables that are difficult to find outside of Vietnam. At times the slugs eat half of our crop, but we do not discriminate. We know they need to live too! Every evening in spring, practitioners go to the greenhouse with their flashlights and pick the slugs off the leaves, put them in a large container, and carry them to the forest, where they can eat the tender leaves there.

In early April of every year, the plum blossoms light up the Lower Hamlet. Looking at the orchard, we feel as though we are looking at the night sky, with millions of tiny stars. Mornings in Plum Village in spring, fall, and winter are usually foggy, and we often have the impression during walking meditation that we are walking among the clouds. Sunsets and full moons are also wonderful occasions for us to practice walking meditation, and they provide inspiration for many to discover their artistic talents. Many Plum Village residents have discovered hidden musical and artistic talents just by living in such a joyful community.

At the request of Western friends, Thầy leads a special retreat every other June in English. The transformation for many Western friends who cannot stay year-round has been great. I have seen people who, after three weeks of strong practice—listening to the teachings and living in the community—have become fresh as flowers. We all need a place we can go to refresh ourselves. I realized that when we were working at the School of Youth for Social Service and I see it today. Plum Village is a joyful, international community, the fruit of many experiences, and we continue to learn and practice.

CHAPTER TWENTY

River Water, Market Rice

On summer mornings, a fine white mist covers the hillsides surrounding Plum Village. Returning from walking meditation this morning, I met young Tho carrying a bucket of water to her three plum trees. A bit further into the orchard, I saw Kim Trang and little Thuc Hien dragging a hose out to water their trees. Here in southwestern France, plum trees flourish with only occasional watering, because the clay in the soil preserves the moisture well. The 1,250 plum trees brought to mind the many Vietnamese children in the West who sent money in 1982 and 1983 to purchase them, knowing that one day the dried plums would be sold to buy food and medicine for hungry children in Vietnam. Today that dream has become a reality.

I helped Tho water her trees. "Dear Tho, do you remember when you first came to Plum Village? I showed you photos of the children in the 'new economic zones' in Vietnam, and you and your sisters decided to save pocket money to help us plant ten plum trees. Do you see how your plum trees have been bearing fruit since the moment you felt a wish to help other children?"

Tho turned her face toward me, her mouth forming a shy smile. How pretty she looks in the pink shirt and black trousers, just like a young girl in Vietnam. Her mother bought these traditional clothes in the Plum Village gift shop.

Tho has returned to Plum Village with her whole family every summer since she was four. The family practices mindfulness together for a month, and the children learn about Vietnamese culture. Now Tho can read and speak Vietnamese, but she is different from the way I was at her age, and even from the youngsters who just arrived from Vietnam. Whenever Tho picks up a French book, she reads it as naturally as drinking a glass of water. But when I give her a book in Vietnamese, she looks at a few pages and then sets it down. When Tho writes me letters in Vietnamese, they are short,

Plum Village orchard.

written just to please me. But when she writes to her friends in French, they continue on for pages. Looking beyond Tho's shy smile, I can see that it is not possible for her to be 100 percent Vietnamese in the same way that Chau is.

Chau is the daughter of a family in South Vietnam that I have been supporting for many years. Chau's father was in a reeducation camp for more than ten years, and her mother, a public health technician, lost her job when it was discovered that her husband had worked for the nationalist regime. When Chau was only two and her brother, Khang, was six, the family was sent to a "new economic zone," a collective farm in a jungle area.

One night Chau fell ill with malaria. Her mother tied her in a sling across her back, and, balancing Khang on the front of her bicycle, pedalled to a city hospital. Halfway there, she met my sister, Thanh, an old friend of hers. Thanh wrote me about Chau's family, and we were able to send modest support, enough to help them survive.

Chau's mother was able to rent a tiny house in a poor section of Saigon, barely big enough for a bed, a table, and a small stove. Every morning she sold rice porridge, and every evening she sold sweet snacks on the street. Working like this day and night, she had no time to care for her children. But with our assistance, Khang was able to attend school.

I often gaze at the photo that Chau's mother sent to me. Chau's tiny face is pale and gaunt, and her legs thin as bamboo. The parcels I send contain medicine that can be sold for rice and vitamins for Chau and Khang. The children don't seem to gain any weight, but at least they haven't succumbed to illness like so many other children in Vietnam.

Reflecting on Khang and Chau's difficult life, my thoughts turned to Vietnamese mothers here in Europe. Like pine trees torn from their native soil and transplanted far away, they have struggled to create stable roots in their new countries. Tho's mother, for example, is overwhelmed by the endless forms and paperwork that she has to complete in a language she does not really understand. She works full-time to support her family, cooks dinner, washes the family's clothes, puts the children to bed, and then attends night school to try to learn French. When she gets home, no matter how tired she is, she tidies the house a bit before going to bed.

She has to be up by six o'clock every morning to prepare breakfast and lunch for the children before putting on several layers of sweaters and heavy boots to brave the snow and catch the bus to work. She and her husband use what little time they have on the weekends to teach their children Vietnamese language and culture. Despite their efforts, Tho still reads Vietnamese hesitantly. She will never be a true Vietnamese daughter like Chau.

Every morning, Chau's mother walks along the streets of Saigon, balancing two big pots of porridge on a bamboo pole, and every evening, she sells a sweet snack, *che*. But even when she sells all that she has, there is barely enough money to buy rice, salt, firewood, coal, and vegetables. Chau's mother never has the luxury of a weekend. A day without work truly means a day without food.

Chau and Khang are left unattended for hours on end. But they live in the cradle of Vietnamese culture, and their mother does not need to do anything to teach them the ways of our people. They learn everything by themselves. It is like having water in the river and rice in the market; they receive their culture every day.

The tiny house of Khang and Chau is next door to the grand house of a professor at Saigon University. But, like Khang and Chau's father, the professor was sent to a reeducation camp. Still, his grown children have been able to support their mother, and together they secretly have preserved their father's collection of books and papers. I cannot imagine how they managed to hide their books from the authorities, but, once in a while, Khang will write to me and say such things as, "Dear Aunt, I've just read *A Rose for Your Pocket*, by Thich Nhat Hanh, and it's wonderful! I felt so much love for my mother after reading it."

Then, a few months later, I received another letter from Khang: "Dear Aunt, I've just read *Mam Forest* and *A Taste of Earth*. They are both so good! I can't understand why such books are censored and burned."

Shortly after that, I received a letter from Chau, written in a delicate and pretty script. Young Chau began by telling me, "Dear Aunt, my mother is terribly sick. Brother Khang must now sell the porridge, or we are afraid we will lose customers. I should go and help him, but Mother is so sick I don't dare leave her alone. Aunt, my old mother is like a ripe banana hanging on the tree. She is so weak, and we are very worried!" Was this letter really from a pale and skinny six-year-old girl, whose dazed eyes seem unable to grasp the harshness of her life? How could she know a beautiful folk expression like "An old mother is like a ripe banana hanging on the tree"? Could the children at Plum Village write like that? They have never seen a banana tree. But when little Chau saw her mother so sick and exhausted, at once she saw the image of a banana so ripe it was about to fall from the tree. No one had to teach this image to her. It was born from her own experience and her own insight.

Chau's letter continued, "Every time Mother coughs, she reminds me of the flickering wick of an oil lamp about to go out. It tears at my heart, dear Aunt!" "Flickering wick" — how could the Vietnamese children in Europe conjure up such an image? They have never lived by the light of an oil lamp and do not know the total darkness that descends when both oil and wick are spent. Do Vietnamese children in the West know that many children's nights in Vietnam are lit by no more than a dim, flickering oil lamp, easily extinguished by a blast of wind? Yes, Chau's mother's health—with no money, no medicine, no hospital—was like a flickering wick.

Even though she had learned Vietnamese from her mother, would Tho be able to read Chau's letter and understand the deep meaning and feeling in her images? I think it is impossible to explain to Tho the terrible darkness that threatens Chau and her brother if their "lamp" goes out.

Chau's letter continued, "Every day, when I return from school, I soak the beans and begin to grate the coconut. When Khang comes home from selling porridge, we cook the sweet che together. I squeeze coconut for milk until late at night. In the morning, I get up early to heat the porridge for Khang to sell. I also chop salted pickles for him to take along. When he returns, we start to cook more porridge and che. We have no time to study.

"Before Mother got sick, I would study every evening, and then help her grate the coconut, and Khang would help her rinse the beans. When we finished, we would go next door and ask Huong if we could borrow one of her father's books. After reading *The Fragrance of Ca Mau Forest*, I loved the land of South Vietnam so dearly that I wanted to read every book by Son Nam. In Huong's library, I found a recent work by him, entitled *Nghe Harbor*. But, I could only read to page thirty. The language was as bland as dried manioc roots. I couldn't swallow any more of it! No wonder it sat openly on the shelf in the living room of Huong's family. When I read the book *Memoirs*, by Vu Bang, affection for the North welled within me. I am not like my friends who hate everything from the North. To reject it all because of the bad deeds of some North Vietnamese doesn't seem right, don't you agree, dear Aunt? But sometimes I wonder, does the lovely North of Vu Bang still exist? Or is the North only filled with reeducation camps, with prisoners like Father?"

Chau daring to write so boldly alarmed me. If this letter had been opened and examined, poor Chau herself would have been sent to a reeducation camp! Could Vietnamese children of the same age in Europe read such books and have such insights? I am reminded again of the phrase, "river water, market rice." Even though little Chau receives no cultural instruction like Tho's lessons, the water and rice of her native country have fed her. The "water" and the "rice" are culture. Books like *A Rose for Your Pocket, Mam Forest,* and *Memoirs,* though hard to come by in Vietnam today, are still understood and appreciated by children like Khang and Chau. They have the passion to read and are nourished by such books.

Tho's mother also has a copy of *The Fragrance of Ca Mau Forest,* but could Tho read it with the same interest? Or would she prefer to spend her time watching TV and videotapes? River water and market rice are more than just books; they are also the folk songs children sing on the street, the lullabies of village mothers, and even the gossip of women at market. Wherever they go, children in Vietnam encounter river water and market rice. Their culture surrounds them.

The water and rice available today in Vietnam are not pure. They are mixed with sand and gravel. Pure water and rice, like good books, have been banned to make room for water and rice that make little Chau feel as if she has eaten tasteless, dry manioc root. Son Nam's writing today is not the same as when he wrote freely about his beloved country in *The Fragrance of Ca Mau Forest.* If Chau wants to taste pure water and fragrant, delicious rice, she has to carefully separate out the pebbles, manioc, and rotten grains. Mixed in with the fine beauties of our homeland—ripe bananas, golden plum flowers, and village mothers' lullabies—are the hardened, cold faces of the communist cadres in their yellow uniforms. They speak the same language, but their rough tone makes it sound like a foreign tongue. These people treat a kind, talented scholar like Huong's father worse than a common pickpocket, so how could the water and rice not be polluted?

Khang wrote to me to describe his neighbor's second arrest: "Twelve cadres searched through every corner of the professor's house, starting at 2:00 in the morning. Two others stood guard in front of our house. I could hear Huong speaking to the cadres, while the professor sat in meditation, as quiet and serene as a Buddha, with a half-smile on his lips. Even as they led him out with handcuffs at 8:00 a.m., his expression was calm and at ease. I never saw such a beautiful scene as that. My heart was filled with love and admiration. My own father is also brave like the professor. He too will never bend his head in the face of violence. That is why, after twelve years, he is still in prison."

Girls at Plum Village.

Vietnam still has many green trees, beautiful "cedars" like the professor and Khang's father. One only has to open his or her eyes to see that the market is still abundant with rice and the rivers are still flowing with clear water. Even rice mixed with gravel still has some delicious, pure rice in it, enough to feed those who know how to select the pure rice and stay in full awareness in their beautiful homeland.

Books like *Mam Forest*, *The Fragrance of Ca Mau Forest*, and *Memoirs* are easily available here in Europe, but do the Vietnamese children raised here care to look at them, drink every line, and appreciate the beauty of each word, the style of each sentence? I feel uneasy when I think of the many refugee children who are drawn in by violent scenes on TV whenever they have free time. These youngsters will never have the occasion to watch the dear professor face the twelve violent cadres with a serene smile. They will never have the chance to hear village mothers singing soft lullabies to their babies on a hot afternoon, nor will they hear the inspiring stories of those sent to "new economic zones" or imprisoned in "reeducation camps" but who continued to be calm and brave in prison. Even if the professor manages to escape and write a book about his experiences, it is unlikely that youngsters overseas will care to read his book. No matter how much time Tho's mother devotes to teaching Vietnamese writings to her children, it is impossible for the children to be in touch with the wondrous reality of Vietnam. For them, it is just a distant land, not at all familiar.

I breathed deeply. At least I have a few photographs of hungry children living in the new economic zones that I can share with the children who come to Plum Village. And there are the 1,250 plum trees to help connect them with children their own age in Vietnam. Looking at the photographs, they can see that they resemble the children in Vietnam more than they look like their classmates in school, even though the children in Vietnam are skinny and live in palm-leaf huts. Every summer, Vietnamese children from all over Europe, America, and Australia can come to Plum Village to discover the richness and the depth of their parents' language, poetry, music, and culture.

I smiled, remembering Vu's Swiss teacher's amazement after reading this essay by him: "A fragrant rose and a heap of garbage are two sides of one living reality. Looking deeply into a rose, I can see the garbage. Looking deeply into the garbage, I can see a rose. It will bloom very soon. When I look anywhere, I see flowers and garbage deeply interconnected. This is necessary for life to be." The Swiss teacher tried to visit Vu's family to understand how such a little boy could have such deep thoughts. Vu visited Plum Village every year. Although Tho may not be as fully Vietnamese as Chau, she will be able to learn many lessons that children in Vietnam cannot because of poverty and the lack of freedom. Refugee children in the West receive the benefits of nutritious food, freedom, and openness. These children will grow up to be healthy offshoots of the "tree of Vietnam." Any child who comes to Plum Village can learn from Thây Nhat Hanh about non-duality and other important aspects of life.

The professor who was arrested cannot teach the children in Vietnam about flowers and garbage. Twenty years ago, the cadres who arrested him might have been like flowers, but because of their victory over the Americans, they have become like garbage, filled with arrogance. What about the beautiful flowers, like the professor or the father of Khang and Chau? Once they get out of jail and are able to emigrate to a free country, will they still be fresh? Will they continue to cultivate their qualities to blossom and give joy, peace, and inspiration to millions of young Vietnamese flowers? Or will the easy life in the West draw them slowly into forgetfulness? Now the professor is not there to teach Khang, so he only sees the communist cadres as garbage to be thrown away. No one is there to teach him the ways to transform garbage back into flowers.

It is so sad to see that thirty years of war followed by eighteen years of dictatorship have transformed the minds of the Vietnamese people into yet another war zone. In the past, Vietnam as a nation had many people who embodied great virtues—people who knew the art of listening, the art of being humble, and the art of looking deeply into each event and each person to see the negative aspect of others as partly their own fault; people who know that if we hurt others, we are only hurting ourselves. Such enlightened persons are more and more difficult to find when war and dictatorship are so prolonged.

Seeds from the bodhi tree in India have been planted throughout the world. Because of different soil and water conditions, each bodhi tree grows a little differently. Some are tall; some are short. But each one contains the essence of the original bodhi tree. Now I see that if Vietnamese children living overseas are lucky enough to have parents who live in awareness, they will thrive, even if they take on a new shape. They will be lovely Vietnamese trees, contributors to the garden of humanity, thriving in France with its own rich heritage, in the lowlands of Holland, among the mountains of Switzerland, the snowy lands of Denmark, Sweden, Norway, and Finland, the wealth and talent of Germany, and the lands of opportunity of America and Australia. For the first time I can see that Vietnam is not just the small dragon-shaped country on the South China Sea. It is now the whole world, extending from the Americas to Europe, and all the way down to Australia.

The challenge is to encourage Vietnamese parents to preserve the beautiful part of the culture of their native land and pass it on to their children. How can I encourage them to give themselves more time to cultivate flowers in themselves and in their children and to cultivate our culture's spiritual depth before everyone in the family gets caught up in selfish concerns? Parents must show an interest in what their children are learning at school, while also sharing with them the delightful customs and traditions of the new land. Looking deeply into each new habit and tradition with their children, they can learn to appreciate the best things about the West and keep them away from the worst habits. Sharing in this way will allow their children to receive and love the culture of their homeland, and plant it intelligently in the rich, new soil.

Parents and children can look deeply together to see why the ancestors took the time to welcome the blooming of a single flower and celebrate the full moon. They can learn to feel within themselves the continuation of their ancestors. They can find ways to stay in touch with those who have no food and no freedom, and ways to celebrate their gratitude to teachers, friends, and all other beings.

Living in awareness, parents will not say or do things that will cause their children to lose faith in their own people. Then there will be hope that the children will want to continue their heritage and study Vietnamese, as they study French, German, and English. In this way, the children will see and understand the joys and pains of their people's 4,000-year history.

No matter how great an effort Tho's mother makes, Tho will be different from Chau. Each girl has her own unique beauty. It is true that Tho looks like an elegant pine from Switzerland, but her dark eyes, her shy smile, and her silky black hair are like the sweet rice and coconut milk of her parents' Vietnam. Her way of speaking, walking, and greeting friends are the fruits of the love and guidance she has received from her parents, grandparents, uncles and aunts, her ancestral heritage.

Suddenly, my thoughts were interrupted by the sweet voice of young Thanh Tuyen, "Who wants bean cakes, who wants coconut cakes?" She is carrying a platter of Vietnamese cakes, calling out like a street vendor. In her brown blouse and black trousers, slightly wrinkled from her noontime nap, Thanh Tuyen sounds just like a vendor from North Vietnam selling cakes along the streets of Saigon. Though her parents are from the South and speak in a southern accent, as a young child in Vietnam Thanh Tuyen often heard vendors from the North. Every summer when she visits Plum Village she is invited to use her voice to sell the traditional cakes. Thanks to the presence of Plum Village, she has a chance to recollect and preserve the image of her homeland. Hopefully in every region where there are Vietnamese people, places like Plum Village will be created where Vietnamese children can come and give new life to these fading images of their homeland. Keeping one foot firmly planted in the old culture and one foot in the new, Vietnamese children can help us all as we create a beautiful garden of humanity for the next century.

CHAPTER TWENTY-ONE

True Emptiness

In June 1982, Thây Nhat Hanh and I went to New York, where Thây spoke at the Reverence for Life Conference. For more than five years, Thây had refused to attend any conferences or to travel in that way, as our experience with the American peace movement and then the World Conference on Religion and Peace in the Gulf of Siam left us unsure if such travels could be of any use. But Thây felt inclined to accept this invitation, and at the conference, we met a number of young American Buddhists who reminded Thây of the novices he had taught in Vietnam.

Thây agreed to accept the invitation of these American Buddhists to come to California the following year to lead two retreats at Tassajara Zen Mountain Center, one on basic Buddhism and the other on working for peace, cosponsored by the Buddhist Peace Fellowship. Also during this visit, Thây Nhat Hanh rekindled his friendship with Thây Tinh Tu, a young Vietnamese monk who admired Thây. Inspired by his meeting with Thây, he vowed to build a practice center for Vietnamese monks and nuns in the U.S. Kim Son Monastery, near Watsonville, California, was founded six months later, and Thây Nhat Hanh agreed to be the head teacher. From that time on, Thây has come to Kim Son every year or two to teach. Since the founding of Kim Son, Thây Tinh Tu, a humble, talented, and wise monk, has been able to link more than twenty temples in Northern California. In the atmosphere of mistrust among Vietnamese refugees because of nearly fifty years of war and dictatorship in Vietnam, Thây Tinh Tu's reconciliation work is most important. These temples organize Wesak, the Buddha's nativity, together, recite the precepts, and organize public lectures and retreats for refugees led by Thây Nhat Hanh and others. Thây Tinh Tu also writes many poems and songs for the practice, and he is now a well-known Dharma teacher among the Vietnamese in North America. During one retreat at Kim Son, Thây Tinh Tu invited me to give a Dharma talk. I had not yet shaved my head and become a formal nun, so it was revolutionary of him to invite me to give a Dharma talk to a large audience of monks, nuns, and laypeople.

Since 1983, Thây Nhat Hanh and I have travelled to many parts of the United States and Canada, throughout Western and Eastern Europe, and to Australia and Brazil, leading retreats for Westerners and also for Vietnamese refugees on the practice of mindfulness. We have led retreats for American Vietnam veterans, artists, environmentalists, psychotherapists, helping professionals, families, and children. In this way, our community of practice continues to grow.

In 1987 in Australia I began to teach the Dharma. When people have mental wounds, they want to share them only with someone they really trust, someone like Thây Nhat Hanh. But Thây cannot see everyone, so when we were in Australia to lead mindfulness retreats for Australians and Vietnamese refugees there, I offered to listen to people's difficulties, report them to Thây, and transmit Thây's advice to them. I listened to so many people that my reports became longer and longer until Thây finally said, "Please look deeply into each person's problem and help him or her yourself. I am sure you can do it." In fact, I was able to see the solutions to many of their difficulties and share them with these friends, thanks to the method of looking deeply taught by Thây. I did my best to "be in the skin" of each person and to help them understand themselves and each other. Thanks to this work, a number of families made peace among themselves for the first time in years, and since then, slowly seeing my ability to help, families have come to me at retreats in the U.S., Europe, and Plum Village for that kind of consultation.

Young people often reveal to me that without the understanding they cultivated at Plum Village or on a retreat, they might have run away from home, taken drugs, or even joined gangs. But after practicing meditation in a supportive community and listening to Thây, they have been able to understand themselves and their parents better, and they have found joy for the first time in their lives. Thây's Dharma talks in Vietnamese often address the cultural and generation gaps between refugees who have grown up in the West and their Vietnamese parents. For the parents as well as the young people, their time on retreat may be the first time they hear their suppressed sufferings stated so skillfully, and in the presence of those who have caused their pain. After Thây's Dharma talks, the parents and young people see how much they do not understand about each other, and they try to learn more. This is also true for couples— Thây devotes a lot of energy to rebuilding stability in relationships and families.

During the summer retreats in the Lower Hamlet, where most of the Vietnamese stay, my Tiep Hien brothers and sisters and I oversee the sitting and walking meditation, eating in mindfulness, cooking, sharing in the communal work, and the many cultural festivals. We also take the time to listen to members of each generation, trying to help them reconcile. We have a staff of young assistants who help by listening to their peers—because we know that many young people will confide only in their friends, not in the adults—and advising them. Slowly, without realizing it, we have become Dharma teachers. The greatest reward is to see those who have been healed later become sources of joy, peace, and generosity for others. Thây Nhat Hanh emphasizes that any teachings must be born from one's own experience, not just by repeating the words of the Buddha or some other authority. Thây shares with us only his own experience, and because it is true, it touches people deeply. To be authentic, our own teaching must also be the fruit of our own looking deeply, not someone else's.

Before the Plum Village summer retreat or before leaving for a long trip to the U.S., Australia, or other countries in Europe, I usually stay up late for several weeks to finish wrapping hundreds of parcels for hungry children in Vietnam. I used to feel a little guilty for leaving the children without help while I joined Thây to lead retreats, but now I see that the work of wrapping parcels and the work of leading retreats are equal. In fact, thanks to the retreat work, we are now in touch with thousands of people in the West— Vietnamese and non-Vietnamese—who are helping our work with hungry children, and the two kinds of work have become one. When someone goes to Vietnam for family reasons or as a tourist, they always offer to take some aid with them, and according to their ability, we can ask them to help us realize a certain project on our behalf. So, even though I left Vietnam in 1968, I have never been gone from that part of the Earth for long. Even as I write these lines, one of our friends is in Kinh Te Moi, a poor jungle area, on our behalf, bringing food and medical supplies to those in need and doing some environmental research to help purify the water.

A number of friends have expressed their sympathy for me, because they know that travelling so much can be exhausting. In fact, besides the work of wrapping parcels and writing letters to each hungry child in Vietnam, I enjoy this work the most. Travelling with Thây and helping to lead mindfulness retreats, I learn so much. I do my best to be awake in every moment, and I fully enjoy meeting many new friends at each retreat. Thây and I learn from their suffering as well as their insights, and Thây has started to adapt his teaching accordingly, emphasizing how to build peace for ourselves and society in practical, concrete ways. For young people of refugee families, Thây always advises them to go back to the roots of their parents' culture and, at the same time, be in harmony with the new culture where the family has settled. For Western friends, Thây always advises them to get in touch with their Christian or Jewish roots. We never wish to "convert" anyone to Buddhism. We only wish to offer everyone the light of awareness ("*buddh*" means aware) to shine onto their own roots so that they understand themselves better and more deeply. In this way, our community of practice gets larger every day. Four thousand people attended a public lecture Thây gave in Berkeley in April 1991, and more than 1,000 attended a Day of Mindfulness with him in northern California a week later. Hundreds of small communities following the way of practice presented by Thây are springing up in towns and cities all over the world.

Listening attentively to practitioners in the West during retreats with Thây Nhat Hanh, I have learned that children here, even though most do not suffer from hunger, suffer greatly from psychological, physical, and sexual abuse inflicted by alcoholic or mentally disturbed parents and other adults. We have been deeply affected many times by the stories we have heard. Reports of childhood sexual abuse and even involvement in the "sex industry" have moved me deeply. After listening to such stories, I have to practice walking meditation for several hours to restore some calm. Without having bombs drop on their heads, these people's hearts are like fields devastated by "bombs" of cruelty and ignorance. I have learned how to relieve suffering by listening attentively to these friends and discussing with them ways to transform their lives. I now see that this kind of suffering can be even greater than the suffering due to the lack of food. The Buddha taught that for his teachings to be authentic, they must be suitable for those who receive them. Thây always does his best to follow that advice of the Buddha, and I always do my best to help him.

I have learned and practiced under the light of the Buddha's teaching for thirty-five years. When I met Thây Thanh Tu in 1958, I began thinking about shaving my head to become a nun, but Thây Thanh Tu thought I was too revolutionary to become a traditional nun, and he agreed to help me set up a new-style community for nuns engaged in social work. From 1964 to 1966, I slowly built up a group of women practitioners devoted to social service guided by the Buddha's teachings. We shared responsibilities for the poor, and all of us lived like nuns. Three friends, for example, were responsible for raising funds to support my trips to Quang Nam to help flood victims living in the war zone. They placed old milk cans as donation boxes in friends' houses and shops, and every week, they brought the donations to Truc Lam Temple.

There we would have Days of Mindfulness in the fresh, cool garden of two monks, Thây Dong Bon and Thây Chau Toan, who loved Thây Nhat Hanh dearly, and who prepared a lovely hut for him to rest in every time he felt tired of working in the city. Days of Mindfulness in the temple were wonderful among huge, beautiful bamboo thickets, jack trees filled with fruit, plumeria blossoms, and bright yellow plum blossoms. After a short report, each practitioner opened the donation box and counted the money we could use to buy food for the flood victims. After that, we chanted, sat together, and then shared a meal in mindfulness cooked by Thây Dong Bon. I remember well the famous dish, *mit kho*, a jack fruit stew with soy sauce. Afterwards, we sang together before Thây Nhat Hanh gave a Dharma talk. Then we shared experiences of our work during the month, listened to Thây's advice, and went back to Saigon in the evening. Even though Truc Lam Temple was far away, the weekly Days of Mindfulness always had at least 100 participants.

When I refused to marry Anh Tran Tan Tram and he suffered, many of his friends said it was my fault for not shaving my head. If I had been a traditional nun, Tram would not have had to undergo such unnecessary pain, they told me. So I told my young Dharma sisters that sooner or later I would have to shave my head. I would ask Thây Nhat Hanh to shave my head and invite Thây Thanh Tu to attend the ordination. I asked my friends if any of them wanted to join me in an ordination, but all of them said they preferred "formless" practice, practicing on the inside in a way that was "invisible" to others. All of them were devoted to mindful, social work, and all lived beautiful lives, but when I mentioned that I would shave my head alone, my Dharma sisters were shocked. "Oh no, please! If you shave your head and become another great superior nun, we will 'die'!" We recalled how hard it had been during our service for the SYSS to work with certain superior nuns.*

In Vietnam, people trust shaven-headed monks and nuns, sometimes to the point of overestimating their real value. Monks and nuns have to be aware of that and try their best to be worthy of this trust. But some unmindful, religious persons become too sure of themselves and lose their ability to listen. My Dharma sisters may have been joking with me, but when I looked deeply into my own nature, I saw the seeds of arrogance. I was not from an aristocratic family, but the fact that I looked so young and yet had a university degree, and my ability to realize many difficult projects in the SYSS, impressed people. I knew that if I was not mindful, I could become arrogant. With my shaven head, people could admire me more than my real value, and I might become a "monster," like the one Thây described in his short story, "The Pine Gate." I was able to imagine the day when members of the younger generation would be frightened even to look at me. So I decided not to shave my

---

* There was one famous superior nun who had been born from an aristocratic family and was highly respected in society before becoming a nun. People treated her like a saint and greatly supported her projects, including setting up several nunneries and day-care centers for poor children in Hue. A few government ministers were even her disciples. Her status increased over time, but when we, the senior students of Thây Nhat Hanh on the staff of SYSS, worked with her during Thây's absence, we were not at all impressed. She imposed difficult and dangerous work on us, like illegally printing and distributing her book, in which she spoke out against the Prime Minister. It was written in a way that did not at all reflect a non-dual understanding of the struggle. If she had been more thoughtful, she could have helped us, but she was so sure of herself that my Dharma sisters opposed my shaving my head, worrying that I might become like her.

Su Ba The Thanh.

head, but instead to continue as a "formless" nun in order to avoid being treated well by some people without earning their respect. I would give my seeds of arrogance a chance to wither and transform themselves. I promised my Dharma sisters I would not shave my head.

I left Vietnam in 1968. Thây Thanh Tu, after three years of retreat from 1968 to 1971, decided to set up a new-style nunnery and monastery in the Vung Tau area of Vietnam. There, monks and nuns did not live on donations as in the past. They farmed, made soy sauce and fermented beans, and practiced sitting meditation. I was very happy to learn about this new-style community, and I felt that I was there with them. We sent medicine, and books and tapes of Thây Nhat Hanh to them regularly. I recently learned that nuns and monks under Thây Thanh Tu also help the sick with acupuncture and other medical care.

But the most significant influence on me was the high nun Su Ba The Thanh. In 1975, around the time the communists came to power, my friendship with her became solidified. During the war, she ran a home for 500 orphans and other children in the Cam Ranh area. From Paris, we sent her regular support, as we did forty-two other groups of Buddhist monks and nuns working under the provincial committees of the UBC. But when the war ended and I was no longer able to send aid directly to hungry children, she was the only nun who dared to correspond with me. In 1976, she sent us names and addresses of hungry children—children of prisoners, orphans, and others in need. Then we heard nothing from her for four years. I learned later that the new authorities, frightened of her popularity, closed her home for children and confiscated her temple. The local people gave her shelter, and the children who had been dispersed by the authorities gathered around her again, and she managed to have enough food for them. Again the communist cadres arrested her, and this time they ordered her to leave Cam Ranh. So she went to Hue to a remote nunnery to restore herself.

Being confined there, Su Ba The Thanh read and practiced the sutras, and she wrote a book on the nuns' precepts that had much the flavor of women's liberation. Then one day, after I had discovered where she was and sent her a book by Thây Nhat Hanh entitled *An Tru Trong Hien Tai* ("Dwelling in the Present Moment"), she wrote to thank me: "After forty years of practice, I have never found any door of practice so simple and profound. Thank you deeply for this wonderful gift." A few weeks later, I received another letter from her: "I know that people in Vietnam today desperately need the simple, profound teachings of the Buddha as taught by Thây Nhat Hanh. I vow that I will practice steadily for the next six months so that new Dharma doors will reveal themselves to me, and then I will teach my students in the nunnery first and then laypeople afterwards."

Just one week later, I received another letter: "I have leukemia. They say I may die within a month. Please wait for me. I will visit you, even without a passport. I am liberated and continue to be liberated, even as I am becoming a cloud." She sounded calm and confident, simply preparing to pass away. She asked one student to photograph her corpse after she passed away to send to Thây and me, so we could see her smiling even after her heart had stopped beating. It turned out to be true! The photo of her face that arrived after her passing away looked fresh and smiling. I knew that she chose to teach liberation through her being, and not just with excellent words! Inspired by her liberation, I decided to shave my head and continue her path, because I know now that every time seeds of arrogance and confusion arise in me, I can think of Su Ba The Thanh, and those seeds will dissolve.

I have been living in the West for twenty-five years, and yet the image of a simple nun wearing peasant-brown robes, walking peacefully or carrying an undernourished baby gently in her arms, is still dear to me. I am always happy to see myself in that way, a nun walking among the poor villagers. For me to become a nun has been to go home, even though my body is still here in the West. So in 1988 I decided to shave my head and wear a humble, brown robe.

In November of that year, thirty-six of us went on a pilgrimage with Thây Nhat Hanh to the sites of the Buddha's life in northeastern India. Thây had just finished writing a biography of the Buddha, *Old Path White Clouds*, and this trip was a celebration of the life of the Buddha. In the Deer Park, the Jeta Grove, by the pool at Lumbini, and many other places, we spent a few days doing sitting and walking meditation. We walked up the hill to Vulture Peak every day we were in the area and stayed until sunset. On the last day we were there, Thây gave an ordination for three nuns, six Tiep Hien brothers and sisters, and several lay practitioners who received the Five Precepts. I was one of the nuns ordained that day.

My Tiep Hien sisters helped me prepare for the ceremony by cutting my long hair and shaving most of it off. Thây Nhat Hanh symbolically cut some of my hair and said, "Shaving the head, all attachments are cut off." On that day, Thây gave me this poem:

Open the Road Wider

Hair which is the color of precious wood
is now offered as incense.
Beauty becomes eternity.
How wonderful the awareness of
impermanence!

Since everything is as a dream,
the true mind is determined to lead the way.
After listening to the voice of the rising tide,

*steps are made in the direction of the
unconditioned.*

*The winds chant this morning on the slope of the
Gridhrakuta.
The mind is no longer bound to anything.
The song now is that of the lovely teaching;
its fragrance is the essence of truth.*

In times past, it was with boket water
that her hair was washed,
then dried in the fragrant breeze of the late
afternoon.
This morning it is the bodhi nectar that she
receives
for the mind of Enlightenment to appear in its
wholeness.*

*For twenty-five years
she has made daily offerings
of loving kindness with her hands.
Compassion has never ceased to grow in her
heart.*

*This morning her hair is shed,
and the Way becomes wide open.
Suffering and illusion, though limitless,
are entirely ended.*

*A heart can touch the world in all the ten
directions.*

In February 1966 when I received the Fourteen Precepts of the
Order of Interbeing with Thây Nhat Hanh, he did not give us

---

* *Gleditsia fera* or *mimosa fera*, a tree of which the fruit is boiled in water and becomes a
fragrant herbal shampoo.

Dharma Lamp Transmission Ceremony, August 1990.

Dharma names right away. My Dharma name, *Diêu Không* (Wonderful Emptiness), given to me by Thây Thanh Tu in 1958, was also the name of a superior nun in Hue, so I rarely used it. Among the leaders of the UBC, there was a kind, humble monk whom I respected very much, named Thây Thiên Hòa. I can still picture him standing in front of An Quang Pagoda, serenely smiling as he approached a pedicab driver. Gently putting his hand on the driver's shoulder, he brought his face close to the driver's and told the man in a quiet voice, "Would you like to carry me to Xa Loi Temple, please?" After a drive, he always gave a double or triple fare to the pedicab driver and bowed deeply to the driver in a sincere way to thank him.

Thây Thiên Hòa visited the SYSS in 1968, after the Têt Offensive. He approved our ideas for helping refugees and nominated me to be vice-president of the Committee to Relieve the War Victims. In 1973, when the Buddhist Committee for Reconstruction and Development was founded to work closely with the SYSS, Thây Thiên Hòa was elected Head of that committee. I was quite pleased, and I wrote him a letter expressing my gratitude. He wrote back to me, referring to me as "*Chu Chân Không* (True Emptiness, young novice monk)." The way he addressed me communicated his respect, so I cherished the name Chân Không, True Emptiness.

In Buddhism, the word "emptiness" is a translation of the Sanskrit *sunyata*. It means "empty of a separate self." It is not a negative or despairing term. It is a celebration of interconnectedness, of interbeing. It means nothing can exist by itself alone, that everything is inextricably interconnected with everything else. I know that I must always work to remember that I am empty of a separate self and full of the many wonders of this universe, including the generosity of my grandparents and parents, the many friends and teachers who have helped and supported me along the path, and you dear readers, without whom this book could not exist. We inter-are, and therefore we are empty of an identity that is separate from our interconnectedness. Following my ordination on Vulture Peak, Thây gave me the same Dharma name, Chân Không, True Emptiness.[*]

Being a nun in the West, I do not carry undernourished babies in my arms, but teenagers and adults do cry silently as they share the stories of their childhoods of sadness and abuse. By listening attentively to their pain and helping them renew themselves, I am able to help heal many of these wounded "children," and this is very close to my ideal of holding the village children in my arms. I am grateful to be able to help in this way.

One day in 1981, seeing how absorbed I was wrapping parcels for hungry children in Vietnam, Thây Nhat Hanh asked me, "If you were to die tonight, are you prepared?" He said that we must live our lives so that even if we die suddenly, we will have nothing to regret. "Chân Không, you have to learn how to live as freely as the clouds or the rain. If you die tonight, you should not feel any fear or regret. You will become something else, as wonderful as you are now. But if you regret losing your present form, you are not liberated. To be liberated means to realize that nothing can hinder you, even while crossing the ocean of birth and death."

His words pierced through me, and I remained silent for several days. No, I was not prepared to die. My work was my life. I had found ways to help the hungry children, despite the difficulties, and

---

[*] From that day on, instead of calling me Chi Chân Không (Sister True Emptiness) in some formal meetings, Vietnamese Buddhists have begun to call me Su Cô Chân Không (Aunt Teacher True Emptiness) or Bhikkuni Chân Không (the mendicant Satyasunya).

I was happy again, knowing how to avoid the restrictions of the authorities in Vietnam. I knew that every time people received one of my packages or some other helping act, new hope was born in them, and also in their sponsors in Europe and America. If I were to die suddenly, who would continue this work?

I contemplated many practical questions like these, while following each in-breath and each out-breath. I was not exactly trying to find a solution. I knew that the ability to find one was in me and that when I was calm enough, an answer would reveal itself. So I continued to breathe and smile, and a few days later, I did see a solution. I knew that the only way I could die peacefully would be if I were reborn in others who wished to do the same work. Then my aspiration could continue even if this body of mine were to pass away. I thought about the young people who came to practice mindfulness with Thây, and I decided to share with them my experiences and deepest desires about helping suffering people. I would teach them how to choose medicines, how to wrap parcels, how to write personal letters to the poor, and how to keep Western people in touch with the suffering of the Vietnamese people. Under my guidance, a few young people were inspired to start their own committees, and today there are thirty-eight committees for hungry children. If I die tonight, by a car accident or a heart attack, these thirty-eight reincarnations will allow me to die in peace.

Nguyen Anh Huong, who arrived in North America in 1981, listened attentively to everything I said and asked me how to start a project. As a newly arrived boat person, she knew better than I the many families in great distress in Vietnam. I encouraged her to prepare her own list of families who needed help and to find sponsors for them. When the hungry children wrote to thank her, she could translate the letters and send them to the sponsors. Slowly, Anh Huong has been able to help almost 100 families. Bui Thanh Vu in Paris has sixty-seven families; Bui Ngoc Thuy in Sceaux, France, has eighty-six families; Annabel Laity at Plum Village is in charge of forty families; and Therese Fitzgerald in California has more than 200. In addition, almost all the Vietnamese sisters of the Tiep Hien Order in Switzerland, Australia, Canada, Germany, and France have been helping groups of hungry families.

Young friends at Plum Village join me wrapping parcels of aid.

· If tonight my heart ceases to beat, you will see me in all these sisters and brothers. There are those who continue my work for hungry children, others who enjoy my work of listening to the suffering of people in order to help them be healed. You can see my smile in their look and my voice in their words. But you will not see my shortcomings in them. The *samsara* of my shortcomings will end the day this body is transformed into ash and then becomes a flower again.

Whenever I do anything, I see the eyes of my parents and grandparents in me. When I worked with villagers, I always had the impression that I was doing the work together with them and also with the loving hands of those friends who saved a handful of rice or a few dông to support the work. My hands were their hands. My love was the wonderful love of the network of ancestors, parents, relatives, and friends born in me. The work I have done is the work of everyone. It is not just my work. As you read these lines and know that, in a remote area of Vietnam, children who are severely malnourished are receiving some funds from Plum Village, you can see that act of love as the collective work of thousands of hands and hearts. All of us, indeed, inter-are. When you hear that my body has ceased to exist, please do not feel sad. Just look deeply and see that my life and work continue in so many friends, so many young people, in their own ways and through their work. I will continue in everyone and everything I have ever touched. I have nothing to fear and nothing to regret.

In July 1992, a friend visited Vietnam and stopped at the War Museum in Ho Chi Minh City, and saw my photograph among the war criminals! In January 1993, another friend saw the same photo there. They were shocked, but they did not dare let people see their emotions, because if the officials knew they were my friends, they could be considered as plotting with war criminals. Me, a war criminal? What amusing news. I learned about that condemnation in 1988 when Thich Tuê Sy, my young brother in the Dharma, was sentenced to death. If Tuê Sy had received such a heavy and unfair sentence, it seemed normal that I could receive the unfair label of "war criminal." I don't feel any anger or hatred towards the rulers of the country. Instead, great pity and sadness arise in me. Their perceptions of millions of Vietnamese are far from reality. Because of erroneous views, they have already killed, tortured, and mistreated millions of people. When will I have a chance to share with them the arts of listening and looking deeply that I have learned from studying with Thây? When will all the world's children, and adults, learn to live together in peace?

Dear readers, I thank you for your patience in reading all of these pages. I am with you just as you have been with me, and we encourage each other to realize our deepest love, caring, and generosity. Together on the path of love, we can try to make a small difference in someone's life. What else is there to do?

AFTERWORD

Afterword

This book could never have reached your hands if it were not for two wonderful friends, Therese Fitzgerald and Arnie Kotler. We three have been assisting Thây Nhat Hanh during his retreat tours in North America since 1983. At every retreat, Thây asked me to share with the participants some of my work during the war. The aim was to let our friends who live in safety and yet suffer with their daily problems be in contact with a larger painful reality. Even though the Vietnam War has ended, the suffering remains, in terms of deprivation of human rights, poverty, and so on. If our friends could touch this large-scale suffering, perhaps they would suffer less from their own daily problems.

During Thây's first tour of North America, we only taped his Dharma talks, not mine. But my experiences watered many seeds of compassion in Therese, who started to record my talks in 1985. Since each retreat drew unique participants, each of my talks differed to fit the audience. Therese proposed that we transcribe these and other tapes of my life story. After a few months, she presented me with a collection of papers and declared, "Here is a book of your experiences." I could never have imagined that one day I would write such a book. The idea had never crossed my mind, even though a number of young people who appreciated my work had asked me to share my experiences in that way. I always had too many things to do, and I could not imagine sitting down and writing. Reading the transcriptions of my tapes, I discovered how poor my English was to communicate the reality of my experiences. Several times I tried to dissuade Therese from publishing my memoirs. I always felt that I could describe my experiences better in a retreat setting where I could share with more than just words, but Therese kept encouraging me. She said, "It could inspire many friends to continue your work. One young woman who helped us transcribe your tapes has already made a vow to work for those who suffer."

If any of the experiences recounted in this book have brought you some insight, have watered your own wonderful seeds, please thank Therese on my behalf, because without her, this book would not be in your hands. Arnie and Therese have spent more time on this book than if they had written a thousand-page book by themselves. Thanks to their friendship and deep wish to let the reader water his or her own wonderful seeds, this book has come to completion.

I tried my best to help them complete this book. Arnie helped me put my stories in a clear order. Both of them continued to ask me questions to help clarify the context of my experiences. As I answered their questions, many other experiences surfaced, and the entire book had to be reorganized again.

In my daily activities, I have always been attracted to giving urgent help to hungry children, flood and typhoon victims, and refugees in camps throughout Asia, revealing to the world human rights violations, sharing with social workers in Central and South Vietnam the art of living in peace in the midst of tumultuous activities. Respecting my wishes to continue to be involved in these realities, Therese and Arnie never pressured me to edit. But slowly, over four years, we finally present this book to you.

Who is Chân Không, Sister True Emptiness? Who is Cao Ngoc Phuong? She is made of her ancestors, the land called Vietnam, the air, the suffering, the friendship, the teachings, the cruel ignorance of the war makers, and the love and understanding of several previous teachers and friends during her first thirty years in that spot of the world, and then another twenty years among many bodhisattvas in the West. The experiences in this book are the collective experiences of all who have shared my life with me.

I would like to further introduce these two wonderful friends to you. Arnie Kotler was a shy, young monk in 1982 when Thây and I first met him at the Reverence for Life Conference in New York, where we joined in a march for disarmament together with one million other people. Seeing Arnie, Thây remembered his own time as a novice, and he asked whether Arnie had enough time to learn the sutras and also get enough sleep. Arnie shyly answered no, so Thây accepted the invitation of Arnie's abbot, Baker Roshi, to come to

Tassajara to teach a course of ten days the following Spring. Thây envisioned many young monks like Arnie who might benefit from his way of practicing the Dharma.

We slowly became great friends, especially when Arnie decided to set up Parallax Press to publish all of Thây Nhat Hanh's books. I remember that everyone tried to dissuade Arnie from setting up a publishing house, especially since Arnie, who had been a monk for fifteen years, had no funds to start a business. But Arnie decided to risk the wonderful adventure anyway. Finances continue to be a big problem, but Arnie is always able to enjoy the sunshine, a cup of tea, and friendship, and try to practice the enlightened path in business. He always breathes between phone calls to calm and renew himself. He tries to live with the friends who help at Parallax Press as brothers and sisters in the community of practice. He is ready to join as many retreats with Thây Nhat Hanh as he can, even though the publishing company calls on him to give his attention. I understand him and Therese deeply in this matter, because we know that being with Thây in retreats is a real "treat" for all of us. Continuously reminded by Thây to be aware of the wonderful teachings of the Enlightened One, we are fresh and renewed after a retreat and know how to cope with difficulties—for Arnie in his poorly-financed press, and me with my increasing responsibilities everywhere.

Fortunately, Therese and another friend, Carole Melkonian, set up a committee in California in 1987 to support our work for hungry children, and, together with others, have shown their ability to continue the work. Now Arnie, Therese, and Carole all help organize retreats with Thây Nhat Hanh in the United States, France, and recently in Eastern Europe. Therese was also the coordinator of several retreats in Plum Village.

If you could visit Therese and Arnie in their humble apartment or visit me and our sisters and brothers in the Dharma in Plum Village, you would see that we don't need much to be happy—a piece of wood on four bricks for a bed, a thin foam mattress, a sleeping bag and a light blanket, several boxes for our files, and a lot of breathing in and out consciously to be aware of our good luck to be in peace and liberty to work for those in need. Letters come every day, bringing good news of inspirational work. But some letters and phone calls bring news that our work has failed in some areas. Conscious breathing always helps us calm and renew ourselves so we can better cope with the difficult situations and transform them. We know that you can do even better than we have. So it is my wish that this book, this work for hungry children, this work of organizing retreats, has been useful to you, as some witness of our practice of interbeing on this wonderful journey together.